A Journey
through Christian Theology

A Journey
through Christian Theology

With Texts from the First
to the Twenty-First Century

Introduced and Edited by
William P. Anderson

Illustrated by
Richard L. Diesslin

Fortress Press
Minneapolis

Scripture translations are from the Revised Standard Version of the Bible, copyright © 1946, 1952, and 1971 by the Division of Christian Education of the National Council of Churches of Christ in the United States of America, and are used by permission.

Interior design: Beth Wright

For reprint permission, the editors and publisher gratefully acknowledge the publishers listed in credit lines accompanying excerpted text. In addition, permission to reprint has been granted for the excerpts from Thomas Aquinas (pp. 78–83) by Benziger Publishing Co.; from Pseudo-Dionysius (pp. 58–60) by Paulist Press; and from Reinhold Niebuhr (pp. 176–79) by Prentice-Hall, Inc., Upper Saddle River, N.J.

Library of Congress Cataloging-in-Publication Data

A journey through Christian theology : with texts from the first to the twenty-first century / edited by William P. Anderson ; illustrated by Richard L. Diesslin
    p. cm.
  ISBN 0-8006-3220-6 (alk. paper)
   1. Theology, Doctrinal—History. I. Anderson, William P.

BT21.2 J68 2000
230'.09—dc 21

                                       00-022303

The paper used in this publication meets the minimum requirements for American National Standard for Information Sciences—Permanence of Paper for Printed Library Materials, ANSI Z329.48–1984.

Manufactured in the U.S.A.   AF 1-3220
04   03   02   01   00   1   2   3   4   5   6   7   8   9   10

To Carolyn, Janice, Bill Jr., and Kevin

and

to Mindy, Grady, Sally, and Neil

CONTENTS

PREFACE

The great two-thousand-year arc of Christian thought stands as a monumental intellectual achievement. Its core ideas have been massively influential on Western and indeed planetary history. Engaging the minds and hearts of dozens of generations, Christian theology has also articulated some of the deepest questions about and conflicts in human existence.

Yet for the novice, theology can be daunting. Its specialized terminology, its heavy use of philosophical concepts, and its sometimes arcane distinctions often fog the live religious questions tackled by Christianity's most illustrious thinkers.

This book issues a hearty invitation to the novice theologian and offers trusty companionship for the journey. We invite the reader to follow along the Christian intellectual quest and to probe some of life's most important questions as they have been posed in the radically different social settings of a two-thousand-year history. To enable the trek, we have created this people-friendly reader, a nonthreatening, sometimes humorous entrance into central texts of Christian theology.

Here we hope you the reader can get some sense of what all the fuss has been about and what has engaged and provoked the chief thinkers in Christian history. Here you will meet the heroes of Christian thought, along with more controversial figures. Here you can experience the thwack and thud of competing theological views—without getting burned at the stake! Most of all, we hope you can gain some sense of the excitement of theology as it addresses perennial concerns and questions that, from the time of Jesus to now, have sparked intellectual creativity and passion, stern invective, and important popular religious movements.

Only a small fraction of theologians can be presented in this format, and the excerpts can only hint at the range and power of their work. Moreover, the selections reflect the largely sexist practice of prior generations of translators and, we fear, of theologians in their noninclusivity. Still, along with the introductions to each period and person, reflections on their main arguments, and study questions, these brief but substantive excerpts should offer some sense of the context, substance, and import of the thinkers. Though spanning twenty centuries, the classic texts we have chosen address five interlocking questions and tensions:

> *Christology:* what is the significance of Jesus? How can one understand his person and work?
> *Ecclesiology:* how does the community of gathered Christians handle questions of power, purpose, and relationship to governmental authority?
> *Faith and reason:* what is a responsible and credible way to reflect on Christian commitment and the host of intellectual problems it raises? How can Christian faith be reconciled with the critical intellectual spirit?
> *Religious experience:* the strong mystical element in Christian experience surfaces in each period. How does this fascinating and unpredictable contemplative strand comport with theology—and with action for social justice?

Social justice: how does Jesus' vision of the reign of God find expression or frustration in the very different circumstances and regimes of Christian history?

We have been gratified by the overwhelmingly positive reception of this project among college and seminary students and adult-education classes. The book can be used by itself or with any of a variety of histories of Christianity or of Christian theology. Augmenting the texts with the cartoons has brought a light and often telling touch to what is perceived as a technical, not to say ponderous, discipline. We hope the cartoons will entertain but also provoke thought and assist in remembering the main points of the texts. A CD-ROM with over one hundred more cartoons on this topic is available from Rich at RLDes@aol.com or the website http://members.aol.com/rldes/index.htm.

Finally, we are grateful to our support team. We would like to thank Mary Ann Boyer for her initial editorial work, Michael West and Beth Wright at Fortress Press, and the host of folks who provided us with reviews and encouragement as we developed and refined the volume.

From Bill: I would be remiss if I did not express my deepest appreciation to my family for their long-suffering support: my wife, Carolyn, for her love, understanding, and tolerance—going on five decades; and my children, Janice, Bill Jr., and Kevin (together with their wide circle of family and friends). Each is a teacher of quality in her or his own chosen field and has engaged me on more than one occasion in thoughtful provocative religious dialogue. To them all, I can only say how happy and blessed I truly am!

From Rich: I am grateful that Bill Anderson was intrigued by my idea for this project and that we were able to work together on it. Bill's depth of knowledge of Christian theology and his sense of humor made working on this project a delight. I would like to thank my wife, Mindy, for her support and encouragement of my cartooning. This goes beyond emotional support, since this past year of cartooning as my full-time vocation has been made possible by her return to full-time teaching. Without that kind of support, this project would still be on the drawing board—literally!

Introducing Adam and Eve

It seemed appropriate to have Adam and Eve as our tour guides on this trip, since, you might say, they got us into this mess! We will use their collective experience to provide commentary on deep theological issues (such as gardening, farming, and childbirth). After all, they should know what not *to do by now!*

Sounds suspect to me!

Never trust a cartoon or serpent, I always say!

PART ONE

THE EARLY CHURCH

A late seventeenth-century thinker described a group of early Christian writers, including such persons as Clement of Rome, Barnabas, the Shepherd of Hermas, Ignatius, and Polycarp, as the "Fathers" who flourished in the times of the apostles. Thereafter these writers have been commonly known and referred to as the Apostolic Fathers. Today the literature ascribed to this period is somewhat extended and includes additional works as *The Epistle to Diognetus, The Didache,* and others.

These writings have some common characteristics. They are: (1) relatively short, (2) preserved for the most part in a very few manuscripts, (3) most likely limited in terms of literary quality, and (4) all generally problematic, in the sense that they all belong to a period in the life of the church for which the records are rather sketchy.

For the religious thinker and for the historian it is only accidentally that these writings form a unity. In some ways they may be compared to old and very dear pieces that one might find in an attic or antique shop. Many times these pieces do not seem to be of much value or significance, and yet, at the same time, they are intriguing. Upon examination we discover that they are in their own way attractive, even though through the centuries many have tried to tinker with them either naively to protect them or intentionally with the purpose of deceiving readers.

The Apologists are a second, later group of important early writers. In this anthology, we shall focus on Justin Martyr, probably the most noted of them all. In turning from a person such as Ignatius of Antioch, with his great desire to be one with Jesus of Nazareth in martyrdom, to a person such as Justin Martyr the Apologist, we enter a

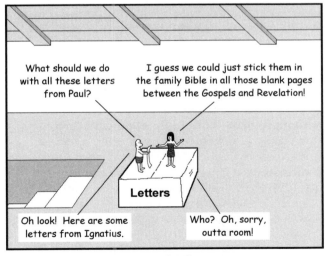

Fan Mail

new and different world. Justin was a philosopher, a man who had reflected seriously on the meaning of the Christian faith and who undertook to demonstrate the validity of that Christian faith to outsiders and to vindicate the right of the Christian community and its faith to exist without persecution. To Justin, and to other Apologists as well (for example, Athenagoras of Athens and Aristides), Christianity was not simply a harmless religious phenomenon; it was a belief system that contained the very best of the elements of Roman civilization and all the best of the Empire. To the mind of the philosophically oriented Christian such as Justin, Christianity and the Empire were ideal "soul-mates"—if only the Empire could understand this reality. Rather than being subversive, as they were accused of being, Christians were ideal Roman citizens. Christian ideas, far from being irreconcilable with Greek philosophy, were the apex of Greek thought. Indeed, Justin saw Christianity as the fulfillment of his Platonism, the completion of his intellectual journey, the key to his understanding of life, which, after all, is one of the functions of philosophy. In the works of the Apologists we find numerous references to great ancient thinkers such as Homer, Sophocles, Socrates, and Plato. Their use of *Logos* made it possible to connect Christian thought to Greek philosophy. The Apologists saw Greek philosophy as incomplete without Christianity. And thus Christianity, for better or worse, became intellectual.

The issues addressed by the Apologists and the answers they offered may differ significantly from the issues that face us in the modern world. Yet there is much of an apologetic nature that occurs today. Theology must continue to defend its right to exist among academic disciplines. Now it is not usually governments that make religion run the gauntlet, but the descendants of the intellectual traditions of ancient Greece, the more recent intellectual communities that in fact originated in, or were at least spawned by, theology, for example, some of the modern empirical sciences.

Other significant figures we shall meet in the early church include: Irenaeus of Lyons, Tertullian, Origen of Alexandria, Arius, Athanasius, Augustine of Hippo, Pseudo-Dionysius, and John Scotus Erigena. We will also examine the Creeds produced by the first ecumenical councils at which fundamental issues were addressed. Although not satisfying everyone, the councils' work provided a theological base for Christian doctrine still in place to this day.

Theologians and philosophers of the early Christian community, such as Justin, not only defended Christianity against the Greeks, Romans, and Jews, but also sought to protect the community from itself, from modification and heresy within the faith. One such person was Irenaeus, bishop of Lyons.

Irenaeus, as a defender of the faith, took on an early formidable foe: Gnosticism, which was a serious threat to the integrity and unity of the emerging church from within its own boundaries. Gnosticism, in part a "mystery rite," in part philosophy (or perhaps better put—theosophy), seemed to be eclectic, synthetic—a little bit of everything. It claimed a special saving knowledge (*gnosis*), available only to initiates, and while doing so was quite divisive and destructive. It was not that the early Christians rejected knowledge outrightly; they rather asserted that the Apostolic Tradition was the only true knowledge.

In the second century Gnosticism became both a friend and a foe to Christianity. Those who saw it as an ally did so because it also spoke of God, human beings, creation, and redemption—all major components of the Christian faith. Those who distrusted it, however, saw it as dangerous because being partly Christian and partly non-Christian, it was capable of seducing the believer. Such deception was far more critical than outright disbelief or skepticism.

Fundamentally, Christian Gnosticism may be said to have at least four principles: (1) the God of the Hebrews is an evil god: this god has disappointed our messianic hopes and aspirations; the Hebrew Scriptures, which present this god, must therefore be rejected; (2) the visible world is evil: this is a world created by the evil god; (3) the God of Jesus of Nazareth is good: this God is completely hidden until revealed in Jesus of Nazareth, who becomes a semi-mythical redeemer of universal or cosmic proportions; (4) the spiritual world is good: it is the creation of the good God who has been revealed (to the Gnostic) in Jesus of Nazareth.

In the early church there were literally dozens of different Gnostic communities—for example, the Nicolaitans, the Cerinthians, the Basilideans, the Satornalians, the Carpocrations, the Valentinians, to name just a few.

On the North African continent, at approximately the same time as Irenaeus, we find Tertullian. Tertullian was the first important theologian to write in Latin rather than Greek, which, up to this time, had been the predominant language of the church.

Often referred to as the father of Latin theology, Tertullian set the course for later Western theological terminology. His scathing attacks against the Roman state, pagans, Jews, and heretics are marked by a vivid and direct literary style that explodes with puns, satire, and all kinds of devastating polemical verbal blasts. His argument in favor of Christianity was as simple as it was clear: it was God's truth handed down by the apostles. All later doctrines were obviously false and must therefore be rooted out and destroyed. The creed, or "Rule of Faith" (regula fidei), was the norm by which heresy was to be judged, and Christians who were tempted into other doctrines only showed that they never really believed correctly in the first place.

Origen of Alexandria stands in grand style among the early theologians and was arguably the very first systematic theologian of the Christian era. Following the Gnostics of the second century and preceding Plotinus (ca. 204–270) and Mani (ca. 216–275), Origen was a defender of orthodoxy and by rational temperament and ecclesiastical discipline in no way inclined toward heretical fancies of the gnostic varieties. When it came to his own attempt at integrating scriptural revelation with independent reason and intuition into a coherent and persuasive whole that meant to embrace the totality of things, all of his care could not prevent him from producing a system that the later church would find necessary to condemn. He is, nevertheless, one of the most important, most prolific, and most interesting figures in all of Christian history.

In the fourth century a new epoch in the history of Christian thought began. The Emperor Constantine in 313 transformed the fortunes of the Christian church by turning it from a persecuted to a tolerated and finally to a favored community. One of the consequences of becoming what we may call "a department of the State" was that the fourth century became an era of great thinkers in the church for the simple reason that the energy expended in defense of the church against outsiders and devoted to martyrdom, that is, to apologetics, refuting accusations of those outside of the Christian community, could now be channeled to different ends. Thus some great theologians and philosophers of religion emerged, such as Arius, Athanasius, and Eusebius of Caesarea. Still other Christians gave themselves over to meditation and contemplation and flocked to the deserts of Egypt.

There was also a negative side to the state-sponsorship of Christianity. First, mass conversions to the now-favored church detracted from the vitality, the depth, and the moral life that had persisted in the time of persecution. There are, of course, parallels to this in the churches of today. Religious faith just simply became easier. Second, when a religious body receives the blessing of government, it also runs the risk of receiving undesired interference or condemnation from that government. Sometimes government will favor one theological position over another; at other times it will interfere in the internal functions of the church itself and by so doing will fuel theological controversy with political dimensions. In the twentieth century we have clearly seen this in the case of Nazi Germany with the Reformed, Lutheran, and Roman Catholic churches caving in to political pressure, and in the former Soviet Union with the capitulation of the Russian Orthodox church. In this early period we shall be looking at some texts from the pens of Arius and Athanasius, as well as the major credal formulations that have remained with the church as normative criteria for doctrine to this very day. In the West we shall be looking at some insights from the great North African theologian, Augustine, bishop of Hippo and a major architect in the development of Western theological thought.

1. IGNATIUS OF ANTIOCH (75–110)

Ignatius, second bishop of Antioch during the reign of Emperor Trajan (98–117), was a unique personality. While functioning as leader of this early Christian community at Antioch, he was condemned for his faith and sentenced to death by Imperial Rome. He was to be sport for the Roman citizenry at the Coliseum, offering his body to the infamous lions. While on his way to execution, he sent letters to other Christian communities from which we may derive useful information about this infant church and the living faith experiences of its leaders and ordinary believers. These letters were sent to Ephesus, Magnesia, Tralles, Philadelphia, and Smyrna; to Polycarp, bishop of Smyrna; and to

Rome. The five cities were Christian communities that had sent representatives to greet him as he passed through on his way to execution.

These letters have some of the most fiery, emotional statements to come out of the early church. They reflect without any doubt the total commitment of Ignatius not only to the church, but, more importantly, to Jesus of Nazareth, the Christ. There were several issues of importance to Ignatius, as a leader in this relatively new religious community, and by way of Ignatius to us as well.

Ignatius had deep concern for the "unity of the church." He is the author of the well-known and often repeated phrase, "where the bishop is, there is the church" (a phrase often misunderstood as well).

He also had a deep and real concern for the *reality* of the humanity of Jesus in opposition to the docetists. Docetists are those who had, and in many cases still have, difficulty seeing Jesus as a real human being. This issue is central to Christian theology. In formal theology this issue is part of Christology, the study of the person and status of Jesus Christ. As the church developed its tradition regarding Jesus, this christological issue became one of the most heated controversies in the church.

Consistent with his opposition to the docetists from a christological point of view, Ignatius also had a *realistic* view of the Eucharist. The theology of the Eucharist is tied very closely to his understanding of the humanity of Jesus. The death of Jesus is real, not mere appearance, as is the celebration of that death on our behalf in the Eucharist.

Further, one cannot consider this fiery Antiochene without considering his preoccupation with his own death, a death that must be significantly related to that of Jesus of Nazareth himself.

Source: The Early Christian Fathers, *edited and translated by Henry Bettenson (Oxford, New York: Oxford University Press, 1956), 41, 42–43, 45, 46, 48–49.*

▼ ▼ ▼

TO THE SMYRNAEANS
Salvation through the Death of Christ, Human and Divine
I perceived that you are settled in unshakable faith, nailed, as it were, to the cross of our Lord Jesus Christ, in flesh and spirit . . . with full conviction with respect to our Lord that he is genuinely of David's line according to the flesh,

son of God according to divine will and power, really born of a virgin and baptized by John that "all righteousness might be fulfilled" (Matt. 3:15) by him, really nailed up in the flesh for us in the time of Pontius Pilate and tetrarchy of Herod—from this fruit of the tree, that is from his God-blessed passion, we are derived—that he might "raise up a standard" (Isa. 5:26, cf. John 12:32) for all ages through resurrection, for his saints and faithful people, whether among Jews or Gentiles, in one body of his church. . . .

[Docetists] have no concern for love, none for the widow, the orphan, the afflicted, the prisoner, the hungry, the thirsty. They stay away from the Eucharist and prayer, because they do not admit that the Eucharist is the flesh of our Saviour Jesus Christ which suffered for our sins, which the Father raised up by his goodness.

Unity under the Ministry: The Supreme Authority of the Bishop
Shun divisions, as the beginning of evil. All of you follow the bishop, as Jesus Christ followed the Father, and the presbytery the Apostles; respect the deacons as the ordinance of God. Let no one do anything that pertains to the church apart from the bishop. Let that be considered a valid Eucharist which is under the bishop or one whom he has delegated. Wherever the bishop shall appear, there let the people be; just as wherever Christ may be, there is the catholic church. . . .

TO THE MAGNESIANS
I advise you, be eager to act always in godly accord; with the bishop presiding as the counterpart of God, the presbyters as the counterpart of the council of apostles, and the deacons (most dear to me) who have been entrusted with the service [diaconate] under Jesus Christ, who was with the Father before all the ages and appeared at the end of time. Therefore do all of

you attain conformity with God, and reverence each other; and let none take up a merely natural attitude towards his neighbor, but love each other continually in Jesus Christ. Let there be nothing among you which will have power to divide you, but be united with the bishop and with those who preside, for an example and instruction in incorruptibility.

Thus, as the Lord did nothing without the Father (being united with him), either by himself or by means of his apostles, so you must do nothing without the bishop and the presbyters. And do not try to think that anything is praiseworthy which you do on your own account: but unite in one prayer, one supplication, one mind, one hope; with love and blameless joy. For this is Jesus Christ, and there is nothing better than he. Let all therefore hasten as to one shrine, that is, God, as to one sanctuary, Jesus Christ, who came forth from the one Father, was always with one Father, and has returned to the one Father.

To the Ephesians

The Incarnation

Avoid heretics like wild beasts; for they are mad dogs, biting secretly. You must be on your guard against them; their bite is not easily cured. There is only one physician [who can cope with it], a physician who is at once fleshly and spiritual, generate and ingenerate, God in man, true life in death, born of Mary and of God, first passible then impassible, Jesus Christ our Lord. . . .

If Jesus Christ should deem me worthy, through your prayers, and if it should be his will, I intend to write you a second pamphlet in which I shall proceed to expound the divine plan [economy] of which I have begun to treat, with reference to the new man, Jesus Christ, which consists in faith towards him and love towards him, in his passion and resurrection; especially if the Lord should make some revelation to me. Meet together in common—every single one of you—in grace, in one faith and

one Jesus Christ (who was of David's line in his human nature, son of man and son of God) that you may obey the bishop and presbytery with undistracted mind; breaking one bread, which is the medicine of immortality, our antidote to ensure that we shall not die but live in Jesus Christ forever.

To the Romans

Martyrdom

I die for Christ of my own choice, unless you hinder me. I beseech you not to show "inopportune kindness" to me. Let me be given to the wild beasts, for by their means I can attain to God. I am God's wheat, and I am being ground by the teeth of the beasts so that I may appear as pure bread. Rather coax the beasts, that they may become my tomb and leave no part of my body behind, that I may not be a nuisance to anyone when I have fallen asleep. Then shall I be truly a disciple of Jesus Christ, when the world shall not even see my body. Entreat the Lord for me that through these instruments I may appear as a sacrifice to God. I do not lay injunctions on you, as Peter and Paul did. They were Apostles; I am a convict. They were free; I am a slave, up till now: but I suffer, then am I a freedman of Jesus Christ, and shall rise free in him. Now I am learning in my bonds to abandon all desire. . . .

My birth pangs are at hand. Bear with me, my brothers. Do not hinder me from living: do not wish for my death. Do not make the world a present of one who wishes to be God's. Do not coax him with material things. Allow me to receive the pure light; when I arrive there I shall be a real man. Permit me to be an imitator of the Passion of my God. . . .

▲ ▲ ▲

Any person who picks up the letters of this ancient church leader and reads them without any preparation will most certainly come to the conclusion that here we must have a man who is not in a proper frame of mind. It is not ordinary for anyone, then or now, to wish to die. And yet, when properly understood, these rather rash statements of Ignatius, on his way to death, make very good sense. How then might we understand what this early bishop is saying to his many friends and colleagues in the faith, both in the second century and for us today?

Arguably, no author early or late, is as eloquent on the imitation of Jesus, the Christ, as Ignatius of Antioch. If anyone wishes to live the life of Christ and/or God, then that person must adopt the principles and virtues of God and Christ. As Christ imitated his Father, reasoned Ignatius, so we must imitate Christ. As he says in his letter to the Philippians (7), "Do as Jesus did, for He, too, did as the Father did." This is not merely lip service, but seen clearly in conforming oneself particularly to the passion and death of Jesus. Thus as we have seen in the text of the letter to the Romans, "Permit me to be an imitator of the passion of Jesus, our God" (Rom. 6).

From this conception of a perfect imitation of Christ springs Ignatius's great enthusiasm for martyrdom. Martyrdom is the perfect imitation of Christ, and only they who are willing to sacrifice their lives for him are true disciples. Today, we have a great many "marginal" Christians. That is, the rolls of the churches are inflated with many who would not, if necessary, take the real risk of "living the faith" of Jesus of Nazareth. To stand for the Christian faith is "costly" as the noted German martyr, Dietrich Bonhoeffer, once said. Bonhoeffer gave his life in opposition to Adolph Hitler and the Third Reich.

In more recent times we may point to the example of Rev. Dr. Martin Luther King Jr., who, in his fight for the civil rights of African Americans and, by virtue of that struggle, the rights of all human beings, was impelled to a large extent by his religious convictions of freedom and love. Joined to these men are thousands of persons who, also sparked by religious convictions, gave of themselves in modern martyriological

St. Ignatius Brand Cat Food

fashion. It may not be as explicit or fiery as that of Ignatius of Antioch, but it is nevertheless equally real and equally valid.

The Jesus to whom Ignatius is so passionately devoted is clearly both human and divine. He vehemently attacks docetists who deny a human nature to the Christ and especially as they deny the suffering of Jesus of Nazareth. This is hardly make-believe to Ignatius. If it is, why would he be so foolish as to be in chains with his own life on the line? Indeed, he argues that the Eucharist is the very flesh of his savior Jesus Christ, who suffered for humanity's sins and who was raised by the Father showing his lovingkindness.

At the same time Ignatius refers to Christ as "timeless" and "invisible," concepts that certainly reflect a being of divine quality. However, nowhere does he try to reconcile these elements of suffering, invisibility, and timelessness. At this stage in the development of Christianity when the so-called end-times were considered imminent, why would there be a need? This problem was left for later generations to solve. It was sufficient at the time for the bishop to affirm the reality of Jesus' humanity against the docetists and the reality of his divinity.

Furthermore, for Ignatius, as it was for other early disciples, something very real occurred in the life of Jesus that affected their lives so dramatically that they were willing to give up their very lives for their personal convictions. No one is willing to die for something that is not very real and true to them.

When Ignatius speaks of imitating the passion of Jesus his God, he would, by later standards, be considered heretical. As the influence of Greek thought begins to take control with such persons as Justin Martyr, the fiery, personal, and dynamic relationship with Christ of which Ignatius speaks becomes more and more problematic. This is clear when Ignatius speaks of the suffering of God—an impossibility for later "orthodox" Christians.

The idea of unity brings all of this together for this first-century martyr. Underlying this sense of unity was the idea that the church was the body of Christ (following Paul), an idea that did not simply mean that unity with the church was unity with Christ, but that without a unity with Christ, unity with the church would not be possible. For Ignatius, Jesus the Christ was the essential link.

The idea of unity is a basic presupposition in Ignatius. How then is it effected? His response is simple and clear. Union with Christ is brought about by participation in the Eucharist. This is what is meant by the phrases "medicine of immortality" and "the antidote by which we escape death." Obviously, Ignatius again has the docetists in mind and, at the same time, reflects some sense of the mystical union that we find in both Paul and John of the New Testament. Ignatius speaks very clearly in physical and human terms of a physical oneness with Jesus, and as we participate in this real, fully human sacrifice, we put on the mantle of immortality.

2. Justin Martyr (100?–165)

From a theological point of view, one of the most important figures of the second century is Justin Martyr. Justin was born of non-Christian parents in Sichem in Palestine and flourished during the period 143–165. He tried many different approaches to find meaning in life, such as the philosophies Stoicism, Pythagoreanism, Aristotelianism, and Platonism, the last of which he ultimately found appealing. It was in the new faith of the Christian community, however, that Justin found his truth, for while Platonism had opened many doors of life to him, it was only Christianity that filled his heart.

Legend has it that an old man at the seashore convinced Justin that Platonism could not fulfill his needs and called his attention to the "prophets who alone announced the truth" (*Dialogue with Trypho*, 8). This old man spoke to Justin of many things and bid him attend to them. From that point on Justin was filled with a desire to pursue this new faith. He found a love for the prophets and a genuine feeling of love and compassion among his newly discovered friends in Christ. It was this Christian philosophy that Justin found to be safe, profitable, and, perhaps most of all, meaningful. In Christianity Justin discovered the fulfillment of his philosophical quest. As he puts it: "It was for this reason that I became a philosopher, and I could wish that all men were of the same mind as myself, not to turn from the doctrines of the Savior" (*Dialogue with Trypho*, 8).

Justin speaks elsewhere of this experience (*Apology II*, 1, 2) where he writes: "I myself used to rejoice in the teaching of

Plato and to hear evil spoken of Christians. But, as I saw that they showed no fear in face of death and all other things which inspire horror, I reflected that they could not be vicious and pleasure-loving." An honest search for truth and humble prayer brought him to accept the faith of Christ: "When I discovered the wicked disguise which the evil spirits had thrown around the divine doctrines of the Christians to deter others from joining them, I laughed both at the authors of these falsehoods and their disguise and at the popular opinion. And I confess that I both prayed and strove with all my might to be found a Christian" (*Apology II*, 13).

After converting to this new Christian philosophy, Justin devoted the remainder of his life to the defense of Christianity. He never relinquished his role of philosopher, however, and continued to wear his philosopher's pallium, a cloak signifying that special status.

He traveled from place to place undertaking the propagation of the only true philosophy, developing his own schools of Christian philosophers. These were the first schools of a Christian nature that were not so-called community church schools. Instead, they were philosophical schools in the old Greek

9

style, groups of young scholars gathered around a master who had the reputation for challenging lectures and exciting classroom dialogue. The schools soon developed a reputation for knowing how to embarrass visiting scholars.

Justin's primary adversaries were Greek philosophers and Roman government officials, personified in the Roman emperor. "Your Majesty," Justin argued, "has seen fit to listen to unpatriotic things about Christians. Let the plaintiffs bring forward their evidence. Your Majesty is herewith guaranteed that the Christian community will not protect the guilty, for the Christians are your Majesty's loyal citizens. And is not your Majesty praised far and wide for his philosophy, for his culture, for his justice? Excellent—now we shall see whether there is a particle of truth in it! Examine the evidence yourself! You can only kill us, you cannot do us harm" (*Apology I, 2*).

When you speak with such audacity to the ruler of the Roman Empire, you can expect not to die with your boots on! As a spokesperson for a group of Christians on trial for refusing to sacrifice to the gods, Justin added characteristically that if he were going to die for the truth, it would be because his judges, blinded by error, were unworthy of the truth. For that kind of holy folly, Justin was beheaded.

Martyrdom or childbirth? Hmmm!

Tilling the soil just started to sound a lot better!

What Justin began in the mid-second century blossomed into a significantly different type of Christianity: intellectual. The Christian-hating emperors were no longer soldiers persecuting an oriental sect, but intellectuals persecuting intellectuals. The philosopher's persecution was nonetheless as bloodthirsty as the soldiers', and the apologists wanted to understand why. Was it merely the name "Christian" that brought down the wrath of the empire on the heads of those who gloried in that name? It was, indeed, claimed the apologists. Discrimination because of a name was discrimination at its most despicable, and the apologists made the entire world aware of this.

There are parallels to this discrimination in modern society. While our political, social, and economic institutions do not put people to death because of their religious views, as was the case in the Roman Empire, they understand that religious values have the capacity to challenge the legitimacy of societal practices and policies and are often disruptive. The ensuing turmoil, within society and within religious communities themselves, can be seen in recent struggles in the United States over civil rights, foreign policy issues, and most recently in the area of sexuality, particularly gay rights. Church stands on government policies or on issues of race, poverty, and sexuality have repercussions for the public's attitude toward the issues and toward religious communities and for membership rolls. Like the early church, the modern church must address societal problems. The challenge is unlikely to result in death, as it did for Ignatius of Antioch or Justin Martyr, but indifference and mockery may be equally powerful chastisements.

We now turn to some of the texts of Justin Martyr for information on the early church and for inspiration for the modern church. As we have stated, Justin is an apologist, that is, he is a person who speaks to those generally outside of the Christian community and in its defense. This will be one area that we shall examine. Another equally significant area in the thought of Justin is his use of *logos*. *Logos* was a term common to both Greek philosophy and Christian theology and denotes the principal of rationality that informs all being. In many Greek philosophical schools (for example, Platonism), it was one of the ways in which humans saw themselves connected to the Creator of the universe. In Christian thought it is very prominent in the literature of the Johannine tradition, especially the prologue to the Gospel of John, where Jesus is first seen as the *logos* personified. We have always translated *logos* in this Gospel with the English term *word,* although it is more technical than that.

In the Apology written around the middle of the second century, Justin undertook to defend Christianity from its detractors and to commend it to the favorable attention of the secular rulers. His *Dialogue with Trypho,* written most likely soon thereafter, is a series of conversations, perhaps even imaginary as we have suggested, with a Jew named Trypho. The aim of the document is to demonstrate from the Hebrew prophets that Christianity, according to God's plan and purpose, has superseded Judaism and that Jews as well as Gentiles may only achieve redemption if they become Christians. (Justin's work here certainly would not be looked upon with much favor today in the dialogues

between Jews and Christians, as it expressed the exclusivity of Christianity, while modern Christianity is trying to advance tolerance and understanding between religions.) While these two works seem to be written from entirely different perspectives, it is clear that both were written not only to convince others of the validity of Christianity but to fortify the faith of fellow Christians as well.

Sources: "The First Apology," "The Second Apology," and "Trypho the Jew," Early Christian Fathers, *translated by Edward R. Hardy (Library of Christian Classics, vol. 1; Philadelphia: Westminster Press, 1953), 46, 242ff.*

▼ ▼ ▼

DEFENSE OF CHRISTIANITY

1. To the Emperor Titus Aelius Hadrianus Antonius Pius Augustus Caesar, and to Verissimus his son, the Philosopher, and to Lucius the Philosopher, son of Caesar by nature and of Augustus by adoption, a lover of culture, and to the Sacred Senate and the whole Roman people—on behalf of men of every nation who are unjustly hated and reviled, I, Justin, son of Priscus and grandson of Bacchius, of Flavia Neapolis in Syria Palestina, being myself one of them, have drawn up this plea and petition.

2. Reason requires that those who are truly pious and philosophers should honor and cherish the truth alone, scorning merely to follow the opinions of the ancients, if they are worthless. Nor does sound reason only require that one should not follow those who do or teach what is unjust; the lover of truth ought to choose in every way, even at the cost of his own life to speak and do what is right, though death should take him away. So do you, since you are called pious and philosophers and guardians of justice and lovers of culture, at least give us a

hearing—and it will appear if you are really such. . . .

9. Certainly we do not honor with many sacrifices and floral garlands the objects that men have fashioned up in temple and called gods. We know that they are lifeless and dead and do not represent the form of God—for we do not think of God as having the kind of form which some claim that they imitate to be honored—but rather exhibit the names and shapes of the evil demons who have manifested themselves {to men}. You know well enough without our mentioning it how the craftsmen prepare their material, scraping, and cutting and molding and beating. And often they make what they call gods out of vessels used for vile purposes, changing and transforming by art merely their appearance. We consider it not only irrational but an insult to God whose glory and form are ineffable, to give his name to corruptible things which themselves need care. You are well aware that craftsmen in these [things] are impure and—not to go into details—given to all kinds of vice; they even corrupt their own slave girls who work along with them. What an absurdity, that dissolute men should be spoken of as fashioning or remaking gods for public veneration, and that you should appoint such people as guardians of the temple where they are set up—not considering that it is unlawful to think or speak of men as guardians of gods.

10. But we have learned [from our tradition] that God has no need of material offerings from men, considering that he is the provider of all. We have been taught and firmly believe that he accepts only those who imitate the good things which are his—temperance and righteousness and love of mankind, and whatever else truly belongs to the God who is called by no given name. We have also taught that in the beginning he in his goodness formed all things that are for the sake of men out of unformed matter, and if they show themselves

by their actions worthy of his plan, we have learned that they will be counted worthy of dwelling with him, reigning together and made free from corruption and suffering.

11. When you hear that we look for a kingdom, you rashly suppose that we mean something merely human. But we speak of a Kingdom with God, as is clear from our confessing Christ when you bring us to trial, though we know that death is the penalty for this confession. For if we looked for a human kingdom we would deny it in order to save our lives, and would try to remain in hiding in order to obtain the things we look for. But since we do not place our hopes on the present [order], we are not troubled by being put to death, since we will have to die somehow in any case.

12. We are in fact of all men your best helpers and allies in securing good order, convinced as we are that no wicked man, no covetous man or conspirator, or virtuous man either, can be hidden from God, and that everyone goes to eternal punishment or salvation in accordance with the character of his actions. If all men knew this, nobody would choose vice even for a little time, knowing that he was on his way to eternal punishment by fire; so as to receive the good things that come from God and avoid his punishments. . . .

13. What sound-minded man will not admit that we are not godless, since we worship the Fashioner of the Universe, declaring him, as we have been taught, to have no need of blood and libations and incense, but praising him by the word of prayer and thanksgiving for all that he has given us? We have learned that the only honor worthy of him is not to consume by fire the things he has made for our nourishment, but to devote them to our use and those in need, in thankfulness to him sending up solemn prayers and hymns for our creation and all the means of health, for the variety of creatures and the changes of the seasons, and sending up our petitions that we may live again in

incorruption through our faith in him. It is Jesus Christ who has taught us these things, having been born for this purpose and crucified under Pontius Pilate, who was procurator in Judea at the time of Tiberius Caesar. We will show that we honor him in accordance with reason, having learned that he is the Son of the true God himself, and hold him to be in the second place and the prophetic Spirit in the third rank. It is for this that they charge us with madness, saying that we give the second place after the unchanging and ever-existing God and begetter of all things to a crucified man, not knowing the mystery involved in this, to which we ask you to give your attention as we expound it.

GOD

6. But to the Father of all, *who is unbegotten,* there is no name given. For by whatever name he be called, he has as his elder the person who gives him the name. But these words, Father and God and Creator and Master, *are not names, but appellations derived from his good deeds and functions . . . the appellation "God" is not a name, but an opinion implanted in the nature of men of a thing that can hardly be explained.*

TRYPHO THE JEW

60. He who has but the smallest intelligence will not venture to assert that the Creator and Father of all things, having left all supercelestial matters, was visible on a little portion of the earth. . . .

127. For the ineffable Father and Lord of all neither has come to any place, nor walks, nor sleeps, nor rises up, but remains in his own place, wherever that is, quick to behold and quick to hear, having neither eyes, nor ears, but being of indescribable might; and he knows all things, and none of us escapes his observation. And he is not moved or confined to a spot in the whole world, for he existed before the world was made. How then could anyone talk

to anyone, or be seen by anyone or appear on the smallest portion of the earth, when the people at Sinai were not able to look even on the glory of him who was sent from him.

THE LOGOS

We have been taught that Christ is the first-born of God, and we have declared that he is the *Logos,* of whom every race of man were partakers, and those who lived according to the *Logos* are Christians even though they have been atheists, as among Greeks, Socrates and Heraclitus, and others like them, and among barbarians, Abraham and Ananias and Azarias and Misael and Elias and many others whose deeds and whose names we refrain from recounting now because it would take too long. And thus those who in other days lived irrationally were wicked and enemies of Christ and murderers of those living rationally. But they that lived and are living in accordance with reason are Christians and fearless and undisturbed.

THE SECOND APOLOGY

10. For whatever either lawgivers or philosophers uttered well, they elaborated by finding and contemplating some part of the *Logos.* But since they did not know the entire *Logos,* which is Christ, they often contradicted themselves. And those who by human birth were more ancient than Christ, when they tried to consider and prove things by reason, were brought before tribunals, as impious persons and busybodies. And Socrates, who was more zealous in this direction than all of them, was accused of the very same crimes as ourselves. For they said that he was introducing new divinity and did not consider those to be gods whom the state recognized. . . . But these things our Christ did through his own power. For no one trusted in Socrates as to die for this doctrine, but in Christ who was partially known even by Socrates, for he was and is the *Logos* who is in every man. . . .

13. Whatever all men have uttered aright is the property of us Christians. . . . For all writers through the implanted seed of the *Logos* which was engrafted in them, were able to see the truth darkly, for the seed and imitation of a thing which is given according to the capacity of him who receives it is one thing, and quite a different one is the *thing itself* of which the communication and the imitation are received according to the grace from God.

▲ ▲ ▲

Justin's Defense of Christianity

To the Greeks and Romans, who were most educated, the religious ideas of this new faith must have appeared to be pure nonsense (not unlike some phenomena we have today, such as Gateway to Heaven). At its very best, the moral sobriety and the devotional piety of the Christians made them appear to be somewhat unconventional. At its very worst, Christian theology made the Christians obnoxious and most likely politically dangerous. To the Romans it might be said that the Christians were in fact atheists because they refused to acknowledge any visible gods. To the Jews, who worshiped a single invisible God, this new faith was clearly a perversion of the religion of the prophets and the patriarchs.

Having been accused of atheism and disloyalty by the Romans and foolishness by the Greeks, Justin tried to clear the name of the Christians by playfully pointing out that a Christian (*Christianios*) is not only a follower of Christ (*Christos*), but is one by necessity or nature (*Chrestos*). The charge of atheism is untenable according to Justin. The heathen are actually the ones who are guilty. It is they who are to be condemned for idol worship. Christians, on the other hand, are those who follow the highest moral standards, the standards of Jesus Christ. Christians are by far the superior citizens of Rome. If they teach some doctrines that are problematic, have these ideas not been offered by other religions and philosophers as well? Whatever good is in the secular world, Justin main-

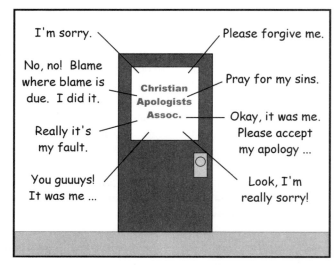

Overheard at a Meeting of Christian Apologists

tains, may be seen in Christianity and not the least from Plato himself. His conclusion is simple. The Christians are being persecuted *merely because they are Christians*. They are being attacked simply because of their name.

Justin argues that Christianity is the realization on this earth of everything that, for the philosophers, Plato and the highly ethical Stoics in particular, was only an *ideal*. In Christianity the ideal becomes real. And so Justin begs the emperor to treat Christians with justice and see to it that all proceedings against them be for real offenses and in regular courts.

Here we see responses to the charges of irrationalism, immorality, political subversion, and atheism, and, from Judaism, apostasy. It is an appeal to the mind rather than the hearts of the antagonists. Justin used philosophical dialectic and rhetoric rather than homily and exhortation (a methodology distinguishing him from Ignatius of Antioch). He has reminded the Romans that the prophets of the Jewish faith, whose authority was accepted by both Christians and Jews, antedated the Stoics, Plato, Aristotle, and Pythagoras. He tried to convince them that these great Hebrew thinkers were wiser than philosophers and even an important source for Greek philosophy itself.

Justin's Theology

Plato taught that God can be known by human beings by way of natural reason, for God and human beings were alike. Justin understood the essence of philosophy to be the knowledge of God and was therefore in fundamental agreement with the great Greek philosophers. Justin's conversion to Christianity, however, led him to deny the philosophers' viewpoint and to argue that God may

only be truly known by revelation (*Dialogue*, 4). Nevertheless, Justin believed that even without revelation, human beings are capable of understanding many things about God. This knowledge is abstract, however, and lacks the clarity and assurance that comes from revelation alone.

Justin's view of God was basically practical and not speculative. It is important to understand that God is an ethical God who requires righteousness and who rewards goodness and punishes evil. Human beings are endowed with freedom and consequently can live properly if they choose to do so. Justin is quite clear about this, as we may see from the following passage:

> God did not make men like other things such as trees and quadrupeds which are unable to act freely. For men would be unworthy of reward or praise if he did right not from choice but because he was made thus: nor would he be justly punished if he did evil not of himself but because he was unable to be other than he was. (*Apology I*, 43)

In Justin's mind we have in our freedom the first step toward leading a Christian life. In this regard Christianity reflects the superiority of this religion compared to other approaches, whether philosophically or politically inspired. Justin emphasizes the excellence of the ethics or moral teachings of Jesus Christ, and he calls attention to the virtuous lives of the Christians contrasting them with the lives of their heathen contemporaries. In particular he stresses the Christians' superiority over the fear of death and their willingness to die for Jesus Christ. This is basic evidence of their high moral character and personal integrity (see especially *Apology I*, 15–17; *Apology II*, 3, 10; and *Dialogue*, 93).

Like Plato, Justin understands God to be a wholly transcendent being (otherworldly), immutable (unchangeable), incorporeal (without body), and uncreated (without origin). This God Justin and the Greeks say is "nameless"; this is a God who by nature could not possibly be in contact with the "created" world, including human beings. The term *God* itself and the designations with which we are so familiar—Father, Creator, Master, etc.—are not names but appellations derived from God's good deeds and functions. Justin argues that in fact *God is not really a name but an opinion implanted in the nature of human beings of something that can hardly be explained.*

Justin's Christology

The concept of the *Logos* played a major role in the life and work of Justin. He called Christ *Logos,* and his use of this term was led to a large degree by his apologetic interests. *Logos* was used frequently by Greek thinkers. The Stoics believed it represented divine forces resident in the world, including human beings, and was the linking device between this world and God. The Platonists thought it referred to the intermediate being or agent that bridged the chasm between God and the world, making it possible for God to relate to this world and act upon it. In Justin's view God is revealed exclusively through the *Logos*.

In a sense the *Logos* is a guide to God and the instructor of all human beings. Originally the *Logos* dwelt within God as a power. Shortly before the Creation, the *Logos* proceeded from God and became the instrument of the creation of the world. The externalization of the *Logos* can be seen in biblical literature as well. For example, for Justin, when God appeared to Moses in the burning bush (Exod. 3:2ff.), it was not really God who was appearing but rather the *Logos*—God's reason, God's creative word. Accordingly, the *Logos* is personalized and identified with the God of the Old Testament theophanies (revelations) and also with Jesus Christ in whom the *Logos* became incarnate (John 1:14). In Justin, who identifies the *Logos* with Christ,

Cross-Eyed

there is a tendency toward a subordination of the *Logos* to God. Sometimes Justin even refers to the *Logos* as a second God, a lesser God (*Dialogue*, 61).

The *Logos* doctrine of Justin is his most important teaching for at least two reasons: (1) it forms the bridge between Greek philosophy and the Christian faith; (2) it is the starting point of a long history to which is attached a great deal of controversy. Although Justin argued that the divine *Logos* appeared fully only in Jesus Christ, a seed [*sperma*] of the *Logos* was scattered among all humankind. It is to the *Logos* that human beings owe their reason and whatever truth they possess. All truth we possess comes from the *Logos*, sometimes directly, sometimes indirectly. The *Logos* spoke in a special way through the figures of the Old Testament and ultimately became incarnate in Jesus Christ. Christ differs from the others because he was in possession of the fullness of the *Logos* and was therefore in possession of all truth, not just a portion of the truth. "The whole *Logos* on our account became Christ, body, mind, and soul" (*Apology II*, 10). Since this is the case, all who are in possession of truth are in possession of Christ and therefore Christians. This enables Justin to argue that Socrates, Plato, Heraclitus, the Greek poets and dramatists, and so forth, who lived according to the direction of the *Logos*, are truly Christians (*Apology I*, 46). This concept enabled Justin to give metaphysical proof for the existence of elements of truth in philosophy and Hebrew literature and to show that there can really be no opposition between any of these divergent positions. Christians alone possess the entire truth, however, because in Christ Truth itself appeared to them. Today we can see some potential for using the concept of *Logos* in ecumenical dialogue and in interfaith discussions, including the religion of humanism.

3. IRENAEUS OF LYONS (140–200)

Irenaeus was from Asia Minor, born somewhere between 130–140 C.E. He states that as a young man he sat at the feet of Bishop Polycarp (purported to have been a disciple of the "beloved" John the Apostle), who was martyred somewhere between 155–156 C.E. By nature Irenaeus was a man of tradition and quite proud of his link to the Apostolic Age. At some point, Irenaeus left Asia Minor for Gaul and most likely spent some time in Rome on his way. In some ways Irenaeus and Gnosticism were both at home in the busy two-way traffic of culture and religious ideas and in different ways were links between the distant parts of the empire, between Gaul and Asia Minor, between the Johannine tradition and the emerging Western Latin Catholic theology.

Irenaeus appealed to the unity and priority of the Christian message while challenging the Gnostics. Gnosticism was a radical dualism; that is, it made a sharp distinction between spirit and matter. The Gnostics took the position that, since God is clearly spiritual and the world is clearly material, the redeeming God could not be the same as the God who created the world. More directly, the God of the Hebrews and the Hebrew Scriptures *was not* the God of Jesus of Nazareth. It is just one step from here to the position that Jesus of Nazareth, the

Christ, must also be purely spiritual or divine and only seemingly human or historical. This is a clear form of docetism that even at this early date the church rejected.

Irenaeus wrote a great number of works, of which only two have survived, but both are extremely important. To the earlier and lengthier of the two he gave the cumbersome title *Five Books of Detecting and Overthrow of the Knowledge Falsely So-Called*. This is usually referred to simply as *Against Heresies.* Briefly stated, in this work Irenaeus affirmed that the God of Creation and the God of Redemption are one and the same God and that Jesus was both *human and divine*. In elaborating on this latter point he made use of Paul's analogy between Adam as the first man and Christ as the second man, that is, the new Creation (1 Cor. 15:21-22). In this manner Christ is the renewer of humanity and, as Irenaeus puts it, the "recapitulation" of God's creative and redemptive purpose. In the preface to his fifth book, Irenaeus sums up what he is suggesting with a now familiar and oft-quoted phrase. This phrase sums up not only his Christology, but indeed his entire theology. "Christ became what we are, in order that we might become what he is" (Book V, *Against Heresies*, Preface).

In these works we see a theology developing that struggled to maintain what was understood to be the authentic form of the century-old Christian tradition against the various forms of Gnosticism. The following selections from Irenaeus's writings give us a picture of one of the earliest formal Christian theologies. In the first century Paul the Apostle wrote letters to respond to specific issues and questions. In the second century other Christians, such as Ignatius of Antioch, Justin Martyr, and others, wrote letters and treatises explaining and defending Christian beliefs and practices. Toward the end of the second century, Irenaeus went well beyond letters and apologies for the faith to create a prototype of Christian theology and what is probably (even if somewhat cumbersome) the most thorough of all the earliest explanations of the Christian faith. (Of course, those who are Origen enthusiasts may have a different view on this matter.)

In our texts we shall focus briefly on a few of the issues of importance to Irenaeus: Gnosticism, his understanding of Christ, and eschatology. In addition, we shall explore his view of evil and his rather positive understanding of the human person. This is significant, as we shall see quite a different theological anthropology coming from the experience and pen of Augustine of Hippo a couple of centuries later.

Source: The Ante-Nicene Fathers: Translations of the Fathers down to AD 325, *vol. 1, The Apostolic Fathers: Justin Martyr—Irenaeus (Grand Rapids: Eerdmans, 1885), 400, 415, 442, 448, 450, 454, 511, 521, 523, 541.*

▼ ▼ ▼

THE INCARNATION, RECAPITULATION, AND REDEMPTION

If anyone says to us "How was the Son produced by the Father?" we reply to him, that no man understands that production or generation or calling by whatever name one may describe his generation, which is in fact altogether indescribable . . . but the Father only who begat and the Son who was begotten. Since, therefore, his generation is unspeakable, those who strive to set forth generations and productions cannot be right in their minds, inasmuch as they undertake to describe things which are indescribable (II, 28, 6).

According to them [the Gnostic heretics], neither the Word nor Christ nor their Savior was made flesh. They hold that neither the Word nor the Christ ever entered this world, that the Savior never really became incarnate or suffered, but that he descended as a dove upon that Jesus who belonged to the dispensation, and then when he had proclaimed the unknown Father, he again ascended into the Pleroma. . . . Others, again, declare that Jesus was born of Joseph and Mary, and that the Christ of the upper realms, being without flesh and the capacity of suffering, descended upon him. But according to no school of the Gnostics did the Word of God become incarnate. For if anyone examines their "rules," he will find that the Word of God is represented in them all as without humanity and the capacity to suffer. Some regard his manifestation as that of a transfigured man, neither born nor incarnate. Others hold that he did not, indeed, assume the figure of a man, but as a dove descended upon Jesus who was born of Mary (III, 2, 3).

They err from the truth because their view is opposed to Him who is truly God, not knowing that His Only-begotten Word, who is always present with the human race, united and blended with his own creatures according to the Father's pleasure, and being made flesh, that he is Jesus Christ our Lord, who both suffered for us and rose on our behalf, and will come again in the glory of the Father to raise all flesh, and to manifest salvation, and to show the rule of a just judgment to all under him. Therefore, there is one God the Father, and one Christ Jesus our Lord who cometh by a universal dispensation, and sums up all things into himself. Man is in every respect the formation of God, and therefore he [Jesus Christ] *recapitulates men into himself*, the invisible becoming

visible, the incomprehensible, comprehensible, the one superior to suffering becoming subject to suffering, and the *Word becoming man*. Thus he summeth up all things in himself, that as the Word of God is supreme in heavenly and spiritual and invisible matters, he may also have the dominion in things visible and material and that by taking to himself the preeminence and constituting himself head of the Church, he may draw all things in due course unto himself (III, 16, 6).

When he [the Son of God] became incarnate and was made man, he recapitulated in himself the long history of man, summing up and giving us salvation in order that we might receive again in Christ Jesus what we had lost in Adam, that is, the *image and likeness of God* (III, 18, 1).

God recapitulated in himself the ancient formation of man, that he might kill sin, deprive death of its power and vivify man (III, 18, 7).

What then did the Lord bring at his coming? Know that he brought *all newness*, by bringing himself, who had been foretold. For this was announced, that a newness would come, to renew and give life to man (IV, 34, 1).

The thing which had perished possessed flesh and blood. For the Lord, taking dust from the earth, molded man; and it was upon his behalf that all the dispensations of the Lord's advent took place. He had himself, therefore, flesh and blood, recapitulating in himself not a certain other, but that *original handiwork of the Father*, seeking out that thing which had perished (V, 14, 2).

ANTHROPOLOGY

Everyone will allow that we are composed of a body taken from the earth, and a soul which receives the spirit from God (III, 22, 1).

This, therefore, was the [object of the] long-suffering of God, that man, passing through all things acquiring the knowledge of moral discipline, then attaining to the resurrection from the dead, learning by experience what is the source of his deliverance, may always live in a state of gratitude to the Lord, having obtained from him the gift of incorruptibility, that he might love Him the more; for "he to whom more is forgiven, loves more (Luke 7:43)" (III, 20, 2).

By this arrangement, therefore, and these harmonies, and a source of this nature, man, a created and organized being, is rendered after *the image and likeness of the uncreated God*—the Father planning everything well and giving His commands, the Son carrying these into execution and performing the work of creating, and the Spirit nourishing and increasing [what is made], but man making progress day by day, ascending towards the perfect, that is, approximating to the uncreated One. . . . Now it was necessary that man should in the first instance be created; and having been created, should receive growth; and having received growth, should be strengthened; and having been given strength, should abound; and having abounded, should recover [from the disease of sin]; and having recovered, should be glorified; and having been glorified, should see his Lord (IV, 38, 3).

If, then, you are God's workmanship, await the hand of your maker which creates everything in due time; in due time as far as you are concerned, whose creation is being carried out [*efficeris*]. Offer to Him your heart in a soft and tractable state, and preserve the form in which the Creator has fashioned you, having moisture in yourself, lest, by becoming hardened, you lose the impression of His fingers. But by preserving the framework you shall ascend to that which is perfect (IV, 39, 2).

▲ ▲ ▲

In considering the theology of Irenaeus, we should keep in mind that we are not dealing with a systematic theologian or philosopher of religion who derives all of his/her conclusions from a few spec-ulative principles. It is best to see theology and religion as a journey, as Irenaeus himself saw it, from creation to consummation.

The God of Irenaeus has existed from eternity and has created all things out of nothing. This is of the utmost importance to Irenaeus because it has great implications for both the world and for humanity. One of his main opponents, as we have noted, was the Gnostics, who were always attempting to absolve God from the responsibility of having made this material world with all of its imperfections. To accomplish this the Gnostics developed complicated theories of how the world came into existence as the result of an error in a long chain of emanations. This was also the reason why Marcion, another early Christian thinker, distinguished between the God of the Hebrew Scriptures and the God of Jesus of Nazareth. In opposition to this, Irenaeus flatly and clearly affirmed that our redeemer God is the very same as the creator God. Here one might also see the influence of the Johannine tradition (especially John 1:1-14) manifesting itself in his work. All things have been created by God, and nothing can exist against the will of God.

For Irenaeus, God has created and rules this world by means of his "two hands": the Son and the Holy Spirit. Most of the texts in which Irenaeus refers to the doctrine of the Trinity are really too brief to allow us to draw conclusions regarding that doctrine (which will become a matter of heated debate in the beginning of the fourth century). He simply bypasses the more subtle aspects of trinitarian theology and affirms, as he must have heard from his leaders in the faith, that God is Father, Son, and Spirit, without ever making specific reference to the relationship between the three. And, indeed, why should he? It was not yet an issue!

In this context, Irenaeus makes use of the doctrine of the *Logos* (Word) as well as his own metaphor of the two hands of God. Nevertheless, when he refers to the Son as "the Word of God," he is not using that term as an intermediate being between God and the world, as Justin did, for example. Rather, Irenaeus is emphasizing the unity between God and God's Word. The Son and the Holy Spirit are the way in which God chooses to relate to the world as God.

To understand Irenaeus is to understand his theory of recapitulation (*anakephalaiosis*). Although the term has a variety of meanings among ancient writers, in Irenaeus the principal and most characteristic meaning of the term is that which sees in it the very best way to express the work of Jesus Christ as the head of a *new humanity*. Even though the plan God had for redemption was in operation from the very beginning, that plan finds its greatest and final expression in the recapitulation of all things by Christ in the incarnation (that is, God entering the human sphere in the person of Jesus of Nazareth). Before that time, while it is necessary to affirm that the Son was present in the actions of God, one cannot speak of a recapitulation in the strictest sense. Recapitulation is a summary and a culmination of what has happened before, and it can be understood only within the context of those previous events.

While recapitulation is to a certain extent a new starting point, it is closely related to what went before it. Even though the incarnation is "a new beginning" in the history of the world, it is not opposed to Creation, but rather is the

continuation and fulfillment of Creation. Christ is the second Adam—the "New Being" to use Paul Tillich's phrase—and the new Creation. In Christ the history of the old Adam is repeated but now in an opposite direction. In Adam, human beings had been created to be like the Son, in Christ the *Son takes humanity to himself*. As a human, Christ is all that Adam should have been had he not succumbed to temptation. Thus in Christ the very image of God is united to humanity, and the world may be overcome.

Irenaeus does not discuss the union of the divinity and humanity in Christ as if these were two opposed natures. Rather, humanity was created to enjoy union with God, and in Christ that union achieves its highest goal. God and humanity are not seen as "two substances" or as "two natures" as they will in the great debates surrounding the Council of Chalcedon a few centuries later (451). It is rather that in Christ divinity is united to humanity because he is the Word that God addresses to humanity and is also the human person who responds to that Word. Irenaeus

My, my. I guess I do look divine tonight!

uses *dynamic* rather than substantialist concepts and language and thus avoids the difficulties that gave rise to those bitter debates from Nicea to Chalcedon and beyond. It is interesting to note that in the so-called modern era of theology, from the time of Friedrich Schleiermacher to the present, there are many theologians who have an unacknowledged debt of gratitude to this ancient theologian of Lyons for his "dynamic" insight, which is, after all, only a return to a more biblically oriented theology.

God, the triune God, creates humanity according to God's own image. Humanity itself is not the image of God, however; that image is the Son, in whom and by whom humanity has been created. "As the image of God hath He made man; and the 'image' is the Son of God, in whose image man was made" (*Ancient Christian Writers*, 16, 61). Thus the image of God is not something to be found in the human person, but rather is the direction in which we are to grow until we attain "to mature manhood, to the measure of the stature and fullness of Christ" (Eph. 4:13). This idea of growth and development is important for understanding Irenaeus. Simply stated, what he means is that Adam was not created as a perfect being in the sense that he was all that God called him to be, but rather was created so that he could develop and grow in the image of God that is the Son. The Son, in other words, becomes a "touchstone," a model, indeed an image for us all.

Irenaeus has no place in his thought for an original state in which Adam, gifted with powers far above our own, wandered around in Eden or Paradise. Rather, Adam was only the beginning of the purpose of God in Creation. Metaphorically speaking, Adam was "childlike," whose purpose was to grow to a fuller, closer, richer relationship with God. This growth is not something Adam achieves on his own, but is a part of the continuing Creation of God.

As creatures of God with the purpose of growth, human beings are free. This freedom, however, is not to be understood in idealistic terms. It is simply the possibility of fulfilling the purpose of God in our lives. Adam's freedom, and of course our freedom, is in no way incompatible with God's omnipotence; it is rather the result of it and its clearest expression.

There is an optimism here that has been generally absent in Western theology, which has been so dominated by the pessimistic views of the human person found in the thought of St. Augustine and later Calvinism. Certainly, Irenaeus's view is more compatible with modern views of progress and development found not only in the areas of process theology and philosophy, but also in developments that have taken place since the enlightenment in the so-called hard sciences. To see that we have responsibility and that God is in this process with us is both refreshing and realistic, not only from our point of view but from the point of view of God as well (if we may so speculate). For what kind of a God would desire a relationship that is based not on freedom of the will but on coercion?

The view of Irenaeus is also useful in dealing with the problem of evil. Since the world is yet in process, moving toward completion, there will be moments of difficulty, periods of despair, as there are in every good growth process. Our confidence is in the knowledge that there is One who is in ultimate control, who will eventually lead us and the Creation itself to its final completion.

John Killinger, a novelist and theologian, captures this thought very clearly in his work *Jessie: A Novel*, in which Jessie is queried by a young friend about all of the evil in the world and how a God who is loving and all-powerful allows it all to happen. Jessie, who is an artist, uses art to answer the question by pointing out that as an artist, in the midst of his or her work, must continue to work on the chaos that sometimes appears on the canvas, so also God works to bring all things to completion while at the same time allowing us to participate freely in the process.

In spite of all our human difficulties, God does not abandon humanity (or the Creation in its entirety for that matter), but loves us continually. In doing this, God is simply carrying forward the plan (like the artist) that God had conceived from the very beginning. The plan is a single one but is made clear to us in a series of particular covenantal events that culminate in Jesus, the Christ, "the express image of God."

The Significance of Irenaeus

It is not really possible to exaggerate the significance of this man Irenaeus.

Like the Gnostics he vindicated what was new in Christian thought, but unlike the Gnostics he preserved the Hebrew Scriptures and the Hebrew tradition for the church. He explained the relationship between Judaism and Christianity and indicated why the Christians were justified in retaining Jewish moral law while abandoning the ceremonial. Irenaeus saw revelation as a *process*; he read the past historically and perceived different stages in its development.

The incarnation of Jesus, in Irenaeus's view, is only the beginning of God's victory over evil and the incompleteness of the world. The life and work of Christ is part of the restoration that continues until the final consummation. After being united to humanity, the Son of God must live a human life and die a human death. He must face temptation—all human temptations. The final fulfillment that we await, when all things will be subject to him, will be Christ's last victory. For now, we who live in the period between the resurrection and the consummation are not living in a period of truce in the struggle of the centuries: We are living precisely at the time in which Christ is making his victory on the cross effective, in order to lead us to the final day.

4. TERTULLIAN (160–220)

In the early church the coast of North Africa produced many defenders of the faith, three of whom achieved theological immortality: Tertullian of Carthage, Origen of Alexandria, and Augustine of Hippo. Directly across the Mediterranean from Rome lay the ancient city of Carthage (modern Tunis) where Tertullian—one of the keenest minds and sharpest tongues in the early church—was born (ca. 160). Son of a proconsular centurion, Tertullian studied law at Rome and as a young man converted to the Christian faith. Perhaps the ramrod discipline of the father and the son's legal training conspired to make Tertullian a stern moralist and precise defender of theological orthodoxy.

Brilliant in his attacks on heretics and vices within and without the church, unsparing in his denunciation against all who departed from the true faith, utterly intolerant of any philosophical intrusion into Christianity—Tertullian was an unyielding authoritarian.

Tertullian was the first important theologian to write in Latin rather than Greek, which up to this time had been the official language of the church. Often referred to as the "Father of Latin theology," Tertullian set the course for later Western theological terminology. His scathing attacks against the Roman state, pagans, Jews, and heretics are marked by a vivid and direct literary style that explodes with puns, satire, and all kinds of devastating polemical blasts. His argument in favor of Christianity was as simple as it was clear: it was God's truth handed down by the apostles. All later doctrines were obviously false and must therefore be rooted out and destroyed.

The creed, or "Rule of Faith" (regula fidei), was the norm by which heresy was to be judged, and Christians who were tempted into other doctrines only showed that they never really believed correctly in the first place.

To guard the faith against perversions and distortions, Tertullian tried to disentangle it from every possible philosophical influence. Faith and reason are as different as day and night; theology and philosophy should not be mixed together; the church is not a Socratic Academy; Jerusalem has absolutely nothing to do with Athens. In one of his more startling paradoxes, Tertullian wrote: "The Son of God died: it is immediately credible—because it is absurd (ineptum). He was buried, and rose again: it is certain—because it is impossible (certum est quia impossible)" (On the Flesh of Christ, chapter 5).

The legal precision of Tertullian's theology and the earnestness of his moral imperative migrated down the centuries in Western thought to reappear in different ways in both Roman Catholic and Protestant faith and life. The mind of Tertullian saw everything sharply defined as white or black, true or false, right or wrong. Such a person makes a powerful advocate for the faithful and a formidable prosecutor of the unbeliever.

▼ ▼ ▼

THE PRESCRIPTIONS AGAINST THE HERETICS
1. The times we live in provoke me to remark that we ought not to be surprised either at the occurrence of the heresies, since they were foretold, or at their occasional subversion of the faith, since they occur precisely in order to prove faith by testing it (Matt. 7:15; 24:4, 11,

24; 1 Cor. 11:19). To be scandalized, as many are, by the great power of heresy is groundless and unthinking.

Fever, for example, we are not surprised to find in its appointed place among the fatal and excruciating issues which destroy human life, since it does in fact exist; and we are not surprised to find it destroying life, since that is why it exists. Similarly, if we are alarmed that heresies which have been produced in order to weaken and kill faith can actually do so, we ought first to be alarmed at their very existence. Existence and power are inseparable.

2. Faced with fever, which we know to be evil in its purpose and power, it is not surprise we feel, but loathing; and as it is not in our power to abolish it, we take what precautions we can against it. But when it comes to heresies, which bring eternal death and the heat of a keener fire with them, there are men who prefer to be surprised at their power rather than avoid it. But heresy will lose its strength if we are not surprised that it is strong. . . . Matched subsequently against a man of real strength, your victor goes off beaten. Just so, heresy draws its strength from men's weakness and has none when it meets a really strong faith.

3. Those who are surprised into admiration are not infrequently edified by the captives of heresy—edified to their downfall. Why, they ask, have so-and-so and so-and-so gone over to that party, the most faithful and wisest and most experienced members of the church? Surely such a question carries its own answer. If heresy could pervert them, they cannot be counted wise or faithful or experienced. . . . Do we test the faith by persons or persons by the faith? No one is wise, no one is faithful, no one is worthy of honor unless he is a Christian and no one is a Christian unless he perseveres to the end.

These [heresies] are human and demonic doctrines, engendered for itching ears by the ingenuity of that worldly wisdom which the Lord called foolishness, choosing the foolish things of the world to put philosophy to shame. For worldly wisdom culminates in philosophy with its rash interpretation of God's nature and purpose. It is philosophy that supplies the heresies their equipment. . . . A plague on Aristotle, who taught them dialectic, the art which destroys as much as it builds, which changes opinions like a coat, forces its conjectures, is stubborn in argument, works hard at being contentious and is a burden even to itself. For it reconsiders every point to make sure it never finishes a discussion.

7. From philosophy come those fables and endless genealogies and fruitless questions, those "words that creep like as doth a canker." To hold us back from such things the Apostle testifies expressly in his letter to the Colossians that we should beware of philosophy. "Take heed lest any man circumvent you through philosophy or vain deceit, after the tradition of men," against the providence of the Holy Spirit (1 Tim. 1:4; 2 Tim. 2:17; Col. 2:8). He had been at Athens where he had come to grips with the human wisdom which attacks and perverts truth, being itself divided up into its own swarm of heresies by the variety of its mutually antagonistic sects. What has Jerusalem to do with Athens, the Church with the Academy, the Christian with the heretic? Our principles come from the Porch (*Stoa*) of Solomon (John 10:23; Acts 5:12), who had himself taught that the Lord is to be sought in simplicity of heart. I have no use for a Stoic or a Platonic or a dialectic Christianity. After Jesus Christ we have no need of speculation, after the Gospel no need of research. When we come to believe, we have no desire to believe anything else; for we begin by believing that there is nothing else which we have to believe. . . .

9. My first principle is this. Christ laid down one definite system of truth which the world must believe without qualification, and

which we must seek precisely in order to believe it when we find it. Now you cannot search indefinitely for a single definite truth. You must seek until you find, and when you find, you must believe. Then you have simply to keep what you have come to believe, since you also believe that there is nothing else to seek, once you have found and believed what he taught who bids you seek nothing beyond what he taught. . . .

13. The Rule of Faith [apostolic tradition; creed]—to state here and now what we maintain—is of course that by which we believe that there is but one God, who is none other than the Creator of the world, who produced everything from nothing through his Word, sent forth before all things; that this Word is called his Son, and in the Name of God was seen in diverse ways by the patriarchs, was ever heard in the prophets and finally brought down by the spirit and power of God the Father into the Virgin Mary, was made flesh in her womb, was born of her and lived as Jesus Christ; who thereafter proclaimed a new law and a new promise of the kingdom of heaven, worked miracles, was crucified, on the third day rose again, was caught up into heaven and sat down at the right hand of the Father; that he sent in his place the power of the Holy Spirit to guide believers; that he will come with glory to take the saints up into the fruition of the life eternal and the heavenly promises and to judge the wicked to everlasting fire, after the resurrection of both good and evil with the restoration of their flesh.

This Rule, taught (as will be proved) by Christ, allows of no questions among us, except those which heresies introduce and which make heretics.

14. Provided the essence of the Rule is not disturbed, you may seek and discuss as much as you like. You may give full rein to your itching curiosity where any point seems unsettled and ambiguous or dark and obscure.

▲ ▲ ▲

Tertullian was not a speculative theologian. In general he followed the thought of the Apologists, Irenaeus of Lyons, and to some degree the tradition of Asia Minor and not quite as much of Stoicism and legal conceptions. Everything he touched, however, he formulated with the clarity of a trained judicial mind and gave precision to many previously vague theological ideas.

Tertullian saw the Christian faith as divine foolishness, wiser than the most sophisticated philosophical speculations of human beings, and in no way to be reconciled with existing philosophical systems (see *De Praescriptione,* 7). In reality, Tertullian looked at Christianity principally through the spectacles of Stoicism. Christianity is primarily knowledge of God. It is based on reason and authority, which is seated in the church alone and only in the "orthodox" church, which solely possesses the truth, expressed in the creed, and alone has the right to use the Scriptures. Like Irenaeus before him, Tertullian saw "true" churches as the ones in agreement with the faith of the apostles, wherein the apostolic tradition has been maintained by episcopal succession. Like Justin and gentile Christianity of the second century, Tertullian identified Christianity as a new law. "Jesus Christ . . . preached the new law and the new promise of the kingdom of heaven" (*De Praescriptione,* 13).

Tertullian also had a deeper sense of sin than any other Christian writer since Paul, and his teachings greatly influenced the development of the conceptions of sin and grace in the Latin church. Though it was not fully developed, Tertullian possessed a doctrine of original sin. "There is, then, besides the evil which supervenes on the soul from the intervention of the evil spirit, antecedent, and in a certain sense a natural evil, which arises from its corrupt origin" (*De Anima*, 41). Nevertheless, "the power of grace is more potent than nature" (*De Anima*, 21). The nature of this grace is nowhere explained, but it evidently included not only the forgiveness of sins, but the grace of divine inspiration, by which the power to do right is infused into the feeble but free human will. This seems to be a legacy of his Stoicism. Though redemption is based on grace, human beings have much to do. Although God forgives previous sins at baptism, satisfaction for those that follow must be made by voluntary sacrifices. The more a person punishes her/himself, then the less God will punish.

Tertullian's most significant work was his *Logos Christology*, although he preferred the designation Son rather than *Logos*. While he may have done little to advance what had been presented by the Apologists and other early leaders, his legal mind gave some clarity to its explanation. He defines the Godhead in terms almost anticipating the Nicene Creed. "All are one, by unity of substance; while the mystery of the dispensation is still guarded which distributes the unity into a Trinity, placing in their order the three, the Father, the Son and the Holy Spirit; three, however . . . not in substance but in form; not in power but in appearance, for they are one of one substance and one essence and one power, inasmuch as He is one God from whom these degrees and forms and aspects are reckoned under the names of the Father, the Son and the Holy Spirit" (*Against Praxes*, 2). He describes then three distinctions of the Godhead as "persona" (*Against Praxes*, 12), meaning by person not our understanding of the word, that is, in the sense of personalities, but objective modes of being. For Tertullian this unity of substance is material, for he was Stoic enough to hold that "God is a body . . . for spirit has a bodily substance of its own kind" (*Against Praxes,* 7). Similarly, Tertullian distinguished between the human and divine in Jesus Christ. "We see his double state, not intermixed, but conjoined in one person, Jesus, God and man" (*Against Praxes*, 27). "Since both Son and Spirit are derived from the Father, in other words, emanate from the Father, both are subordinate to Him" (*Against Praxes,* 7, 9). This subordination doctrine, already seen in the Apologists, was characteristic of the pre-Nicene, pre-Chalcedonian periods.

Tertullian himself broke with the Roman church around 200. He was attracted to the puritanism of Montanism, an otherworldly, ascetic movement, and founded a sect of his own.

Ingredients: Oil, vinegar, water, hydrogenated Aristotle, lecithin of Tertullian, essence of Plato, and cream of Martyr.

5. ORIGEN OF ALEXANDRIA (185–254)

In majestic terms Dante Aligheri described a panoramic view of human destiny that he called a "comedy." Posterity has added the term *divine*. This combined title suggests several things:

1. It is a drama with one pervading plot;
2. In contrast to tragedy, which ends in disaster, this action moves to a serene ending;
3. And finally, while focusing on human beings, it is more than that limited scope. In fact it is God's great interaction with humanity, in which the divine cause is at stake.

As we view the stage on which the drama unfolds or is enacted, we observe that it is not a one-storied plane, but rather multi-leveled—hell, earth, heaven—through which the action moves up and down, as does the journey of Dante himself.

This cosmic spiritual drama can be traced back to the early stages of the Christian era. During the first centuries there burst forth—partly inspired by the general philosophical climate of the age, partly by the Christian message—a surprising efflorescence of bold visionary and speculative constructions of the total scheme of things, many Christian at least in name, others pagan, all of them reaching for an ultimate truth by which humanity could understand its own con-

dition and goal. These speculations with their ever-shifting versions of the cosmic drama of redemption were followed in the third century by the more rigorously constructed systems of the mythology of Mani and the philosophy of Plotinus.

Standing in grand style among these early system builders was Origen of Alexandria, perhaps the very first systematic theologian of the early Christian era. Following the Gnostics of the second century and preceding Plotinus (ca. 204–270) and Mani (ca. 216–275) slightly, Origen was a defender of orthodoxy and by rational temperament and ecclesiastical discipline in no way inclined toward heretical fancies of the gnostic varieties. Yet when it came to his own attempt at integrating scriptural revelation with independent reason and intuition into a coherent and persuasive whole that meant to embrace the totality of things, all of his care could not prevent him from producing a system that the later church would find necessary to condemn.

In his epoch-making work, *On First Principles [peri archon/de Principiis],* we see an explicit attempt to rally philosophical support for theology—the first such in the history of Christian thought. This *First Principles* sought to unite Greek philosophy with Christian thought without subordinating either to the other. Origen was neither a nineteenth-century Idealist ranking religion below philosophy nor a twentieth-century theologian, such as Karl Barth, vowing to use philosophy only on the rare occasion necessary and, for the rest, keeping it at a distance.

Origen demonstrated, throughout the course of his enormous production and with notable ease and competence, his fundamental conviction that Christianity meshed with many ideas from contemporary philosophy. Gregory Thaumaturgus (that is, the "wonderworker"), an ardent admirer of Origen, demonstrates the exacting formation in Greek philosophy that Origen demanded of his students in his work *Panegyric*.

Sources: Origen: On First Principles, translated by G. W. Butterworth (New York: Harper and Row, 1966), 2, 9–10, 52, 56–57, 70, 76, 125–26, 134, 251, 313, 326.

▼ ▼ ▼

ON GOD

The kind of doctrines which are believed in plain terms through the apostolic teaching are the following: First, God is One, who created and set in order all things, and who, when nothing existed, caused the universe to be. . . . [Preface, 4]

[God is] a simple intellectual existence, admitting of himself no addition whatever, so that he cannot be believed to have in himself a more or less, but *is unity, or if I may say so Oneness throughout.*

[God is] the fount from which originates all intellectual existence or mind . . . the first principle of all things. . . . [I,1,6]

ON THE HOMOOUSION OF ALL MINDS

All rational creatures, that is: the Father, Son, and the Holy Spirit, all angels, authorities, dominions, and other powers, and even man himself in virtue of his soul's dignity are of one substance. [III, 4, note 1]

Every rational creature can, in the process of passing from one order to another, travel through each order to all the rest and from all to each, while undergoing the various movements of progress or reverse in accordance with its own actions and endeavors and with the use of its power of free will. [I, 6, 3]

[These] different movements (i.e. of the rational natures) result in the creation of different worlds, and after this world in which we live there will arise another world quite unlike it. [III, 5, note 6]

[The demons] themselves and the rulers of the darkness in any world or worlds, if they desire to turn to better things, become men and so revert to their original condition, in order to be disciplined by the punishments and torments which they endure for a long or short period while in the bodies of men they may in time reach the exalted rank of angels. [I, 6, note 4]

All rational beings existed as minds bodiless and immaterial without any number or name, so that they all formed a unity by reason of the identity of their essence and power and activity and by their union with and knowledge of the Word of God. [II, 8, 3]

They were seized with weariness of the divine love and contemplation and turned toward the worse. [II, 8, 3]

Now since the world is so varied and comprises so great a diversity of rational beings, what else can we assign as the cause of existence except the diversity in the fall of those who decline from unity in dissimilar ways? [II, 1, 1]

This was the cause of diversity among rational creatures, a cause that takes its origin not from the will or judgment of the Creator, but from the decision of the creature's own freedom. . . . And these were also the reasons which gave rise to the diversity of the world. [II, 9, 6]

ON THE DEVIL

Our contention is, however, that among all rational creatures there is none which is not capable of both good and evil . . . not even the devil himself was incapable of good. [I, 8, 3]

[The devil and a host of kindred minds] of their own fault have departed from holiness and descended to such a pitch of negligence as to be changed into opposing powers. [I, 5, note 1]

The devil was not created as such, but he fell to this state as a result of his own wickedness. [I, 8, 3; Greek fragment]

[After] many ages and the one restoration of all things, Gabriel will be in the same state as the devil, Paul as Caiaphas, and virgins as prostitutes. [I, 6, note 1]

[The contrary powers:] even an archangel may become a devil as on the other hand the devil may turn again into an angel. [I, 6, 3]

ON THE APOKATASTASIS
[THE RESTORATION OF ALL THINGS]

Out of all the original unity of rational beings one mind (at the time of the general fall) remained steadfast in the divine love and contemplation, and he, having become Christ and king of all rational beings, created all bodily nature. [II, 8, note 3]

[Now this mind] because he pitied the various falls that had happened to those who originally belonged to the same unity, and wished to restore them, went through all modes of being and was invested with different kinds of bodies and took different names, becoming all things to all, being changed into an angel among angels, into a power among powers, and into other ranks or species of rational beings according to the necessities of each particular case, and then at last shared in flesh and blood like us and became a man among men. [IV, 4, note 1]

[Even the kingship of Christ will one time come to an end;] one day he will lose his kingship. [III, 6, note 3]

All beings are equal and each, even the devil will be restored to his ancient rank . . . and Jesus will then together with the devil be reigned over by God. [III, 5, note 1]

The heavenly powers and all men and the devil and the spiritual hosts of wickedness are as unchangeably united to the Word of God as the mind itself which is called Christ and which was in the form of God and emptied himself; and there will be an end to the Kingdom of God. All rational beings will form one unity, hypostases and numbers alike being destroyed; and knowledge of rational truth will be accompanied by a dissolution of the worlds, an abandonment of bodies and an abolition of names; and there will be an identity of the knowledge as well as of the hypostases; and in the state of restoration only the bare minds will exist. The life of the spiritual [minds] will be the same as it formerly was, when they had not yet descended or fallen, so that the beginning is the same as the end, and the end is measure of the beginning. [III, 6, note 3]

▲ ▲ ▲

For Origen of Alexandria the divine One, which is "Unity Absolute," stands at the peak of the scale of being, devoid of all diversity in its own essence. Considered purely by itself, the Godhead is "One," "Simple," "Unity," or "Oneness." Moreover, God is "mind or even beyond mind and being," and at least for human thought—incomprehensible. Only God, as Father (in traditional terms), is uncreated. The obvious implication of this insight is that it suggests that the other two hypostases or persons of the traditional Godhead are creatures. God is never alone, however. Even as God is primordial mind, God is the source of all intellectual existence; in other words, God is the first principle of all things. In this creative process or procreative role, God is likened to the sun, with its rays emanating forth from it—a simile widely used in Origen's time. This lends an aspect of natural necessity to divine creativity—whose Creation, therefore, at least in its original form, must be "eternal Creation"—as distinct from the biblical simile of the free fiat by a purposeful maker and shaper of things, which issues in a temporally unique act. Adhering to his principle, Origen derives the Trinity from this creativity of God by whose radiance it is generated and sustained, as an aura is generated and sustained by a source of light.

The immediate splendor of God is the Son. As Origen puts it, "the only-begotten Son is the brightness of this light proceeding from God without separation; as brightness from light and enlightening the whole Creation" (*On First Principles,* Book I, 2, 7). Radiating from this first brightness and mediated by it, the Holy Spirit subsists as God's brightness at a second remove. Both realities or hypostases, as they are traditionally called, are *creations*, but they are creations from eternity as the light simile implies: eternal radiances of the eternal light (cf. *On First Principles,* I, 3, 3 and I, 2, 11). But perhaps even more significant than the dogmatically delicate points of createdness within the Trinity is the subordinationism that the light simile imparts into the *internal relations of the Trinity* establishing a very clear *vertical, linear, descending order of divine natures* that accords well with the vertical structure of reality. Origen's view reveals the dominating influence of Neoplatonic philosophy and echoes many of the thoughts contained in the writings of the secular philosopher Plotinus in his work *Enneads.* In Origen's day this was less a problem than it would be about a cen-tury later in the Arian crisis, when the co-equality of the Son with the Father was demanded for purposes of achieving redemption.

Origen suggests to us that before all Creation God was surrounded by a "world" of pure rational beings or natures whose primary characteristic or essence was that of being "free" or "rational." This was the goal of God's creativity. Everything that comes into existence does so out of the initiative of these "free, rational beings." For Origen they are all equal and free because within God's Self nothing existed that could give rise to diversity. Here we may see reflections or shadows of the influence of Middle Platonism and Neoplatonism in the thought of the great Alexandrine. Origen also suggests that only a certain number of these natures exist, basically a number that the divine essence would be able to control. This implies that Origen believed in divine finitude.

A question that arises is this: "How did the spirits or minds begin to move?" To put it simply: into this realm of blessed tranquility and continued enjoyment of God, movement entered through the freedom of the will with which the minds were endowed. And since they were in union with God, the only movement that could occur would be movement away from God. Origen is almost tantalizing in his indication of motive at this critical point. They were simply seized with weariness of divine love and contemplation and turned toward the worse. In other words, they grew tired of too good a situation.

There is also a neat play on words in this context, for when Origen speaks of a turning away, he speaks of a "cooling" of love's ardor, and we are in consequence called souls. The Greek word for "cooling" is *psychros*, while the Greek word for soul is *psyche*. Thus the conception of the human soul is that it is a deteriorated, lessened, cooled off condition of "original mind."

Given the initial equality of all rational Creation combined with the absolute freedom of the will, there had to be one who, in the exercise of that freedom, was the first to turn away from God and in its continued exercise moved farthest away. To that being we attribute the name of the devil or Satan for as long as that being occupies that place and role in the hierarchy of beings. Rehabilitation is open to that being, however, as it is to any other being, and indeed in some other world cycle another may take that being's place. In the thought of Origen there is no eternal principle of evil opposing the goodness of God.

In Origen we see two fundamental ideas at work: (1) that diversity as such (subjects being of this kind or that) is a faulty condition—a defect brought about by themselves in the first place— and a condition that remains a function of their own will throughout their career; and (2) the complementary notion that the deed of differentiation— that is, these distinctions—can be undone, and that its undoing *is the final goal*. This is the central principle of Origen's theological system.

Origen's teaching on Satan or the devil is truly indicative of the radicalism of his thought. The devil belonged to the same unity of minds as all rational creatures. But the devil and a host of minds due to the exercise of their free will "descended to such a pitch of negligence" that they were changed into opposing powers. It is easily the greatest triumph of the absoluteness of the will that it can lead to the extreme opposite of the original unity, while at the same time *retaining its essential nature*, namely, its freedom for good and evil. As a result, it also retains the freedom to restore itself to its original state. So the devil and those of the devil's ilk can rise again to the highest level, and the ultimate consummation includes the restoration of the devil, who will be redeemed along with the Christ in the restored unity of all minds.

One may ask what role the Christ plays in all of this for Origen. Origen's peculiar Christology, which lies almost entirely outside the doctrine of the Trinity, connected only by the most slender

Life Is Hell

of threads, is perhaps the most offensive of Origen's theological opinions for those of an orthodox position. Issues of Christology and universal restoration were central to Origen's condemnation in the fifth and sixth centuries.

The main point is that the Christ is not the *Logos*, that is, not the second person of the Trinity, but rather that Christ is a rational creature who is called "mind" in the sense that only Christ preserved his original status unimpaired while the others were forfeiting theirs through their defection, in other words through their fall. It was neither predictable which of the equally endowed minds would remain faithful on that occasion, nor predictable which will remain so in coming and ever new beginnings. Therefore, it appears that Christ is no less an exchangeable figure than the devil; Christ is Christ because he happens to be the non-fallen mind of the time. He too exemplifies the general principle of the equality of all natures combined with the limitless mutability of the will—the principle that admits no unique individual figures, thus no real proper names, into the system but knows only role and rank designations.

Pursuing this yet further, we find that through the steadfastly maintained knowledge of God the "One," this mind was made Christ; in particular he has before all ages been so intimately united with God the Word (the second person of the Trinity) that "by a misuse of language" this too is called "Christ," whereas the name genuinely pertains to the mind thus clinging to him. This mind pitied our situation and so goes through all modes of being; it was invested with different kinds of bodies—changed into everything from angel to human being—for the redemption of all. Of such a role the divine *Logos* was incapable because of its immutability (unchangeability).

In general terms, the role and function of the Christ is to help fallen minds, by instruction and by example, to find their way back. The doctrine of his suffering many times in many different spheres and forms means that the uniqueness of his one appearance, on which the message of the New Testament grounds itself, somehow dissolves into the universality of a process in which "Christ" is a function rather than a unique event.

Finally, in view of all this it is not surprising to have it made known that even the kingdom of Christ will one time come to an end. The kingdom will end since it is just the aim of Christ's mission that in the end, when all beings are again equal to each other as they were in the beginning, even the devil will be restored to his ancient rank.

Today it might seem as if we have nothing in common with Origen and the people of his age. We certainly do not share their metaphysics, nor do contemporary biblical scholars utilize his allegorical method of scriptural interpretation to any large degree. At the same time, we should be aware that some two thousand years from now those who look at the work we do will likely have similar reactions to those we have to Origen and his colleagues. This should give us some pause, at least, in our criticism of the great Alexandrine.

6. Arius (250–330) and the Arian Controversy

Arius was a presbyter in the Alexandrine church. He had been a follower of the teachings of Lucian of Antioch, who, advocating the more radical views of Origen of Alexandria, viewed Jesus Christ as subordinate to rather than equal with the Father. Subordinationism was contrary to the teaching of Arius's bishop, Alexander, who, while also an Origenist, did not follow the more radical views of the great Alexandrine teacher and theologian. Arius apparently possessed impressive leadership skills and gifts and used them to attack the position held by his bishop.

Arius taught that the Word, the *Logos,* was radically different from the Father. Arius was an absolute monotheist, as may be seen quite easily in his letter to Eusebius of Nicomedia. "And before he was begotten or created or appointed or established, he did not exist; for he was not unbegotten." In the logic of Arius, the Son cannot be without a beginning, for then he would be a brother of the Father and not a Son. Therefore, the Son has a beginning, and he was created out of nothing by the Father. Before that creation the Son did not exist, and it is inappropriate, inaccurate, and incorrect to affirm that God is eternally Father.

Arius does not mean to suggest that there was not always a *Word/Logos* in God, that is, an immanent reason. But Arius makes a distinction between this immanent *Logos/Word/Reason* and the *Son,* who was later created. In this sense when anyone suggests the Son is the Wisdom or the Word of God, this is only correct on the basis of that distinction between the Word that always was or always exists, as God's reason, and the

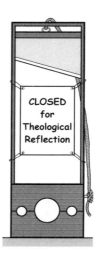

other Word that is "the first-born of all creation" (Col. 1:15). Even though all things were made by him, he himself was created by the Father and is consequently a creature and not strictly speaking God. This is essential Arianism and the point that, when clearly expounded and understood, created havoc among many Christians of his day. The Savior is not God, but a creature. Certainly it raised the proverbial "hair on the neck" of Athanasius (see chapter 7), who became his chief opponent.

In defense of Arius it can be argued, and it was argued, that his position was not without historical precedent. It appears certainly in Christian thought wherever the Word is interpreted in a Platonic sense, as a "craftsperson" or "demiurge," that exists between a divinity that is immutable and a world that is filled with change and diversity. As we have already pointed out, Justin Martyr, almost two centuries earlier, had argued that the Word was "another god," a "second god"; this argument, in view of

Christian monotheism, would imply that the Word was God only in a relative sense. Furthermore, there is biblical support for the view of Arius in the letter to the Colossians, traditionally attributed to the apostle Paul, and so strictly speaking the idea was hardly new.

Source: Documents of the Christian Church, *edited by Henry Bettenson (Oxford: Oxford University Press, 1961), 54–56.*

▼ ▼ ▼

THE LETTER OF ARIUS TO EUSEBIUS, BISHOP OF NICOMEDIA (CA. 321)

To his dearest lord, the man of God, faithful and orthodox, Eusebius, Arius, unjustly persecuted by Pope Alexander on account of that all-conquering truth which you also champion, sends greeting in the Lord.

Since my father Ammonius is going into Nicomedia, I thought it my duty to salute you by him, and at the same time to advise that naturally charitable disposition of yours, which you display toward the brethren for the sake of God and his Christ, how grievously the bishop attacks and persecutes us, and comes full tilt against us, so that he drives us from the city as atheists because we do not concur with him when he publicly preaches. "God always, the Son always; at the same time the Father, at the same time the Son; the Son not born-by-begetting; neither by thought nor by any moment of time does God precede the Son; God always, Son always, the Son exists from God himself."

Eusebius, your brother Bishop of Caesarea, Theodotus, Paulinus, Athanasius, Gregory, Aetius, and all the other bishops of the East, have been condemned for saying that God existed, without beginning, before the Son; except Philogonius, Hellanicus, and Macarius, men who are heretics and unlearned in the faith; some of whom say that the Son is an effluence, others a projection, others that he is co-unbegotten.

To these impieties we cannot even listen, even though the heretics threaten us with a thousand deaths. But what we say and think we both have taught and continue to teach; that the Son is not unbegotten, nor any part of the unbegotten in any way, nor is he derived from any substance; but that by his own will and counsel he existed before times and ages fully God, only-begotten, unchangeable. And before he was begotten or created or appointed or established, he did not exist; for he was not unbegotten. We are persecuted here because we say that the Son has a beginning, but God is without beginning. For that reason we are persecuted, and because we say that he is from what is not. And this we say because he is neither part of God nor derived from any substance. For this we are persecuted; the rest you know.

I trust that your are strong in the Lord, mindful of our afflictions, a true-fellow disciple of Lucian, Eusebius.

THE SO-CALLED ARIAN SYLLOGISM (FROM A FIFTH-CENTURY ACCOUNT)

After Peter, Bishop of Alexandria, who was martyred under Diocletian, Achillas succeeded to the see, and after Achillas, Alexander succeeded in the above-mentioned period of peace. He, by his fearless conduct of affairs, welded the church together. On one occasion, at a gathering of his presbyters and the rest of the clergy, he essayed a rather ambitious theological disquisition on the Holy Trinity, a metaphysical explanation of the Unity in Trinity. But one of the presbyters of his diocese, Arius by name, a man not lacking in dialectic, thinking the bishop was expounding the doctrine of Sabellius the Libyan, from love of controversy espoused a view diametrically opposed to the teaching of the Libyan, and attacked the statements of the bishop with energy. "If," said he, "the Father begat the Son, he that was begotten had a beginning of existence; hence it is clear that there was [a time] when the Son was not *(en hote ouk en)*. It follows then of necessity that he had his existence from the non-existent."

▲ ▲ ▲

In 325 the Christian church formally and officially adopted a "doctrinal" or "dogmatic" definition initiating a new path in its history. The doctrine formulated at that crossroad, called the Council of Nicea, is the formal doctrine of the Trinity. To a very large extent, Arius is responsible for precipitating this specific doctrinal statement and for the way in which doctrine would be formulated in the future.

Arius preached the theology of his mentor, Lucian of Antioch—basically an "adoptionist" view that God raised up the man Jesus of Nazareth to be Son of God not by nature but by this adoption. This was combined with Arius's unique view of the *Logos*/Word incarnate, which was a word that was not identical with the divine *Logos* (or Reason). By propounding this viewpoint, Arius came into conflict with his bishop Alexander, who was a staunch defender of the deity of Christ.

Arius was more a rationalist than a mystic, and his primary interests were intellectual rather than religious. In some ways his view is a foreshadowing of the conflicts over faith versus reason in more recent centuries. God, Arius argued, is *one* both in substance and in person. God's nature is indivisible and therefore cannot be shared by any other being. For Arius, God is self-existent and eternal. Therefore everything else has been created out of nothing and had its beginning in time. Consequently the Son is not eternal; on the contrary, the Son was created in time by an act of God's will.

The significance of this position is clear. God is immutable, eternally perfect; the Son is subject to change and advances in wisdom and in knowledge. The essence of the Son is his own and is identical with neither God nor humans. The firstborn of all creatures (Col. 1:15ff.), the Son belongs to a higher order of being than any other creature whether angelic or human. The Son became incarnate in Jesus Christ, was born of a virgin,

Theology with Punch

but did not take a human soul. The soul of Christ was the *Logos;* only Christ's body was human. All that Christ did and suffered was done and suffered by the *Logos.* Arius's way of preserving monotheism appeared to impugn the divine character and status Christians had long affirmed in Jesus.

It is interesting to note here how different Arius's view is from that of Ignatius of Antioch and Irenaeus of Lyons, for example. There was no union of divine with human substance effected by the incarnation. There was no deification such as we find in Irenaeus. The most that Christ could do to redeem humanity was to announce the divine judgment and thus lead humanity to repentance and obedience.

7. ATHANASIUS (295–373)

Unlike Origen of Alexandria, Athanasius was not a "scientific theologian"; unlike Justin Martyr, he was not a philosopher of religion. In the words of J. K. Mozley, speaking of Athanasius's famous treatise on the incarnation, Athanasius's works are rather paeans of victory, hymns singing the praises of religion, and in this specific case, the Christian faith. Athanasius does not contribute much, therefore, by way of speculation; he does not develop any system of theology, nor does he invent new terminology. Yet, at the same time, Athanasius is one of the most significant personalities in the history of doctrine in the fourth century.

Perhaps Athanasius's greatest merit, or his greatest contribution to Christian theology, was his defense of the faith against the radical Hellenization of the faith in the person of Arius and his followers. His primary focus and purpose were to substantiate the faith that was given from the very beginning by the apostles and that had been maintained by the leaders of the early Christian community. Against the rationalists he established the priority of faith over reason (not unlike Karl Barth and other neoorthodox thinkers of the twentieth century). Reason cannot be the sole judge in metaphysical matters.

When Athanasius did make use of philosophy (with which he was quite familiar), he did so to unfold and clarify the teachings of the church and not to penetrate the divine essence with human reason. Athanasius knew how to separate Greek thought from Christian revelation whenever there was a danger that the truth of the faith was threatened. In his giving priority to faith we can anticipate the thought of the great medieval thinker St. Anselm of Canterbury and his most noted theological principle, *fides quarens intellectum* (faith seeking understanding). In these texts we find Athanasius trying to articulate (against Arius) a way in which all that is affirmed of Jesus Christ (and the Spirit) can be reconciled with classical Greek notions of the unity and eternity of God.

Source: Johannes Quasten, Patrology, *vol. 3 (Utrecht/Antwerp, Neth.: Spectrum Publishers, 1963), 66–67, 69–70, 71–72.*

▼ ▼ ▼

ON GOD AND TRINITY

The Letter to Serapion

There is then a Triad, holy and complete, confessed to be God in Father, Son, and Holy Spirit, having nothing foreign or external mixed with it, not composed of one that creates and one that is originated, but all creative; and it is consistent and in nature indivisible, and its activity is one. The Father does all things through the Word and in the Holy Spirit. Thus the unity of the Holy Triad is preserved. Thus one God is preached in the church "who is over all" (Eph. 4:6), and through all, and in all—over all as Father, as beginning, as fountain; "through all," through the Word; "in all," in the Holy Spirit. It is a Triad not only in name and form of speech, but in truth and actuality. For as the Father is he that is, so also his Word is one that is and God over all. And the Holy Spirit is not without actual existence, but exists and has true being. Less than these [Persons] the Catholic church does not hold, lest she sink to the level of the modern Jews, imitators of Caiaphas, and to the level of Sabellius. Nor does she add to them by speculation, lest she be carried into the polytheism of the heathen.

Contra Arianos

If they shall assign the toil of making all things as the reason why God made the Son only, the whole creation will cry out against them as saying unworthy things of God; and Isaiah too who said in Scripture "the Everlasting God, the Lord, the Creator of the ends of the earth, fainteth not, neither is weary; there is not searching of his understanding" (Isa. 40:28). And if God made the Son alone, as not deigning to make the rest, but committed them to the Son as an assistant, this on the other hand is unworthy of God, for in him there is no pride. Nay the Lord reproves the thought, when he says, "Are not two sparrows sold for a farthing?" and "one of them shall not fall on the

ground without your Father that is in heaven" (Matt. 10:29). . . . If then it be not unworthy of God to exercise his providence, even down to things so small, a hair of the head, and a sparrow, and the grass of the field, also it was not unworthy of him to make them. For what things are the subjects of his providence, of those he is maker through his proper Word (2, 25).

For they are one, not as one thing divided into two parts, and these nothing but one, nor as one thing twice named, so that the same becomes at one time Father, at another His own Son, for holding this Sabellius was judged a heretic. But they are two, because the Father is Father and is *not* also Son, and the Son is Son and *not* also Father; but the nature *(physis)* is one; (for the offspring is not unlike its parent for it is his image), and all that is the Father's is the Son's (2,25).

The Synodical Letter

For only to say "like according to essence" *(homoios kat' ousian)*, is very far from signifying "of the essence" *(ek tes ousias)*, by which . . . the genuineness of the Son to the Father is signified. Thus tin is only like to silver, a wolf to a dog, and gilt brass to true metal; but tins is not from silver, nor could a wolf be accounted the offspring of a dog. But since they say that he is "of the essence" and "like-in-essence," what do they signify by these but consubstantial? For while to say only "like-in-essence" does not necessarily convey "of the essence," on the contrary, to say "consubstantial," is to signify the meaning of both terms, "like-in-essence" and "of the essence." And, accordingly, they, the semi-Arians themselves, in controversy with those who say that the Word is a creature, instead of allowing him to be a genuine Son, have taken their proofs against them from human illustrations of son and father, with this exception that God is not as man, nor the generation of the Son as an issue of man, but such as may be ascribed to God, and is fit for us to think. Thus they have called the Father the Fount of Wisdom and Life and the Son the Radiance of the Eternal Light, and the Off-spring from the Fountain, as he says, "I am the Life," and "I Wisdom dwell with Prudence" (John 14:6; Prov. 8:12). But the Radiance from the Light and Offspring from the Fountain, and Son from Father, how can these be so fitly expressed as by "consubstantial."

REDEMPTION

On the Incarnation

9. The Word, perceiving that no otherwise could the corruption of men be undone save by death as a necessary condition, while it was impossible for the Word to suffer death, being immortal, and Son of the Father; to this end he takes himself a body capable of death, that it, by partaking of the Word who is above all, might be worthy to die instead of all, and might because of the Word which was come to dwell in it, remain incorruptible, and that henceforth corruption might be stayed from all by the grace of the resurrection. . . . For being over all, the Word of God naturally by offering his own temple and corporeal instrument for the life of all satisfied the debt by his death. And thus, he, the incorruptible Son of God, being conjoined with all by a like nature, natu-rally clothed all with incorruption by the promise of the resurrection.

54. He was made man that we might be made God *{theopoiethomen}* and he manifested himself by a body that we might receive the idea of the Unseen Father; and he endured the inso-lence of men that we might inherit immortality.

The Synodical Letter

51. By partaking of him, we partake of the Father; because the Word is the Father's own. Whence, if he was himself too from participa-tion, and not from the Father his essential Godhead and Image, he would not deify being

deified himself. For it is not possible that he, who merely possesses from participation, should impart of that partaking to others, since what he has is not his own, but the Giver's; and what he has received, is barely the grace suffi-cient for himself.

CHRISTOLOGY

For just as he is Word of God, so afterwards "the Word was made flesh"; and while "in the beginning was the Word," the Virgin at the consummation of the ages conceived, and the Lord has become man. And he who is indicated by both statements is one person, for "the Word was made flesh." But the expressions used about his Godhead, and his becoming man, are to be interpreted with discrimination and suitably to the particular context. And he that writes of the human attributes of the Word also knows what concerns his Godhead; and he who expounds concerning his Godhead is not ignorant of what belongs to his coming in the flesh: but discerning each as a skilled and "approved money-changer," he will walk in the straight way of piety; when therefore he speaks of his weeping, he knows that the Lord, having become man, while he exhibits his human char-acter in weeping, as God raised up Lazarus; and he knows that he used to hunger and thirst phys-ically, while divinely he fed thousands of persons from five loaves; and knows that while a human body lay in the tomb, it was raised as God's body by the Word himself (*de sent. Dion.,* 9).

Being Son of God in truth, he became also Son of Man, and being God's only-begotten Son, he became at the same time "firstborn among many brethren." Wherefore neither was there one Son of God before Abraham, another after Abraham: nor was there one that raised up Lazarus, another that asked concerning him; but the same it was that said as man, "Where does Lazarus lie?" (John 11:34), and as God raised him up: the same that as man and in the body spat, but divinely as Son of God opened the eyes of the man blind from his birth; and while, as Peter says (1 Pet. 4:1), in the flesh he suffered, as God he opened the tomb and raised the dead (*Tom. ad Ant.*, 7).

The Savior had not a body without a soul *{ou soma apyschon}*, not without sense or intelligence; for it was not possible, when the Lord had become man for us, that his body should be without intelligence: nor was the salvation effected in the Word himself of the body only, but also of the soul (*Tom. ad Ant.*, 7).

We do not worship a creature. Far be the thought. For such an error belongs to the heathen and Arians. But we worship the Lord of creation, incarnate, the Word of God. For if the flesh also is in itself a part of the created world, yet it has become God's body. And we neither divide the body, being such, from the Word, and worship it by itself, nor when we wish to worship the Word do we set him far apart from the flesh, but knowing, as we said above, that "the Word was made flesh," we recognize him as God also, after having come in the flesh. Who is so senseless as to say to the Lord: "Leave the Body that I may worship Thee" (*Ep. ad Adelph.*, 3).

The Word was not impaired in receiving a body, that he should seek to receive a grace, but rather he deified that which he had put on, and more than that, gave it graciously to the race of man (*Or. Arian.*, I, 42).

▲ ▲ ▲

God and the Trinity

Athanasius's understanding of the Godhead shows the balance and fine perception that make him one of the greatest theologians of all time. God is, for him, transcendent, and yet this is not to be interpreted in such a way that God cannot enter into direct contact with God's creatures. Even though God exists above and beyond the world, God has established a direct relationship with the world in the work of creation itself. This understanding of the relationship of God to the world is significant, for it is no longer necessary to posit the Word as an *intermediate* being between God and the world. Those who posit the *absolute* transcendence of God make the Word

God on the Lookout

into a subordinate being, that is, a subordinate deity, serving as an intermediary between God and the World. This subordination is one of the consequences of the interaction of the Christian faith with Greek philosophy, especially Platonism, which Athanasius is addressing. In other areas, such as his understanding of the immortality of the human soul, he himself mirrors the very same Platonism.

This God is also Triune, for God exists as Father and as Son and as Holy Spirit. Athanasius's insistence on the divinity of the Son was one of the major factors that led to the defeat of one of the most significant heresies in Christian history, namely, Arianism. Athanasius devoted his full attention to the relationship between the Father and the Son in his struggle against Arianism. This preoccupation with the relationship between the Father and the Son pushed any discussion of the Holy Spirit into the background. It simply was not an issue at the time. When a group known as the Pneumatomachians arose accepting the divinity of the Son but denying the divinity of the Spirit, however, Athanasius developed his doctrine on this point and affirmed the divinity of the Spirit as well. This doctrine was one of the additions to the Niceno-Constantinopolitan Creed of 381.

Athanasius never developed any fixed terminology for his trinitarian thought, although he was aware of the need for such terminology. This project was left for later thinkers such as the great Cappadocians. Without Athanasius one might suggest that the work of the Cappadocians would have been impossible, and without the Cappadocians the work of Athanasius would have been incomplete.

Redemption

Two fundamental issues occupied the mind of Athanasius: (1) monotheism and (2) redemption or salvation. To him they were issues of vital significance both before, during, and after the Arian crisis.

For Athanasius the redemption of which human beings are in need is continuous with creation, for it is in fact a re-creation of fallen humanity. God, who is a loving God, in creating human beings did not create them to return to nothingness. To avoid this, God created humans according to God's own image, so that being a participant in the Word/*Logos* would also be a participation in being and reason. Thus, although humans are by nature mortal beings, in their very creation they have received the gift of immortality that would be retained as long as they duly reflected the image according to which they had been made.

Of course, humans did not cooperate in their continued reflection of the image of God and have been prisoners of death ever since this failure. As a result sin is not simply a mistake or a debt that needs to be repaid; it is not even that humans have forgotten the way and need to be reminded—in other words, receive a restoration of knowledge (perhaps in the fashion of the Gnostics). On the contrary, sin has disrupted the very integrity of creation by introducing an element of disintegration that leads human beings toward destruction. The only way possible to rectify this is by a new work of creation.

The solution is clear, and it becomes the core of the doctrine of redemption in Athanasius. Only God can redeem humankind. If the redemption we need is really a new creation, only God the

Creator can bring it to us. Furthermore, as the immortality we have lost consisted of existence according to the image of God and was therefore an existence similar to that of God, the salvation we need now is a kind of divinization. This requires that the Redeemer be God, for only God can grant an existence similar to God's own. In the *Treatise on the Incarnation,* Athanasius reflects the thought of Irenaeus on this point when he writes, "For He was made man that we might be made God." This is a position very typical of early Eastern Christian thought.

The Christology Texts

As far as the relationship between the Word/*Logos* and the human nature of Jesus Christ is concerned, the Christology of Athanasius is typically Alexandrine. In this regard he is somewhat similar to his major opponent, Arius. That is, they both interpret the union of that Word/*Logos* in a similar way. For Athanasius, the Word is united to the flesh (and the Johannine tradition with its familiar emphasis on the Word becoming flesh is a favorite of Athanasius and most other Alexandrines, if not all). However, in making this claim, one never finds a clear affirmation that the term *flesh* had to do with both the body and the soul. It seems that Athanasius takes for granted that in Jesus there was no human rational soul, and the Word/*Logos* took the place of that soul. This is the doctrine of Apollinaris of Laodicea and was condemned at the Council of Constantinople in 381. Although he does not seem to be aware of it, Athanasius's interpretation of the person of Christ does not agree with his

own concerns over redemption. Later, in addressing this issue principally against Apollinaris, who was originally a close colleague and friend of Athanasius, the Cappadocians would point out that the Word/*Logos* took human nature in order to free it from sin, and since the soul is involved in this dilemma, the Word/*Logos* must also have taken a soul in order to save it as well. This is their famous "therapeutic" argument: that which has been assumed has been healed; hence body, soul, and mind must all be assumed in order to provide the complete base for the redemption of humankind.

When Athanasius discusses the unity between the two natures (the divine and human), he does so again in typical Alexandrine fashion. In the union the divinity becomes the subject of all the actions of Christ. It is an unbreakable unity. In the incarnation of Christ, the flesh becomes the instrument of the Word/*Logos.* That which is properly said of one of the terms of the union may be transferred to the other. This is the doctrine usually referred to as the "communication of properties" *(communicatio idiomata).* It is therefore proper to worship the man Jesus, although worship properly belongs to God alone.

It is from this understanding that another issue will arise. For in this way of thinking Mary is the God-Bearer *(theotokos* in the Greek) or Mother of God *(mater dei* in the Latin). Athanasius believes that this title is to be given to Mary as a clear consequence of the indivisible union between divinity and humanity in Jesus Christ and because of his understanding of the communication of these properties one to the other. To deny Mary this would be to deny that God was born of Mary and that in turn would be a denial of the incarnation of the Word/*Logos,* according to Athanasius (and all other traditional Alexandrines, as we shall see later).

Conclusions

Athanasius is significant for his contributions to the development of the doctrine of the Trinity at Nicea, for his treatment of the question of the *Logos,* or who Jesus Christ is, from a principally religious perspective, and for his formidable opposition to the theology of Arius.

Although Athanasius may not have been a great speculative thinker, he had a lucid and direct mind and the unique ability to distinguish the essential from the non-essential and get to the heart of the matter under discussion. Moreover, he had profound religious convictions that he felt distinguished Christianity from all other religions the world had known and that he believed to be threatened by Arius and his followers.

To Athanasius the incarnation was central. This was the theme of one of his earliest essays and recurs in his work over and over again. Athanasius had an incarnational understanding of redemption, unlike the cosmological interests of a great many Alexandrine thinkers such as Origen. Not creation, but redemption was all important to Athanasius. And redemption to him *demanded* the incarnation. Only as God became human could a union between God and humanity be accomplished and thus secure our redemption.

In Jesus Christ there was not incarnate some subordinate divine being. In Jesus Christ there was incarnate the very *nature of God.* Although the divine nature is One and indivisible, it is eternally shared by both the Father and the Son. Furthermore, it was the Son and not the Father who became incarnate in Christ. Untroubled by the philosophical tribulations and logical issues that confronted people like Justin Martyr, Origen, and many others, for Athanasius the incarnation of the Son, who was of the same nature as the Father, was as effective as even the incarnation of the Father could have been.

We should notice here that the mystery of the doctrine of the Trinity, as held by Athanasius, lay not in the possession of a common divine nature by the Father, the Son, and the Holy Spirit. The mystery lay rather in the claim that the Father, Son, and the Holy Spirit each possesses the *whole* divine nature and that though equally God and equally self-existent with the Father, the Son and the Holy Spirit are subordinate to the Father. This subordination is hardly more than verbal for Athanasius.

The doctrine of redemption as interpreted by Athanasius is principally and primarily a religious phenomenon. It was based upon the recognition of the need for human redemption, and the essence of it was the deity of Jesus Christ. His view contained a philosophical element, but this was of secondary importance. Athanasius's quarrel was not with those who denied or minimized the distinction between the Father and the Son, but with those who denied the deity of Jesus Christ. For him, to deny the deity of Jesus Christ was tantamount to denying the very first and foremost purpose of the incarnation, which is redemption.

8. THE ECUMENICAL COUNCILS AND CREEDS (325–451)

As we have indicated, the subordinationism in the teaching of Arius was not without historical and even biblical support. Nor was the response of Alexander, bishop of Alexandria, unexpected. The radical Hellenism of Arius was not acceptable to Alexander, and so he convened a synod in Egypt, consisting of almost one hundred bishops who condemned and deposed Arius.

Not to be out-maneuvered, Arius appealed to his "fellow Lucianists" (Lucian of Antioch), gaining their support for his position. Especially significant was the support of the influential bishop of Nicomedia, Eusebius. Eusebius granted Arius support over the vehement objections of the Alexandrines, thereby causing the theological dispute that became the schism or break that appears in the history of theology whenever and wherever the issues of trinitarianism and Christology are discussed.

Emperor Constantine, although granting Christianity favored status, was still a politician—one who perceived Christianity as the "cohesive force" that would hold his empire together. His task was not easy, however. He had just dealt with another schism, Donatism, on the Western North African continent—a dispute over the validity or invalidity of the sacraments, especially the sacrament of Baptism. This new split in the East, with its complex theological fine points, caused him great concern. In light of this he dispatched his religious advisor, Hosius of Cordova, to resolve the controversy in as peaceful a manner as possible. Hosius advised the emperor that the issues at stake in this controversy were much too intricate and complex to be so easily reconciled. Constantine had little choice, and so he convened a council of bishops who were to deal with the problems raised by the teaching of this presbyter from Alexandria, that is, Arius.

Hosius Can You See . . . ?

The council called by Constantine, now known as the First Ecumenical Council, met in Nicea in Bythinia in 325 with more than three hundred bishops from vast regions of the church in attendance. Given the history of persecution in the church, this first council was considered by many of those in attendance, a number of whom had experienced persecution firsthand, to be somewhat of a miracle. We should not be so naive, however, as to credit the emperor with noble theological concerns for the church. Rather, Constantine was certainly far more interested in the "unity of his empire" than in the "unity of God." The problems and issues raised by Arius were having a disruptive impact on the empire. They were divisive, and Constantine sought to find a solution that would be acceptable to the greatest number of bishops possible, thereby securing stability for him in his realm.

Truly, then, for Constantine this was really a "political" assembly, even though for the bishops present, at least those who understood what the issues were, it was of extreme religious or theological significance. Ultimately the question of the validity and the surety of human redemption was at stake, for if the Christ was not in some way *substantially* equal with God the Father, then would we sinful human beings in fact be redeemed? This is a question that would repeat itself over and over again in the history of theology.

Source: Documents of the Christian Church, *edited by Henry Bettenson (Oxford: Oxford University Press, 1961), 34–38, 72–73.*

▼ ▼ ▼

THE CREED OF CAESAREA (EUSEBIUS'S CREED)

We believe in one God, the Father All Governing *{pantokratora}*, Creator *{poieten}* of everything visible and invisible.

And in one Lord Jesus Christ, the Word [*Logos*] of God, God from God, Light from Light, Life from Life, the only-begotten Son, the first born of all creation, begotten of the Father before all time *{pro panton aionon}*, by whom also everything came into being, who for our salvation became incarnate and lived among men. He suffered, and rose the third day, and ascended to the Father, and will come again in glory to judge the living and the dead.

We believe also in the Holy Spirit.

THE CREED OF NICEA (325)

We believe in one God, the Father All Governing *{pantokratora}*, Creator *{poieten}* of all things visible and invisible.

And in one Lord Jesus Christ, the Son of God, begotten of the Father as only begotten, that is, from the essence [reality] of the Father *{ek tes ousias tou patros}*, God from God, Light from Light, true God from true God, begotten not created *{poiethenta}*, of the same essence [reality] as the Father *{homoousion tou patri}*, through whom all things came into being, both in heaven and in earth; who for us men and for our salvation came down and was incarnate, becoming human *{enanthropesanta}*. He suffered and the third day he rose, and ascended into the heavens. And he will come again to judge both the living and the dead.

And [we believe] in the Holy Spirit.

But those who say, once he was not, or he was not before his generation, or he came to be out of nothing *{ex ouk onton}*, or who assert that he, the Son of God, is of a different *hypostasis* or *ousia,* or that he is a creature, or changeable, or mutable, the catholic and apostolic church anathematizes them.

THE CONSTANTINOPOLITAN CREED (381)

We believe in one God, the Father All Governing {pantokratora}, Creator {poieten} of heaven and earth, all things visible and invisible;

And in one Lord Jesus Christ, the only begotten Son of God, begotten from the Father before all time {pro panton ton aionon}, Light from Light, true God from true God, begotten not created {poiethenta}, of the same essence [reality] as the Father {homoousion to patri}, through whom all things came into being, who for us men and because of our salvation came down from heaven, and was incarnate by the Holy Spirit and the Virgin Mary and became human {enanthropesanta}. He was crucified for us under Pontius Pilate, and suffered and was buried, and rose on the third day, according to the Scriptures, and ascended to heaven and sits on the right hand of the Father, and will come again in glory to judge the living and the dead. His Kingdom shall have no end {telos}.

And in the Holy Spirit, the Lord and life-giver, who proceeds from the Father, who is worshipped and glorified together with the Father and Son, who spoke through the prophets; and in one, holy Catholic, and Apostolic Church. We confess one baptism for the remission of sins. We look forward to the resurrection of the dead and the life of the world to come.

THE DEFINITION OF CHALCEDON (451)

Therefore, following the holy fathers, we all with one accord teach men to acknowledge one and the same Son, our Lord Jesus Christ, at once complete in Godhead and complete in manhood, truly God and truly man, consisting also of a reasonable soul and body; of one substance {homoousios} with the Father as regards his Godhead, and at the same time of one substance with us as regards his manhood; like us in all respects, apart from sin; as regards his Godhead, begotten of the Father before all the ages, but as regards his manhood begotten, for us men and for our salvation, of Mary the Virgin, the God-bearer {Theotokos}; one and the same Christ, Son, Lord, only-begotten, recognized in two natures, without confusion, without change, without division, without separation; the distinction in no way annulled by the union, but rather the characteristics of each nature being preserved and coming together to form one person, and subsistence {hypostasis}, not as parted or separated into two persons, but one and the same Son and only-begotten God, the Word, Lord Jesus Christ; even as the prophets from earliest times spoke of him, and our Lord Jesus Christ himself taught us, and the creed of the Fathers has handed down to us.

▲ ▲ ▲

The position of Arius presented before the Council was very clear and straight to the point: *before Christ was begotten, he simply did not exist* and therefore logically is a creature, albeit a very special creature, but yet a *creature*. Arius's famous syllogism was recorded for all time by the historian Socrates:

If the Father begat the Son, he that was begotten *had a beginning of existence;* hence it is clear that there was when he was not *[en hote ouk en]*. It follows then *of necessity* that he had his existence from the non-existent. [emphasis added]

Such an audacious statement with its serious implication for redemption scandalized the bishops who were present, and they responded by attempting to produce a document, based in Scripture, that would declare without reservation, without exception, that the Son *is not a creature*. But, as we well know, biblical texts are subject to multiple interpretations, and the Arian supporters were certainly not lacking in skill to present theirs. Furthermore, the Arians could always point to the Letter to the Colossians for definitive support wherein we read that:

> [Son:] . . . in whom we have redemption, the forgiveness of sins. He is the image of the invisible God, the *firstborn of all creation:* for in him all things in heaven and on earth were created. . . . (Col. 1:14-15)

In light of all these confusions and difficulties, Emperor Constantine (perhaps at the suggestion of his religious advisor, Hosius) intervened and suggested the word *homoousios* be used in the creed in order to make certain the conviction of the divinity of the Son. Taking this suggestion into account, a group of anti-Arians were asked to write a statement of faith, the result of which is the first Ecumenical Creed of the Church, the Creed of Nicea (325).

The significance of this creed is found in the anathemas attached to the end of the document and the following clauses:
1. that is, from the substance of Father *[ek tes ousias tou patros]*, and
2. true God from true God, begotten not created, of one substance *[homoousios]* with the Father.

Clearly this creed leaves no room for Arianism, which was soundly condemned as being heretical.

The creedal development that took place at Nicea in 325 and continued through the councils that were held in Constantinople in 381 and Chalcedon in 451 issued in new tests for orthodoxy in belief and were to be authoritative for the entire church. These creeds, although subject to continued controversy even in their own day, are still major documents in theological discussion today.

There were indications of this type of development earlier; it was not the total invention of Nicea. For example, the regional council held at Antioch in 268 had prepared statements of belief, and local creeds had been regarded as containing the Christian faith as well. Nicea was considerably different, however. The issues raised by Arius that the Word/*Logos* was a creature, that the Word/*Logos* was created/made by God, and that the Word/*Logos* had a beginning had serious implications for the Christian faith. Simply put, these views of Arius and his followers meant that in Jesus Christ, humanity was not really confronted by God, at least according to the leaders of Nicea. As we have seen above in the texts themselves, the Nicene Council insisted God had fully come into human history in Jesus Christ. This was made absolutely clear in the phrase cited: "of one substance [reality] with the Father *[homousion to patri]*."

Theologically, the assertion that the Word/*Logos* is less than equal with God in substance (reality) undermined the Christian community's faith and conviction about the finality of Christ. The claim that the Word/*Logos* was less than God left open the possibility that another more like God might appear. In this case, Christianity would then only be one more religion among others. If God is incarnate in Jesus Christ, however, then we have the definitive word. Nothing more needs to be said!

The Niceno-Constantinopolitan Creed of 381 is essentially Nicene, that is, the same as the Creed of 325. It goes beyond Nicea in that it amplifies the position of the church with respect to the Holy Spirit, but does so in biblical/doxological language rather than with the philosophical invention *homoousios*. The clause "who is worshipped and glorified together with the Father and Son" leaves no doubt as to the authentic deity of the Holy Spirit.

This creed, which is widely used in liturgy, such as in the Roman Catholic Church, may have developed precisely in that context. It was employed early on as a baptismal creed and by the sixth century was used in conjunction with the celebration of the Eucharist as well. Moreover, it did not have the same difficulties attached to it as did the term *homoousios*, the philosophical term used at Nicea to accomplish the same task with respect to the person of Jesus Christ in his relation to God.

9. AUGUSTINE OF HIPPO (354–430)

By any standard, Augustine of Hippo is one of the greatest theologians, if not *the* greatest, of the early church. He is far superior to his contemporaries and towers over even the great company of Apologists. He is perhaps only rivaled by Origen of Alexandria, whose greatness is dampened by his being twice condemned.

Looking back through history, we can see Augustine's link with the great Apostle Paul; if we look forward, he is the architect of theology in the Western world, both Roman Catholic and Protestant. In a sense he appears to stand with one foot in the age of the great thinkers of the early church while his other foot is poised to enter the medieval world.

Defender of the faith, scholar, preacher, teacher, administrator—Augustine was all of these and more. Coming out of paganism and encircled with the prayers of his beloved mother, Monica, Augustine ran through a succession of philosophies and religious experiments. Augustine was always searching for the truth and was fundamentally unsatisfied in his early explorations. While studying first in Rome and later in Milan, Augustine was finally converted to Christianity (an answer to his mother's prayers?).

Augustine describes this experience himself in his *Confessions* in what some have argued is one of the most dramatic conversions to the faith since that of the Apostle Paul on the road to Damascus. Ultimately appointed bishop of Hippo Regius, a harbor city several miles west of the famous city of Carthage, Augustine consolidated the church against schismatic groups and set up a clerical training center that was famous throughout the Roman world.

Augustine's work is comprehensive. He was drawn into almost every conceivable theological and ecclesiastical dispute possible, and when challenged he used his pen like a sword, cutting through all sorts of opposition with decisiveness. Toward the close of his life he wrote a review of his own work (the *Retractiones*) and found there were 232 works on all sorts of subjects and issues. Less dogmatic than his predecessor Tertullian, he was also less speculative than Origen. Not so systematic in his work and frequently laborious in his style, he practically always wrote in response to some specific issue at hand, yet he also produced two of the greatest systematic theological treatises, *The City of God* and *The Trinity*.

Selecting a few passages from his massive collection is a difficult task, but we have included here some from *Confessions*, including his famous prayer and his account of a youthful prank, from *Enchiridion*, and from *The City of God*. These works include his summary of doctrine, an autobiographical account of his conversion, and his speculative discussion of time and eternity. In *The City of God* Augustine defended Christians against the charge that their betrayal of the Roman gods was the cause for the downfall of Rome. As in many of his writings, in this treatise he also digresses into many related subjects, such as foreknowledge and free will, the mediatorial role of Christ, the relation of this world to other possible worlds, and the nature of the church in a world in which we encounter both good and evil.

Augustine is one of a handful of philosopher-theologians through whom we must pass if we are to gain an understanding of the nature and development of the Christian faith.

Sources: The Confessions, *translated by A. Outler (Library of Christian Classics, vol. VII; Philadelphia: Westminster Press, 1955), 31ff., 50ff., 175ff.; "The City of God" and "Admonition and Grace" in* Writings of St. Augustine, *translated by Demetrius Zema, John Courtney Murray, et al. (The Fathers of the Church series; Washington, D.C.: Catholic University of America Press, 1950), 245ff., 262ff.*

▼ ▼ ▼

THE RESTLESS HEART

I.1.1. "Great art thou, O Lord, and greatly to be praised; great is thy power, and infinite is thy wisdom" (Ps. 145:3). And man desires to praise thee, for he is a part of thy creation; he bears his mortality about with him and carries the evidence of his sin and proof that thou dost resist the proud. Still he desires to praise thee, this man who is only a small part of thy creation. Thou hast prompted him, that he should delight to praise thee, for thou hast made us for thyself and restless is our heart until it comes to rest in thee. Grant me, O Lord, to know and understand whether first to invoke thee or to praise thee; whether first to know thee or call upon thee. But who can invoke thee, knowing thee not? For who knows thee not may invoke thee as another than thou art. It may be that we should invoke thee in order that we may come to know thee. But "how shall they call on him in whom they have not believed? Or how shall they believe without a preacher?" (Rom. 10:14). Now, "they shall praise the Lord who seek him" (Ps. 22:26), for "those who seek shall find him" (Matt. 7:7), and finding him, shall praise him. I will seek thee, O Lord, and call upon thee. I call upon thee, O Lord, in my faith which thou hast given me, which thou hast inspired in me through the ministry of thy preacher [Bishop Ambrose of Milan].

I.5.5. Who shall bring me to rest in thee? Who will send thee into my heart so to overwhelm it that my sins shall be blotted out and I may embrace thee, my only good? What art thou to me? Have mercy that I may speak. What am I to thee that thou shouldst command me to love them, and if I do not, art angry and threatenest vast misery? Is it, then, a trifling sorrow not to love thee? It is not so to me. Tell me, by thy mercy, O Lord, my God, what art thou to me? "Say to my soul, I am your salvation" (Ps. 35:3). So speak that I may hear. Behold, the ears of my heart are before thee, O Lord; open them and "say to my soul, I am your salvation." I will hasten after that voice, and I will lay hold upon thee. Hide not thy face from me. Even if I die, let me see thy face, lest I die.

I.5.6. The house of my soul is too narrow for thee to come in to me; let it be enlarged by thee. It is in ruins; do thou restore it. There is much about it which must offend thy eyes; I confess and know it. But who will cleanse it? Or, to whom shall I cry but to thee? "Cleanse thou me from my secret faults," O Lord, "and keep back thy servant from strange sins" (Ps. 19:12, 13). "I believe, and therefore do I speak" (Ps. 116:10). But thou, O Lord, thou knowest. Have I not confessed my transgressions unto thee, O my God; and hast thou not put away the iniquity of my heart? I do not contend in judgment with thee, who art Truth itself; and I would not deceive myself, lest my iniquity lie even to itself. I do not, therefore, contend in judgment with thee, for "if thou, Lord, shouldst mark iniquities, O Lord, who shall stand?" (Ps. 130:3).

I.15.24. Hear my prayer, O Lord; let not my soul faint under thy discipline, nor let me faint in confessing unto thee thy mercies, whereby thou hast saved me from all my most wicked ways till thou shouldst become sweet to me beyond all the allurements that I used to follow. Let me come to love thee wholly, and grasp thy hand with my whole heart that thou mayest deliver me from every temptation, even unto the last. And thus, O Lord, my King and my God, may all things useful that I learned as a boy now be offered in thy service—let it be that for thy service I now speak and write and reckon. For when I was learning vain things, thou didst impose thy discipline upon me; and thou hast forgiven me my sin of delighting in those vanities.

EARLY FASCINATIONS WITH SIN

II.1.1. I wish now to review in memory my past wickedness and the carnal corruptions of my soul—not because I still love them, but that I may love thee, O my God.

II.2.2. But what was it that delighted me save to love and to be loved? Still I did not keep the moderate way of the love mind to mind— the bright path of friendship. Instead, the mists of passion stemmed up out of the puddly concupiscence of the flesh, and the hot imagination of puberty, and they so obscured and overcast my heart that I was unable to distinguish pure affection from unholy desire. Both boiled confusedly within me, and dragged my unstable youth down over the cliffs of unchaste desires and plunged me into a gulf of infamy. Thy anger had come upon me, and I knew it not. I had been deafened by the clanking of the chains of my mortality, the punishment for my soul's pride, and I wandered farther from thee, and thou didst permit me to do so. I was tossed to and fro, and wasted, and poured out, and I boiled over in my fornications—and yet thou didst hold thy peace, O my tardy Joy! Thou didst still hold thy peace, and I wandered still farther from thee into more and yet more barren fields and restless lassitude.

II.2.3. If only there had been someone to regulate my disorder and turn to my profit the fleeting beauties of the things around me, and to fix a bound to their sweetness, so that the tides of my youth might have spent themselves upon the shore of marriage? They might have been tranquilized and satisfied with having children, as thy law prescribes, O Lord—O thou who dost form the offspring of our death and art able also with a tender hand to blunt the thorns which were excluded from thy paradise! For thy omnipotence is not far from us even when we are far from thee. Now, on the other hand, I might have given more vigilant heed to the voice from the clouds: "Nevertheless, such shall have trouble in the flesh, but I spare you" (1 Cor. 7:28), and, "It is good for a man not to touch a woman" (1 Cor. 7:1), and "He that is unmarried cares for the things that belong to the Lord, how he may please the Lord; but he that is married cares for the things that are of the world, how he may please his wife" (1 Cor. 7:32, 33). I should have listened more attentively to these words, and thus having been "made a eunuch for the Kingdom of

Heaven's sake" (Matt. 19:12), I would have with greater happiness expected thy embraces.

II.2.4. But, fool that I was, I foamed in my wickedness as the sea and, forsaking thee, followed the rushing of my own tide, and burst out of all thy bounds. But I did not escape thy scourges. For what mortal can do so? Thou wast always by me, mercifully angry and flavoring all my unlawful pleasures with bitter discontent, in order that I might seek pleasures free from discontent. But where could I find such pleasure save in thee, O Lord—save in thee, who dost teach us by sorrow, who woundest us to heal us, and dost kill us that we may not die apart from thee. Where was I, and how far was I exiled from the delights of thy house, in the sixteenth year of the age of my flesh, when the madness of lust held full sway in me—that madness which grants indulgence to human shamelessness, even though it is forbidden by thy laws—and I gave myself entirely to it? Meanwhile, my family took no care to save me from ruin by marriage, for their sole care was that I should learn how to make a powerful speech and become a persuasive orator.

II.3.5. Now, in that year my studies were interrupted. I had come back from Madaura, a neighboring city where I had gone to study grammar and rhetoric; and the money for a further term at Carthage was being got together for me. This project was more a matter of my father's ambition than of his means, for he was only a poor citizen of Tagaste.

To whom am I narrating all this? Not to thee, O my God, but to my own kind in thy presence—to that small part of the human race who may chance to come upon these writings. And to what end? That I and all who read them may understand what depths there are from which we are to cry unto thee. For what is more surely heard in thy ear than a confessing heart and a faithful life? . . .

II.3.6. During that sixteenth year of my age, I lived with my parents, having a holiday from school for a time—this idleness imposed upon me by my parents' straitened finances. The thornbushes of lust grew rank about my head, and there was no hand to root them out. Indeed, when my father saw me one day at the baths and perceiving that I was becoming a man, and showing signs of adolescence, he joyfully told my mother about it as if already looking forward to grandchildren, rejoicing in that sort of inebriation in which the world so often forgets thee, its Creator, and falls in love with thy creature instead of thee—the inebriation of that invisible wine of the perverted will which turns and bows down to infamy. But in my mother's breast thou hadst already begun to build thy temple and the foundation of thy holy habitation—whereas my father was only a catechumen, and that but recently. She was, therefore, startled with a holy fear and trembling: for though I had not yet been baptized, she feared those crooked ways in which they walk who turn their backs to thee and not their faces.

II.3.7. Woe is me! Do I dare affirm that thou didst hold thy peace, O my God, while I wandered farther away from thee? Didst thou really then hold thy peace? Then whose words were they but thine which by my mother, thy faithful handmaid, thou didst pour into my ears? None of them, however, sank into my heart to make me do anything. She deplored and, as I remember, warned me privately with great solicitude, "not to commit fornication; but above all things never to defile another man's wife." These appeared to me but womanish counsels, which I would have blushed to obey. Yet they were from thee, and I knew it not. I thought that thou wast silent and that it was only she who spoke. Yet it was through her that thou didst not keep silence toward me; and in rejecting her counsel I was rejecting thee—I, her son, "the son of thy handmaid, thy servant" (Ps. 116:16). But I did not realize this, and rushed on headlong with such blindness that, among my friends, I was ashamed to be less shameless than they, when I heard them boasting of their disgraceful exploits—yes, and glorifying all the more the worse their baseness was. What is wrong, I took pleasure in such exploits, not for the pleasure's sake only but mostly for the praise. What is worthy of vituperation except vice itself? Yet I made myself out worse than I was, in order that I might not go lacking for praise. And when in anything I had not sinned as the worst ones in the group, I would still say that I had done what I had not done, in order not to appear contemptible because I was more innocent that they; and not to drop in their esteem because I was more chaste.

CONFESSIONS AND ENCHIRIDION
"Tolle, Lege; Tolle, Lege"

VIII.12.28 Now when deep reflection had drawn up out of the secret depths of my soul all my misery and had heaped it up before the sight of my heart, there arose a mighty storm, accompanied by a mighty rain of tears. That I might give way fully to my tears and lamentations, I stole away from Alypius, for it seemed to me that solitude was more appropriate for the business of weeping. I went far enough away that I could feel that even his presence was no restraint upon me. This was the way I felt at the time, and he realized it. I suppose I had said something before I started up and he noticed that the sound of my voice was choked with weeping. And so he stayed alone, where we had been sitting together, greatly astonished. I flung myself down under a fig tree—how I know not—and gave a free course to my tears. The streams of my eyes gushed out an acceptable sacrifice to thee. And, not indeed in these words, but to this effect, I cried unto thee: "And Thou, O Lord, how long? How long? Wilt thou be angry forever? Oh, remember not against us our former iniquities" (Ps. 6:3; 79:8). For I felt that I was still enthralled

by them. I sent up these sorrowful cries: "How long, how long? Tomorrow and tomorrow? Why not now? Why not this very hour make an end to my uncleanness?"

VIII.12.29 I was saying these things and weeping in the most bitter contrition of my heart, when suddenly I heard the voice of a boy or girl—I know not which—coming from the neighboring house, chanting over and over again, "Pick it up, read it; pick it up, read it." {*Tolle, Lege; Tolle, Lege.*} Immediately I ceased weeping and began in earnest to think whether it was usual for children in some kind of game to sing such a song, but I could not remember ever having heard the like. So, damming the torrent of my tears, I got to my feet, for I could not but think that this was a divine command to open the Bible and read the first passage I should light upon. For I had heard how Anthony, accidentally coming into church while the gospel was being read, received the admonition as if what was read had been addressed to him: "Go and sell what you have and give it to the poor and you shall have treasure in heaven; and come and follow me" (Matt. 19:21). By such an oracle he was forthwith converted to thee.

So, I quickly returned to the bench where Alypius was sitting, for there I had put down the apostle's book when I had left there. I snatched it up, opened it, and in silence read the paragraph on which my eyes first fell: "Not in rioting and drunkenness, not in chambering and wantonness, not in strife and envying, but put on the Lord Jesus Christ, and make no provision for the flesh to fulfill the lusts thereof" (Rom. 13:13). I wanted to read no further, nor did I need to. For instantly, as the sentence ended, there was infused in my heart something like the light of full certainty and all the gloom of doubt vanished away.

VIII.12.30 Closing the book, then, and putting my finger or something else for a mark, I began—now with a tranquil countenance—to tell it all to Alypius. And he in turn disclosed to me what had been going on in himself, of which I knew nothing. He asked to see what I had read. I showed him, and he looked on even further than I had read. I had not known what followed. But indeed it was this, "Him that is weak in the faith, receive" (Rom. 14:1). This he applied to himself, and told me so. By these words of warning he was strengthened, and by exercising his good resolution and purpose—all very much in keeping with his character, in which, in these respects, he was always far different and better than I—he joined me in full commitment without any restless hesitation.

Then we went in to my mother, and told her what happened, to her great joy. We explained to her how it had occurred—and she leaped for joy triumphant; and she blessed thee, who are "able to do exceeding abundantly above all that we ask or think" (Phil. 3:20). For she saw that thou hadst granted her far more than she had ever asked for in all her pitiful and doleful lamentations. For thou didst so convert me to thee that I sought neither wife nor any other of this world's hopes, but set my feet on that rule of faith which so many years before thou hadst showed her in her dream about me. And so thou didst turn her grief into gladness more plentiful than she had ventured to desire, and dearer and purer than the desire she used to cherish of having grandchildren of my flesh.

FOREKNOWLEDGE AND FREE WILL

V.10. If by necessity we mean one that is in no way in our power, but which has its way even when our will is opposed to it, as is the case with the necessity to die, then, our choices of living well or ill obviously are not subject to this kind of necessity. The fact is that we do many things which we would most certainly not do if we did not choose to do them. The most obvious case is our willing itself. For, if we will, there is an act of willing; there is none if we do not want one. We would certainly not make a choice if we did not choose to make it. On the other hand, if we take necessity to mean that in virtue of which something must be so and so or must happen in such and such a way, I do not see that we should be afraid of such necessity taking away our freedom of will. We do not put the life of God and the foreknowledge of God under any necessity when we say that God must live an eternal life and must know all things. Neither do we lessen his power when we say that he cannot die or be deceived. This is the kind of inability which, if removed, would make God less powerful than he is. God is rightly called omnipotent, even though he is unable to die and be deceived. We call him omnipotent because he does whatever he wills to do and suffers nothing that he does not will to suffer. He would not, of course, be omnipotent, if he had to suffer anything against his will. It is precisely because he is omnipotent that for him some things are impossible.

So with us, when we say we *must* choose freely when we choose at all, what we say is true; yet, we do not subject free choice to any necessity which destroys our liberty. Our choices, therefore, are our own, and they effect, whenever we choose to act, something that would not happen if we had not chosen. Even when a person suffers against his will from the will of others, there is a voluntary act—not, indeed, of the person who suffers. However, a human will prevails—although the power which permits this is God's. (For, wherever there is a mere will without power to carry out what it chooses, it would be impeded by a stronger will. Even so, there would be no will in such a condition unless there were a will, and not merely the will of another but the will of the one choosing, even though he is unable to carry out his choice.) Therefore, whatever a man has to suffer against his will is not to be attributed to the choices of man or of angers or of any created spirit, but to God's choice who gives to wills whatever power they have.

It does not follow, therefore, that there is no power in our will because God foreknew what was to be the choice in our will. He who had this foreknowledge had some foreknowledge. Furthermore, if God foresaw not nothing, but something, it follows then that there is a power in our will, even though God foresaw it.

The conclusion is that we are by no means under compulsion to abandon free choice in favor of divine foreknowledge, nor need we deny—God forbid!—that God knows the future, as a condition for holding free choice. We accept both. As Christians and philosophers, we profess both—foreknowledge, as a part of our faith; free choice, as a condition of responsible living. It is hard to live right if one's faith in God is wrong.

Far be it from us, then, to deny, in the interest of our freedom, the foreknowledge of God by whose power we are—or are to be—free. It follows, too, that laws are not in vain, nor scoldings and encouragements, nor praise and blame. He foresaw that such things should be. Such things have as much value as he foresaw they would have. So, too, prayers are useful in obtaining these favors which God foresaw he would bestow on those who should pray for them. There was justice in instituting rewards and punishments for good and wicked deeds. For, no one sins because God foreknew that he would sin. In fact, the very reason why a man is undoubtedly responsible for his own sin, when he sins, is because he whose foreknowledge cannot be deceived foresaw, not the man's fate or fortune or what not, but that the man himself would be responsible for his own sin. No man sins unless it is his choice to sin; and his choice not to sin, that, too, God foresaw.

GRACE, FREE WILL, PREDESTINATION

I.2. The Lord Himself not only shows us the evil we are to avoid and all the good we are to do (which is all that the letter of the law can do), but also helps us to avoid evil and to do good—things that are impossible without the spirit of grace. If grace is lacking, the law is there simply to make culprits and to slay; for this reason, the Apostle said: "The letter killeth, the spirit giveth life" (2 Cor. 3:6). He, therefore, who uses the law according to the law learns from it good and evil, and, trusting not in his own strength, has recourse to grace, which enables him to avoid evil and to do good. But when has a man recourse to grace, except when the steps of a man are directed by the Lord and he delighteth in His way? Therefore, even the desire for the help of grace is itself the beginning of grace; about it he said: "And I said: Now have I begun; this is a change due to the right hand of the Most High" (Ps. 76:11).

It must, therefore, be admitted that we have a free will to do both evil and good; but, in doing evil, one is free of justice and the slave of sin; on the other hand, in the matter of good no one is free unless he be freed by him who said: "If the Son makes you free, you will be free indeed" (John 8:36). Not, however, as if one no longer needed the help of his liberator, once he has been freed from the domination of sin; rather, hearing from God: "Without me you can do nothing" (John 15:5), one must say: "Be thou my helper, forsake me not" (Ps. 26:9). I am happy to have found this faith in our brother Florus; it is indubitably the true, prophetic, apostolic, and Catholic faith.

II.3. This is the right understanding of the grace of God through Jesus Christ our Lord, by which alone men are freed from evil, and without which they do no good whatsoever, either in thought, or in will and love, or in action; not only do men know by its showing what they are to do, but by its power they do with love what they know is to be done.

II.4. Accordingly, let no one deceive himself saying, "Why are we preached to, and given commandments, in order to have us avoid evil and do good, if it is not we ourselves who do these things, but God who effects in us the will and the deed?" Let them rather grasp the fact that, if they are the sons of God, they are acted on by the Spirit of God in order that they may do what ought to be done, and when they have done it, give thanks to him by whom they did it; for they are acted on, in order that they may act, not in order that they may have nothing to do. And to this end it is shown them what they ought to do, in order that, when they do it as it ought to be done—that is, with love and delight in justice—they may rejoice in the experience of the sweetness which the Lord gave, that their earth might bring forth its fruit. On the other hand, when they fail to act, either by doing nothing at all, or by not acting out of charity, let them pray to receive what they do not yet have. For what will they have, except what they shall receive? And what have they, except what they have received? (1 Cor. 4:7).

VII.13. As for those who by the bounty of divine grace are singled out of that original body of the lost {massa perditionis}, (Rom. 9:21), there is no doubt that the opportunity to hear the Gospel is arranged for them; and, when they hear, they believe, and persevere unto the end in the faith which worketh by charity; and if ever they go off the track, they are chastised by admonitions; and some of them, even though they are not admonished by men, return to the path they had abandoned; and some too, having received grace at various ages, are withdrawn from the dangers of this life by a swift death. All these things are done in them by him who made them vessels of mercy, and who also chose them in his Son before the foundation of the world by a gracious choice. "And if out of grace, then not in virtue of works; otherwise grace is no longer grace" (Rom. 11:6). For they are not so called, as not to be chosen; for which reason it is said, "Many are called, but few are chosen" (Matt. 20:16). But, since they are called according to God's purpose, they are surely chosen by the choice which we have termed gracious; it is not made in view of their preceding merits, because their every merit is a grace.

VIII.17. At this point, if I am asked why God does not give perseverance to those whom he once gave the love whereby they lived a Christian life, I answer that I do not know. Not with arrogance, but in the recognition of

Graceful Winner

my condition, I heed the Apostle's words: "O man, who art thou to reply to God?" (Rom. 9:20). "O depth of the riches of the wisdom and of the knowledge of God! How incomprehensible are his judgments, and how unsearchable his ways" (Rom. 11:33)! Insofar as he has deigned to manifest his judgments to us, let us give thanks; insofar as he has hidden them, let us not murmur against his will, but let us believe that this, too, is most salutary for us.

But you—the enemy of his grace, who put the question—what do you say? I suppose you will not deny that you are a Christian, but will boast of being a Catholic. If, therefore, you admit that perseverance in good to the end is a gift of God, I dare say you are as ignorant as I am of why one receives this gift and another does not; neither of us can penetrate the inscrutable judgments of God in this regard. Or, if you say that it depends on the free will of man (which you defend, not in its harmony with the grace of God, but against his grace), whether one perseveres or does not persevere in good, and that it is no gift of God if one perseveres, but the work of the human will, how shall you get around the words: "I have prayed for you, Peter, that your faith may not fail" (Luke 22:32)? You will hardly dare to say that, even after the prayer of Christ that Peter's faith should not fail, it might have failed, if Peter had wished it to fail—that is, if he had been unwilling to have it persevere to the end. This would mean that Peter would will something else than what Christ prayed that he should will. Obviously, Peter's faith would collapse if his will to believe were to fail; and it would stand firm, if that will stood firm. But, since "the will is prepared by the Lord" (Prov. 8:35), the prayer of Christ for him could not be in vain. When, therefore, Christ prayed that Peter's faith might not fail, what else did he pray for, except that Peter might have an entirely free, strong, unconquerable, and persevering will to believe? This is the way in which the freedom of the will is defended in harmony with the grace of God, and not against it. The fact is that the human will does not achieve grace through freedom, but rather freedom through grace, and through grace, too, joyous consistency, and invincible strength to persevere.

▲ ▲ ▲

The *Confessions*, completed in 397, is Augustine's most well-known work. It is an address to God, and in addressing God, Augustine discovers his own human identity. Since it contains many reflections on his life, there is a temptation to call this work autobiographical, albeit a "spiritual" biography. At the same time much about the life of Augustine is omitted, and any attempt to view this work as historical deserves serious qualification.

The drama begins immediately when one opens the work, for we are greeted with Augustine's response to God: "for thou hast made us for thyself and restless is our heart until it comes to rest in thee." These reflections led Augustine to the question of the finite mind's capability for containing the infinite. The answer given by Augustine is that only paradoxically through divine grace and human faith can humanity know God.

The problem with humanity is its yielding to the temptation and love of finite objects. Ultimately this results in a rather pessimistic anthropology (understanding of the human) from which there is no escape save divine grace. Augustine places so much emphasis on the grace of God that he has been given the honorific title "Doctor of Grace" by the church. In this scenario the human self finds God not through memory or any other human intellectual exercise, and Augustine himself tried many, but by preparing itself for God's self-revelation.

Another of Augustine's classic works, *The City of God*, created between 413 and 426, is most likely the first major philosophy of history and theology. It is monumental in scope. It seeks no less than to define God, humanity, and the world. The city is Augustine's metaphor of choice simply because in his day the city was the cultural and political model.

Augustine speaks of two cities: the City of God and the earthly city, which currently co-exist side by side and are inseparable. Those who truly believe in the true God may now enter into that heavenly city, even though such belief does not guarantee preferential treatment of any type whatsoever during this life (here are some hints at a perennial issue in theology, that is, election, predestination, and their recognition; being one of God's chosen does not exempt a person from the trials and tribulations of this life). What characterizes each city, and each person in the city, is the direction of love—whether that love is directed toward God (the heavenly city) or toward the material world (the earthly city). As Augustine implies in his opening prayer in the *Confessions*, we are made for God, and our true happiness materializes when we are made aware of that true disposition.

Probably one of the best works to examine when beginning to study Augustine is the *Enchiridion* (*Handbook*), written around 421 in response to a request by a certain Laurentius to provide him with a Christian "handbook." Responding to the challenge, Augustine took the Apostles' Creed and the Lord's Prayer as his framework and demonstrated that the principles of the Chris-

tian life are to be found in faith, hope, and love. Some of the principle ideas elucidated in this marvelous little book are the idea of the precedence of faith over reason and ascribing to reason the role of aiding our understanding of that which has been previously apprehended by faith; these themes were the precursor to Anselm's famous *fides quarens intellectum* (or *credo ut intelligam*). We also find his classic summary regarding the problem of evil, which became the standard response in the Christian community for centuries and in the eyes of many is yet the best response. Evil was an issue that frequently taxed his mind and brought him through stages of belief, as he embraced Manichaeism, Neoplatonism, and finally Christianity (tinged of course with much Neoplatonism). With regard to evil, Augustine argued: whatever is, insofar as it is, is good; evil is simply a privation of the good and is dependent on the good for its very existence, and hence, evil does not exist.

Augustine, with his pessimistic anthropology and strong emphasis on God, saw original sin as the introduction of evil into human life. Humans are born with free will, but we should not delude ourselves. Our free will has been corrupted by "original sin," that is, the fall of Adam, and our redemption becomes effectual only through divine predestination. We can do nothing on our own; only by God's grace are we redeemed. Our sin is understood in terms of pride, or self-elevation, and its consequences are ignorance and lust. This view has penetrated the heart of Christianity and dominated it through history, even into the twentieth century in such a person as Reinhold Niebuhr. Niebuhr articulates this view extraordinarily in his

Gifford lectures, *The Nature and Destiny of Man* (1941–1943). The resolution to this human dilemma comes to us from the divine side by faith through the grace of God—a grace fully manifest in the person and work of Jesus of Nazareth, the Christ.

The importance of Augustine, whether one agrees or disagrees with him, cannot be overestimated. For example, in the days of the Reformation almost all the actors in this great historical drama were Augustinians, even though adversarial. Thus can Martin Luther, John Calvin, Huldrych Zwingli, and the theologians of the Roman Catholic Church be so described. And that has always been the case; Augustine is all-pervasive in the history and development of Western Christian thought.

10. PSEUDO-DIONYSIUS (CA. 500)

There appeared, late in the fifth century, as if from nowhere, an unknown genius of the highest order, a Neoplatonist destined to exercise a massive influence on all Christian theology. Following a received custom of the time, he used a *nom de plume* (pseudonym). He chose a name already respected by his audience in order to win a favorable reading, convinced that the reader would receive such great benefits by the truth of his writing that no real deception would have taken place.

The writer succeeded so well, with both pseudonym and presentation of what he saw as the truth, that the entire cadre of church leaders after him not only reverenced his purloined identity (the Apostle Paul had a convert named Dionysius the Areopagite, mentioned in Acts 17:34) but accepted his strange mystical doctrine as well, even if they had to purify it of unorthodox elements. Perhaps the greatest of his disciples would be his orthodox interpreter, Maximus of Chrysopolis (better known as Maximus the Confessor). Thomas Aquinas is another of his orthodox re-interpreters. Only in the modern period was the dat-

ing deception detected, and the writer once thought to be Dionysius is now called "Pseudo-Dionysius."

The actual author remains unknown, although it has been reasonably suggested that he flourished toward the end of the fifth century, probably in the vicinity of Syria where speculative mysticism abounded. He was widely read in the Eastern church, and when John Scotus Erigena translated his work in the ninth century, a series of important commentaries began in the West that extended his already vast influence.

Source: "Mystical Theology 1, 3," The Mystical Theology and the Celestial Hierarchy of Dionysius the Areopagite, *translated by Fintry, Brook, and Godalming (Surrey, Eng.: Shrine of Wisdom, 1949), 9, 11, 15–17.*

▼ ▼ ▼

WHAT IS THE DIVINE DARKNESS?

(1) Supernal Triad, Deity above all essence, knowledge, and goodness; Guide of Christians to Divine Wisdom, direct our path to the ultimate summit of Thy mystical Lord, most incomprehensible, most luminous, and

most exalted, where the pure, absolute, and immutable mysteries of theology are veiled in the dazzling obscurity of the secret Silence, outshining all brilliance with the intensity of their Darkness, and surcharging our blinded intellects with the utterly impalpable and invisible fairness of glories surpassing all beauty.

Let this be my prayer; but do thou, dear Timothy, in the diligent exercise of mystical contemplation, leave behind the senses and the operations of the intellect, and all things sensible and intellectual, and all things in the world of being and non-being, that thou mayest arise, by unknowing towards the union, as far as is attainable, with him who transcends all being and all knowledge. For by the unceasing and absolute renunciation of thyself and of all things, thou mayest be borne on high, through pure and entire self-abnegation, into the supercelestial radiance of the Divine Darkness.

It was not without reason that the blessed Moses was commanded first to undergo purification himself and then to separate himself from those who had not undergone it; and after the entire purification heard many voiced trumpets and saw many lights streaming forth with pure and manifold rays; and that he was thereafter separated from the multitude, with the elect priests, and pressed forward to the summit of the divine ascent. Nevertheless, he did not attain to the Presence of God himself; he saw not him (for he cannot be looked upon), but the Place where he dwells. And this I take to signify that the divinest and highest things seen by the eyes or contemplated by the mind are by the symbolical expressions of those that are immediately beneath him who is above all. Through these, his incomprehensible Presence is manifested upon those heights of his Holy Places; that then It breaks forth, even from that which is seen and that which sees, and plunges the mystic into the Darkness of Unknowing, whence all perfection of understanding is excluded, and he is enwrapped in that which is altogether intangible and noumenal, being wholly absorbed in him who is beyond all, and in none else (whether himself or another); and through the inactivity of all his reasoning powers is united by his highest faculty to him who is wholly unknowable; thus by knowing nothing he knows that which is beyond his knowledge.

WHAT ARE THE AFFIRMATIONS AND THE NEGATIONS CONCERNING GOD?

(3) In the *Theological Orations* we have set forth the principal affirmative expressions concerning God, and have shown in what sense God's Holy Nature is One, and in what sense three; what is within It which is called Paternity, and what is Filiation, and what is signified by the name Spirit; how from the uncreated and indivisible Good, the blessed and perfect Rays of Its Goodness proceed, and yet abide immutably one both with Their Origin and within Themselves and each other, co-eternal with the act by which They spring from It (Comment 10); how the superessential Jesus enters an essential state in which the truth of human nature meet; and other matters made known by the Oracles are expounded in the same place.

Again, in the treatise on *Divine Names*, we have considered the meaning, as concerning God, of the titles of Good, of Being, of Life, of Wisdom, of Power, and of such other names as are applied to him; further, in *Symbolical Theology*, we have considered what are the metaphysical titles drawn from the world of sense and applied to the nature of God; what is meant by the material and intellectual images we form of him, or the functions and instruments of activity attributed to him; what are the places where he dwells, and the raiment in which he is adorned; what is meant by God's anger, grief, and indignation, or the divine inebriation; what is meant by God's oaths and threats, by his slumber and waking; and all sacred and symbolical representations. And it will be observed how far more copious and diffused are the last terms than the first, for the theological doctrine and the exposition of the *Divine Names* are necessarily more brief than the *Symbolical Theology*.

For the higher we soar in contemplation the more limited become our expressions of that which is purely intelligible, even now, when plunging into the Darkness which is above the intellect, we pass not merely into brevity of speech, but even into absolute silence, of thoughts as well as of words. Thus, in the former discourse, our contemplations descended from the highest to the lowest, embracing an ever-widening number of conceptions, which increased at each stage of the descent; but in the present discourse we mount upwards from below to that which is the highest, and according to the degree of transcendence, so our speech is restrained, until, the entire ascent being accomplished, we become wholly voiceless, inasmuch as we are absorbed in him who is totally ineffable. "But why?" you will ask, "does the affirmative method begin from the highest attributions, and the negative method with the lowest abstractions?" The reason is because, when affirming the subsistence of that which transcends all affirmation, we necessarily start from the attributes most closely related to It and upon which the remaining affirmations depend; but when pursuing the negative method to reach that which is beyond all abstraction, we must begin by applying our negations to things which are most remote from It.

For is it not more true to affirm that God is Life and Goodness than that he is air or stone; and must we not deny to him more emphatically the attributes of inebriation and wrath than the applications of human speech and thought?

▲ ▲ ▲

According to this influential writer of the late fifth century, the names given to God cannot literally represent God, for God is nameless. The understanding and contemplation of the "actual"

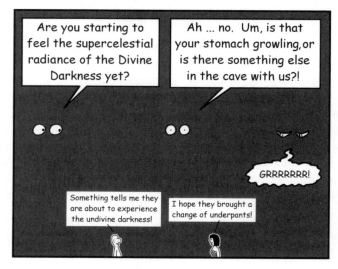

The Divine Lion

nature of God are inaccessible to any being; thus names for God can only be used symbolically. Unlike Paul Tillich, for example, who uses the text in Exodus, "I am Who I am," and treats it as a disclosure of the divine name as "Being" itself, Dionysius would suggest that the real meaning of that text is precisely the opposite; namely, that God's name is never apprehendable.

Dionysius begins then with the assumption that no proper concept of God can be formed or expressed in speech. The One, as God is referred to by this Neoplatonist, is beyond utterance and surpasses the reach of all human vocabulary. Yet human beings must do their best to discourse about God. The ineffability of the One, that is, God, is partly due to the fact that the One is beyond existence; the One is the very cause of existence while not existing itself. This paradox results from the attempt to understand God by the use of names.

Dionysius must, as a Christian, also meet the challenge of the Trinity. He clearly appears to prefer unity to trinity as an ultimate concept, although he attributes a trinitarian nature to his Godhead as a natural consequence of its supernatural richness or fecundity. Speaking generally of God's fecundity (richness or productivity) does not enjoy much orthodox status in Christianity, since the Trinity must remain as an inexplicable doctrine, an outpouring of a nature essentially beyond distinctions.

Since the divine being transcends all being, all knowledge is obviously transcended; the divine being may be symbolized by terms, but not grasped by them. In a word, we cannot put "God in a box." On the one hand, we use the *via negativa,* the negative way, and deny all attributes as being inappropriate to God. At the same time, we draw upon the whole of creation to properly characterize God. Like biblical literature, Dionysius celebrates the One by every name while yet calling it nameless. Such a transcendent cause must both be nameless and, at the same time, in some sense the source of the meaning of all names.

Thus, in typical Neoplatonic fashion, Pseudo-Dionysius conceives the world in hierarchical fashion in which all things come from God and all things lead to God, each according to its position in the hierarchical order. God is One in the absolute sense; God totally transcends every category of human thought. God is even beyond essence. God is not, but rather all that is derives its being from God. God is unknowable as such, although all beings reveal and lead to God. As is readily seen, the work of this unknown author contributed greatly to the influence of Neoplatonism on Christian theology. Throughout the Middle Ages the West would cite him as a faithful interpreter of the Pauline message, and his work is a high point in the long and rich Christian mystical tradition.

11. John Scotus Erigena (ca. 817–877)

Johannes (John) Scotus Erigena, born somewhere around 817 is known generally as Erigena—probably because he was Irish-born of Scottish parents. Most of what we know about the circumstances of Erigena's life is conjectural. It seems that after some schooling at home in Ireland, he went to France where he was attached as director of the palace school of Charles the Bald around the year 847. He enjoyed a position of prestige and protection under the court of the king.

In 851 at the request of Hincmar, archbishop of Reims, Erigena wrote a treatise on predestination in which he defended the freedom of the will, a treatise that later received conciliar condemnation. His participation in this debate, however, reflects the substantial respect he commanded in his own times. He was respected for his philosophical acumen, for his erudition, but he was also regarded with some amount of suspicion because of his love of Greek philosophy, from which he drew what were often considered unorthodox conclusions. For these reasons he had no real "followers," although he was employed as a source of information and of ideas by many of his contemporaries as they pursued their own theological endeavors. He was frequently cited during the three succeeding centuries, even though those who cited him cautioned and reminded their readers about his theology.

Early in the thirteenth century his major work, *On the Division of Nature*, was condemned with charges of pantheism and freethinking, which have never been entirely dispelled. Nevertheless, his influence continued through his translation of the work of Pseudo-Dionysius.

Regardless of his controversial ideas, many concede that he possessed the finest philosophical mind of his day. And even though his work was condemned by Pope Honorius III in 1225 (coincidentally the birth year of Thomas Aquinas), *On the Division of Nature* may be considered as the first real *Summa* in Western theological thought.

Sources: "On the Nature of Paradise," Periphyseon: Liber Quartus, *edited by Edouard A. Jeanneau, translated by John J. O'Meara (Dublin: Institute of Celtic Studies, 1995), 161; and* Periphyseon: Liber Secundus, *edited by I. P. Sheldon-Williams (Dublin: Dublin Institute for Advanced Studies, 1983), 9, 10.*

▼ ▼ ▼

On the Nature of Paradise

[Therefore] the praise of the life of humanity in paradise must refer to the future life that would have been ours if Adam had remained obedient, rather than to the life which he had only just begun, and in which he did not continue. For if he had continued in it for even a brief period, he must have achieved some degree of perfection, and in that case perhaps his master would not have said, "He began to live (*vivebat*)" but "He lived (*vixit*)," or "He had lived (*vixerat*)." However, if he had used the past or pluperfect tenses in this way, or if he used them like this somewhere else, I would have thought that he was using the past tense to refer to the future, rather than meaning that Adam had continued for a space of time in the blessedness of paradise before the Fall. My reason for doing so is that he was giving the expression to the predestined and foreordained blessedness, which was to be ours if Adam had not sinned, as though it had already happened—when, as a matter of fact, it was still among the things which were destined to be perfect in the future, and which have yet to take place. Now I say this because often when he is writing about Paradise, he does not use the past and pluperfect tenses. . . . This is not surprising, in that the most wise divine authority often speaks of the future as though it had already taken place.

THE FORMS OF CREATION

Let us make an "analytical" or regressive collection of [the four forms of nature: creating and not created, created and creating, created and not creating, and not creating and not created]. The first, then, [and] fourth are one since they are understood of God [alone]. For he is the Principle of all things which have been created by him, and the end of all things which seek him so that in him they find their eternal and immutable rest. For the reason why the Cause of all things is said to create is that it is from it that the universe of those things which have been created after it [and by it] proceeds by a wonderful and divine multiplication into genera and species and individuals, and into differentiations and all those other features which are observed in created nature; but because it is to the same Cause that all things that proceed from it shall return when they reach their end, it is therefore called the end of all things and is said neither to create nor to be created. For once all things have returned to it nothing further will proceed from it by generation in place and time [and] genera and forms since in it all things will be at rest and will remain an indivisible and immutable One. For those things which in the processions of natures appear to be divided and partitioned into many are in the primordial causes unified and one, and to this unity they will return and in it they will eternally and immutably remain.

But this fourth aspect of the universe, which, like the first also, is understood to exist in God alone, will receive a more detailed treatment in its proper place, as far as the Light of Minds shall grant [us].

▲ ▲ ▲

Much of the work of John Scotus Erigena consisted of translating the writings of earlier Eastern theologians. This was of particular value since the Greek language

Pluperfect Paradise

had fallen into disuse and oblivion in the West.

Erigena stands in the tradition of Clement of Alexandria, Origen, and Pseudo-Dionysius. His philosophy, as can be seen from these readings, is one of high speculative flights in which dialectics and the art of precise definition are paramount and in which everything is included in a vast vision of God and the universe.

Erigena spiritualized the idea of paradise; he denied that paradise is a specific place. Part of his argument, reflecting his penchant for precise definition, rested on an appeal to the specific tenses associated with the verbs found in Scripture. While theologians such as Augustine understood paradise as a specific location in space and time, Erigena argued that paradise is perfect human nature. Thus we read: ". . . the praise of the life of humanity must refer to the future life that would have been ours if Adam had remained obedient, rather than to the life which he had only just begun, and in which he did not continue." This line of thought can also be found not only in Clement, Origen, and Pseudo-Dionysius, but also in Gregory of Nyssa and Maximus the Confessor.

Furthermore, for Erigena everything came from God and returns to God. He argued that God has made all things out of nothing, but this nothing is not the absolute denial of being, not a total vacuum, but rather God who is not and God who can therefore be called nothing. For Erigena, the traditional doctrine *creatio ex nihilo* became *creatio ex Deo*. Ultimately the entire creation returns to God in a great process of final restoration—the ancient Greek doctrine of *apokatastasis*. Although this process implies the disappearance of corruptible bodies, even those things that now exist in such bodies will return to God. Their existence is spiritual, and they will therefore be restored. Each thing will be taken up into another higher than it, until all things return to God and God becomes "all in all." The vast cycle of Erigena's philosophy is thus completed.

His importance stems from his independent thinking and the impressive vastness of his theological system. Erigena influenced the future of Christian theology primarily through his introduction of earlier Eastern theology into the medieval West.

PART TWO

THE MIDDLE AGES

The thousand-year period from the time of Augustine until the rise of the Protestant reformers is generally referred to as the "Middle Ages." The term *Middle Ages* is a fairly ambiguous term—middle of what? Supposedly it is the period between classical antiquity and its rediscovery in the Renaissance, or perhaps the Reformation, or even the period known as the Enlightenment.

The Middle Ages was the time of the emergence of modern Europe: Christian culture (the *Corpus Christianum*) became visible and viable; marvelous architecture, including the great cathedral tradition, appeared; universities were established. It was, in the eyes of some, the "golden age of faith."

On the other hand, the Middle Ages may look like the "Dark Ages." The intellectual confusion within Christian thought brought about by the dominance of Aristotle over the Apostles, the endless bickering between popes and princes, the metaphysical remoteness of the scholastics, the world resignation of the mystics—to the sixteenth-century Reformers, these were symptoms of chronic theological disease. The ambitious so-called medieval synthesis was short-lived, the Renaissance was soon to distill out and revive the Greco-Roman strain, while the Reformation would try to reintroduce the Hebrew-Christian biblical tradition.

Modern scholarship does not tend to debate these two views of the medieval period because it sees the intellectual and cultural dimensions of this time in more balanced terms. Clearly, the medieval period cannot be reduced to simple epithets, for here labels turn into libels. The Medieval Age was a complex period, characterized as

Men in Tin

much by inner tensions as by overarching faith. An excellent example of this point is the co-existence of scholasticism and mysticism.

Scholasticism has been given a negative or pejorative slant by moderns. The term simply refers, however, to the life and thought of the scholastics—that is, the scholars who lived, worked, worshipped, and studied in the medieval schools. The schools began modestly, inside or alongside the cathedrals. Gradually they emerged as the modern universities, of which Paris and Oxford were probably the most famous. If there was darkness in the period, the lamp of learning was kept burning by the schools. Here Greek and Roman classics, as well as the writings of the early church, were studied, codified, and copied.

When Aristotle was rediscovered with the help of Arab translators, scholars applied his syllogistic method to theology as well as to everything else in view. When the realms of nature and grace expanded almost beyond control, the scholastics constructed a massive synthesis as impressive intellectually as the great cathedrals were architecturally. When the theological initiate was on the verge of being overwhelmed by the sheer mass of accumulated doctrines from the past, the dialectical pattern of questions (investigations, problems for debate) and "sentences" (opinions, theses) was devised. If all this took on a metaphysical accent, it did so only because Christian philosophy was understood as the unifying factor in an age of speculative stress and strain (the *Summa* of Thomas Aquinas is perhaps the best illustration of this process).

While scholastics were spinning their systems and constructing their *Summae*, mystics were pursuing a very different course of life and thought in their monasteries. If Aristotle was the "patron" of the scholastics, Plato was the philosopher of choice for Medieval mysticism. As Socrates had argued, the human soul is of divine origin; it not only knows and remembers its source, but seeks to be reunited with it. The desire for reunion with eternal Being and the consequent renunciation of every finite, material, mundane restriction upon that effort thus becomes the chief end and purpose of the religious life.

Augustine, who could be quoted by the scholastics on the relation between reason and revelation, was equally useful to the mystics. For example, Augustine wrote: "My mind in the flash of a trembling glance came to Absolute Being—That Which Is" (*Confessions*, VII, xvii). Put in its simplest terms, medieval mysticism was merely an extended gloss upon the intuitive experience. The search for immediate awareness of the One, the Absolute, the consciousness of Divine Presence, the patient pilgrimage of the soul, the ladder of ascent from earth to heaven, the sequence of purgation, illumination and union—these became the characteristics of the way of the mystics.

As theological distinctions, the interrelations of scholasticism and their effect upon medieval life and culture are significant. The polarity principle that operated here was at work in many creative ways in this period. It was a time when Plato and Aristotle both felt at home, when church and state engaged in ceaseless struggle, when realism and nominalism split the schools, when Dominicans and Franciscans squared off in mendicant rivalry.

The dialectic of such opposing forces gave the medieval period its stimulating intellectual climate. These forces were in the land—in both the schools and the monasteries—if not so often in the towns or on the farms. It must have been an exciting time to be alive.

12. ANSELM OF CANTERBURY (1033–1109)

Between the twin peaks of Augustine and Aquinas stands the not as well-known yet eminent Anselm of Canterbury. The forerunner of scholastic theology, he is closer to Aquinas than to Augustine. Nevertheless, the reputation of Anselm is by no means derivative; Anselm deserves to stand on his own because of his significant contributions to the field of Christian "philosophy." Some today would consider this field at the least problematic and even, perhaps, contradictory.

Born in Aosta in Northern Italy near modern-day Turin, Anselm entered the monastery at Bec in Normandy, of which he eventually became abbot. For nearly thirty years Anselm lived and worked, gathering around him a distinguished circle of disciples and admirers. It was during this period that he wrote some of his most important and celebrated works, such as *Proslogion*, with its much debated and highly celebrated argument for the existence of God.

At the age of sixty, after a long drawn-out exchange with authorities of both church and state in France, England, and Rome, he was appointed archbishop of Canterbury. While temporarily in Rome on official business, he prepared his well-known doctrinal masterpiece, the *Cur Deus Homo?*, on the nature of the atonement. Both the arguments for the existence of God and his theory of atonement are theological treatises carefully studied to this day. Anselm died during Holy Week on April 21, 1109, and was buried at Canterbury Cathedral.

The subtitle to the *Proslogion* gives us an insight into his theological principle: namely, *fides quarens intellectum* (faith seeking understanding). To believe in order to understand *(credo ut intelligam)* was a sequence first enunciated by Augustine (and perhaps even Tertullian); Anselm extended this principle in order to clarify the relation between faith and reason. Later Thomas Aquinas would magnify this position into his lofty system of theology, *Summa Theologiae*. Reason or thinking is not the way to faith, but faith is the way the believer takes in order to understand. Reason can function within as well as outside faith, and while dialectic cannot be the source of faith, it can serve as the instrument of faith.

Anselm's ontological argument for God's existence exemplifies his notion of reason in the service of faith. Thus, the very idea of God, even in the denial of the fool, implies divine thought; if God existed only as an idea, God could be superseded by any being who existed in reality as well as thought—but this is impossible. God, in the view of Anselm, "is that than which nothing greater can be conceived"; the essence of God necessitates the existence of God. The significance of this argument may be seen in the attention it has received by such notable scholars as: René Descartes, Baruch Spinoza, Gottfried Leibniz, Immanuel Kant, and in more recent times Karl Barth and Charles Hartshorne.

The doctrinal discussion of the why and how of redemption is contained in Anselm's closely reasoned dialogue, *Cur Deus Homo?* (Why did God become human?). If Christians were to explain their redemption in Christ to a non-believer, Anselm asked, how would they go about it? Operating within his cultural milieu, the feudal system of the Middle Ages with such symbols as honor, dishonor, satisfaction, obedience, and reward, Anselm constructed an Aristotelian syllogism with cumulative impact. It is as follows: sin is an affront to God and God's honor and majesty. God's justice requires full satisfaction for this offense given. Human beings already owe God total obedience, however, and cannot make up, ever, for their disobedience. Naturally, God could arbitrarily cancel the debt, but that would contravene against divine justice. Human beings must atone for their own sin, but unfortunately they cannot. God, of course, can, but must not. Consequently, the divine-human God, Jesus Christ, lives the life and dies the death of a perfect obedience and satisfies the requirements of justice. As a result a reward is owing Jesus Christ, the divine-human, for his perfect satisfaction. God needs nothing, however, and so the reward is transferred to sinful humanity. In this manner, three things are accomplished: (1) God's honor is restored; (2) sin is forgiven; and (3) atonement is achieved. There are, of course, problems with this system that would have made sense to the people of his day since it was culturally situated.

It would also be imprudent to assume that medieval thinkers believed that such reasoned arguments would actually persuade non-believers to become believers. It is hardly that simple. They did, however, maintain that such reasoning could at least "demonstrate" that Christian faith—whether we are speaking of the existence of God or of the redemption of humankind that takes place in Jesus Christ—is neither nonsensical nor irrational. Anselm, whether we agree with him or not, is quite clear and we are always aware of exactly what his intent is.

Source: "Philosophical Theology" from Proslogion (The Ontological Argument for the Existence of God), *translated by Eugene R. Fairweather (Library of Christian Classics, vol. X: A Scholastic Miscellany; Philadelphia: Westminster Press, 1956), 73ff.*

▼ ▼ ▼

O Lord, since you give understanding to faith, help me to understand—as far as you know it to be good for me—that you do exist, as we believe, and that you are what we believe you to be. Now we believe that you are a being than which no one greater can be thought. Or could it be that there is no such being, since "The fool has said in his heart, 'There is no God'" (Ps. 14:1)? But when this same fool hears what I am saying—"A being than which no one greater can be thought"—he understands what he hears. What he understands is in his understanding, even if he does not understand that it exists. For it is one thing for an object to be in the understanding, and another thing to understand that it exists. For example, when a painter considers beforehand what he is going to paint, he has it in his understanding, but he does not suppose that what he has not yet painted already exists. But when he has painted it, he both has it in his understanding and understands that what he has now produced exists. Therefore, even the fool must be convinced that a being than which no one greater can be thought exists at least in his understanding, since when he hears this he understands it, and whatever is understood is in the understanding. But clearly that than which a greater thing cannot be thought cannot exist in the understanding alone. For if it is actually in the understanding alone, it can be thought of as existing also in reality, and this is greater. Therefore, if that than which a greater thing cannot be thought is in the understanding alone, this same thing than which a greater cannot be thought is that than which a greater can be thought. But obviously this is impossible. Therefore, there certainly exists, both in the understanding and in reality, something than which a greater thing cannot be thought.

Certainly it exists so truly that it cannot be thought of as nonexistent. For something can be thought of as existing, which cannot be thought of as not existing, and this is greater than that which can be thought of as not existing. Thus, if that than which a greater thing cannot be thought can be thought of as not existing, this very thing than which a greater cannot be thought is not that than which a greater cannot be thought. But this is contradictory. Therefore, there truly is a being than which a greater cannot be thought—so truly that it cannot even be thought of as not existing.

And *you* are this thing, O Lord our God! You so truly exist, O Lord my God, that you cannot even be thought of as not existing. And this is right. For if some mind could think of something better than you, the creature would rise above the Creator and judge its Creator; but this is altogether absurd. Indeed, whatever is can be thought of as not existing, except you

The Nature of Reality

alone. You alone of all beings have being in the truest and highest sense, since no other being so truly exists as you do, and thus every other being has less being. Why, then, has "The fool said in his heart, 'There is no God,'" when it is so obvious to the rational mind that, of all beings, you do exist supremely? Why indeed, unless he is a stupid fool?

GAUNILO'S RESPONSE TO ANSELM

To illustrate my argument (that the idea of something does not necessitate its actual existence), people say that somewhere in the ocean is an island which some have called the "Lost Island" because of the difficulty, and indeed the impossibility, of finding it. They say that it has all kinds of priceless riches and abundant delights. . . .

Now, if someone were to tell me about this island, I would easily understand what they said, because it is not difficult. But suppose that someone else told me, as if it were a direct result of this, "You cannot any more doubt that this island that is more excellent than any other land does in fact exist in reality, than you can doubt that it is in your mind. Since it is more excellent for it to exist in reality than just in your mind, therefore it must exist in reality." I say that if someone tried to convince me in this way that this island really exists beyond any doubt, I would think that they are joking with me. Or I would wonder which of us is a bigger fool: I myself, if I agreed with them, or they, if they thought that they had certainly proved the existence of this island.

SOTERIOLOGY (REDEMPTION)
[FROM CUR DEUS HOMO?]

Anselm: Tell me what you think still remains to be answered of the question you posed at the beginning, which forced so many other questions on us.
Boso: The heart of the question was this: Why did God become human, to save humans by his death, when it seems that he could have done this in some other way? You have answered this by showing, by several necessary reasons, how it would not have been right for the restoration of human nature to be left undone, and how it could not have been done unless humankind paid what it owed to God for sin. But the debt was so great that although humankind alone owed it, only God could pay it, so that the person who paid it must be both human and God. Thus God had to take human nature into the unity of the divine, so that humankind who in its own nature ought to pay the debt was in a person who could pay. Then you showed that the person who also was God had to be born from a Virgin in the person of the Son of God, and how he could be taken from the sinful mass of humankind without sin. Also, you have proved most clearly that the life of this Man was so wonderful and valuable that it can suffice to pay what all humankind owes for its sins, and infinitely more. Now it remains to be shown how it is paid to God for the sins of humankind.
Anselm: There is no need to explain what a great gift the Son gave freely.
Boso: That is very clear.
Anselm: You will not think that he who gives such a great gift to God ought to go unrewarded.
Boso: Not at all! I see how necessary it is for the Father to reward the Son. . . .
Anselm: He who rewards someone either gives what the other does not have or gives something that he can expect of him. But before the Son did this great work, all that belonged to the Father belonged to him. What can be given to him as a reward, when he needs nothing and has nothing to be forgiven for? . . . It must be paid to someone else, since it cannot be paid to him. . . . To whom would it be more fitting for him to give the fruit of his death than to those for whose salvation (as true reasoning has taught us) he made himself human, and to whom by dying he gave an example of dying

for justice's sake? They will imitate his death in vain if they do not share in his merit.

▲ ▲ ▲

These two major works, *The Proslogion* and *Cur Deus Homo?* have had a lasting impact on the development of theology in the West. Indeed, no less an authority than Karl Barth argued that Anselm's ontological argument in the *Proslogion* was the best demonstration for the existence of God in Western theological literature. *Cur Deus Homo?* is significant in that it replaced the long-standing Greek "ransom" theories as the most appropriate explanation for the incarnation and atonement.

With respect to God's existence, Anselm resolved to formulate a brief, lucid, and irrefutable argument for the existence of God as the supreme good. The alternate title to his book—*Faith Seeking Understanding*—indicates Anselm's conviction that although reason or dialectics is not the source of faith, faith seeks to go beyond belief to understanding. (In this he is following in the footsteps of Augustine.) It would seem that Anselm's purpose in the argument is to nurture faith from its simple form as belief to its more mature form as understanding. There are also some suggestions that the argument may lead from non-belief to belief.

The basic thrust of Anselm's argument is that God is that being than whom none greater can be conceived. Such a being must be conceived of as existing in reality and not merely in thought, for that which is conceived of as having real existence is greater than that which is thought of as only a concept. In short, the very idea of such a perfect being necessitates the actuality of that being. One cannot understand, according to Anselm, what the term God means and think of God as not being. Since God cannot be thought not to be, God necessarily is!

Anselm's most notable adversary was Gaunilo, a Benedictine monk from Marmoutier near Tours. In a brief reply to Anselm titled "In Behalf of the Fool," Gaunilo contends that Anselm's argument does not refute atheism. If it is true that God cannot be thought not to be without God's actual existence being understood, then, Gaunilo argues, no argument for God's existence would be necessary, for God's existence would be a proven fact as soon as one's understanding possessed the concept of God. And yet, Gaunilo continues, Anselm distinguishes between having a thing in mind as an idea and then later the idea of the actual existence of the thing.

Gaunilo's oft-cited illustration was the "imaginary isle of bliss." Just because we can conceive of such an isle does not necessitate the existence of that isle. Consequently, Anselm's argument is really absurd, concludes Gaunilo.

Although people are yet debating this issue, it is more than fair to say that Gaunilo misses Anselm's main point. Only of God can it be concluded that it is impossible to conceive of God's non-existence. The argument applies to God only; God is Being itself. Of God alone is existence a predicate. Consequently, the nature of God's existence is sharply different from that of isles, or any other kind of finite reality.

With respect to theories of atonement, Anselm, in opposition to Greek ransom theories, elaborated an understanding of atonement within the context of God's relationship with human beings. Anselm was trying to demonstrate the unfathomable depth of God's love and, simultaneously, to suggest the horrendous character of human sin, the gravity of sin. In his theology, he introduces two ideas that have had lasting influence in the subsequent history of salvation (soteriology): (1) the idea of satisfaction and (2) the idea of the absolute necessity of the atonement.

Anselm argues that the necessity of the incarnation can be demonstrated by the use of reason alone, apart from any reference to a knowledge of Christ. Anselm's argument runs as follows: human beings are rational beings whose purpose is to find happiness in fulfilling the will of God. Human sin is humanity's disobedience wherein God's honor is tarnished. It would not be fitting for God to remit sins unless punishment is inflicted or satisfaction rendered, since this would introduce anomaly into God's domain. Punishment, however, would ruin humanity, and satisfaction cannot be rendered by one who already is under the obligation of total obedience.

As a result, humanity must pay a debt to God, which, in reality, only God can pay. Therefore, out of love for humanity and in congruity with God's own nature, God wills to become human in order that the necessary satisfaction may be rendered; hence the answer to the question in the title *Cur Deus Homo?*

The God-human, who is the incarnate Son of God, offers up a sinless life to pay the debt of sinful humankind and to restore God's honor. Since God cannot allow this deed to go unrewarded and since the Son needs nothing, the reward accrues to the advantage of those for whom the Son died. At times this is referred to as the "objective-satisfaction theory" and has had a long history in the West.

13. PETER ABELARD (1079–1142)

If ever there was a "soap opera" in the history of theology, it would have to be about Peter Abelard and his beloved Heloise. Indeed, not many theologians have been immortalized for their tragic love affairs along with their theology. Abelard had an enormous thirst for knowledge, a very critical mind, and great audacity. He was the subject of repeated charges of heresy (which certainly makes him interesting, for, as P. T. Forsyth once said, "A live heresy is better than a dead orthodoxy") and has been influential long after his death.

Abelard was born near modern Nantes in western France and entered the cathedral school of Notre Dame in Paris at an early age. He quickly became as skilled as his teachers and wandered from school to school debating the theological and philosophical issues of his day. He established a new school near Paris independent of the cathedral and sometimes is given credit for laying the foundation of what would later become the University of Paris. His fame as a teacher was unparalleled, and many of his students went on to significant positions in the church, including the papacy.

Characteristic of Abelard's method of teaching was his well-known work *Sic et Non (Yes and No)*, in which he compiled apparently contradictory opinions of the theologians of the early church on a variety of theological issues. It was his intention not to disparage the orthodoxy of the early church but rather to force critical evaluation on his contemporaries. Peter Lombard, one of his famous pupils, extended this method further, and, ultimately, Thomas Aquinas's work demonstrates his dependence on Abelardian dialectics.

Many were fearful of Abelard's teaching and methods. Saint Bernard of Clairvaux, who was perhaps the most significant of his critics, suspected Abelard of heresy in a number of areas, including the doctrine of the Trinity. On his way to Rome to defend himself against the charges of Bernard, Abelard fell ill and retired to the monastery at Cluny, where he died the following year. At the time of his death he was an embittered and disheartened man.

Abelard was not a systematic theologian, but rather a brilliant teacher. His most important contribution to doctrinal theology is his challenge to and dismissal of Anselm's theory of the atonement. In place of Anselm's objective-satisfaction theory already discussed, Abelard offered what has been described as the "moral influence" or "subjective influence" theory. His argument was that the death of Christ was not so much a forensic satisfaction of the affronted honor of God as it was a magnificent and supreme manifestation of the love of God. Abelard was subjective and personal, not objective and legalistic in his presentation. It is tempting to speculate that Abelard's concern for the place of love in his theory might just be related to his

St. Bernard Contemplates Abelard's Theology

own deep, passionate nature and his tragic affair with Heloise.

The theory was never worked out in detail by Abelard. It can only be reconstructed from incidental discussions from his commentary on the Epistle of Paul to the Romans. Anselm's theory prevailed until more recently when, because of intellectual developments of the nineteenth century (for example, the social sciences), Abelard's self-sacrificial Christ found a more congenial audience. One might say simply that Abelard was centuries ahead of his time.

Source: "Exposition of the Epistle to the Romans" translated by J. P. Moffat, Library of Christian Classics, *vol. 10, A Scholastic Miscellany: Anselm to Ockham (Philadelphia: Westminster Press, 1956), 283–84.*

▼ ▼ ▼

It seems to us that we have been justified by the blood of Christ and reconciled to God (Rom. 3:24-25) in this way: through this unique act of grace manifested to us—in that his Son has taken upon himself our nature and persevered herein in teaching us by word and example even unto death—he has more fully bound us to himself by love; with the result that our hearts should be enkindled by such a gift of divine grace, and true charity should not now shrink from enduring anything for him.

And we do not doubt that the ancient Fathers, waiting in faith for this same gift, were aroused to very great love of God in the same way as men of this dispensation of grace, since it is written: "And they that went before and they that followed cried, saying: 'Hosanna to the Son of David'" (Mark 11:9). Yet everyone becomes more religious—by which we mean a greater lover of the Lord—after the Passion of Christ than before, since a realized gift inspires greater love than one which is only hoped for.

Wherefore, our redemption through Christ's suffering is that deeper affection in us which not only frees us from slavery to sin, but also wins for us the true liberty of sons of God, so that we do all things out of love rather than fear—love to him who has shown us such grace that no greater can be found, as he himself asserts, saying, "Greater love than this no man hath, that a man lay down his life for his friends" (John 15:13). Of this love the Lord says elsewhere, "I am come to cast fire on the earth, and what will, but that it blaze forth?" (Luke 12:49). So does he bear witness that he came for the express purpose of spreading this true liberty of love amongst men.

The apostle, closely examining this great fact, exclaims further on: "Because the charity of God is poured forth in our hearts, by the Holy Spirit, who is given to us. For why did Christ . . ." (Rom. 5:56). And a few verses later, "God commendeth his charity toward us; because when as yet . . ." (Rom. 5:8). But these utterances we shall expound more fully when we come to them. Now, as befits brevity of exposition, let the foregoing suffice as a summary of our understanding of the manner of our redemption.

▲ ▲ ▲

Although Peter Abelard had many controversial theological positions, some of which we shall characterize shortly, our focus here will be on his theory of the atonement, a theological doctrine for which he is well noted. Traditionally, Abelard's theology of the work of Jesus (which is the doctrine of the atonement, that is, soteriology) has been classified as being either "subjective" or "moral" and is generally seen in opposition to the work of Anselm of Canterbury, whose work has been characterized as being "juridical" or "objective." Whether these designations are all correct or incorrect is highly debatable. Nevertheless, while perhaps not doing justice to either of these theologians, they clearly point to their radically differing points of view on this fundamental issue. Peter Abelard rejected outrightly what has sometimes been referred to as the "classic" theory of the atonement, which held that Jesus as the Christ had come to pay a debt or a "ransom," as it is sometimes called, to the Devil as well as his rejection of the view of Anselm that he had come to pay a debt to God (a theory predicated on the system of punishment and payment in the medieval feudal system and one that many people would have easily understood).

In opposition to these views, Abelard argued that the work of Jesus as the Christ consisted in providing an example and teaching, both factual and verbal, of God's love for humanity. This example of Jesus was so poignant and so powerful, in the mind of Abelard, that it had the capacity to lead human beings to love God. On the basis of that love, and in response to the intercessory prayers of the resurrected Jesus offered in our behalf, God forgives humanity.

Abelard, powerful teacher and dynamic personality that he apparently was, evoked strong responses both from those who were in support of his views and equally from those who were opposed to him. As may be seen in our brief excerpt from the commentary on the Romans, Abelard gave much responsibility to the human person as that person shared in the work of redemption.

The views most characteristic of this daring dialectical teacher, when applied to the mysteries of the faith, resulted in his being twice condemned by the church. In 1121 his trinitarian views were rejected (although modern scholarship suggests that he was misunderstood). Again in 1141, to a large degree due to the influence of the most powerful man of the day, Bernard of Clairvaux, many of Abelard's other theological positions were rejected without allowing him the opportunity to debate or defend himself. He was given only the opportunity to recant. Some of these views are: (1) that Christ did not take flesh in order to free us from the yoke of the Devil; (2) that the power to bind and unbind was given to the apostles only, and not their successors (clearly this must have been upsetting to the hierarchy); (3) that free will in and of itself suffices to do good; (4) that we have not received the guilt of Adam, but only the penalty; and (5) that those who crucified Christ did not sin, for they did not know what they were doing, and that there is no guilt in that which is done in ignorance. It took Christian theologians until the latter part of the twentieth century to catch up with Abelard on this last point.

14. Thomas Aquinas (1225–1274)

To many people, Thomas Aquinas is the most magnificent architect of the discipline known as systematic theology, especially when viewed in terms of size, scope, and consistency. The systematics of Thomas paralleled the great Gothic cathedrals that enshrined the medieval era's unified view of the world. The cathedrals were built of stone, Thomas's system of enduring ideas.

Thomas was born in the town of Aquino, midway between Rome and Naples. His early studies were pursued at the Benedictine monastery at Monte Cassino, which was close by. He later joined the Dominican Order and became the prize pupil of St. Albert the Great. Subsequently he studied and lectured at Rome, Bologna, Pisa, and Naples.

Though involved in many civil and church affairs, Thomas was first and foremost a theologian. The only figure comparable in previous history is Augustine, and Thomas quotes his distinguished predecessor more frequently than he does any other authority. Unlike Augustine, however, Thomas was a systematizer with a neat, clear, and orderly mind that delighted in logical and dialectical coherence. Aristotle, newly discovered, whom he usually refers to simply as "the philosopher," aided him in the development of his theological system. Aristotle's precise definitions and syllogistic distinctions provided Thomas with the philosophical instrument needed for his theological work. Thus in Thomas both Augustine and Aristotle meet, and the synthesis adds an astonishing brilliance to the ongoing problems of the relation of revelation and reason.

Two clear lines of development may be seen in Christian theology. One comes from the Hebrew-Christian tradition and the other from the Greco-Roman philosophy and culture. The synthesis of Thomas brought the two into functional coexistence. This relationship was interpreted later by Reformation thinkers as implying that reason was either above or on a par with revelation. However, this was not part of the apologetic purpose of Thomas. In Thomas's system, reason is not by itself sufficient for redemption or even for the understanding of the cardinal doctrines of the Christian faith. Reason is of little use in coming to grips with issues such as those raised by the Trinity, the incarnation, or the resurrection. On the other hand, reason is a God-given faculty that should be used and not abused. Thomas accepted Anselm's dictum: "I believe in order that I may understand" (credo ut intelligam). This means that the Christian believer may discover that reason can demonstrate such theological propositions as: God exists; the divine attributes include, for example, omnipotence; and so forth.

The all-inclusive purpose of Thomas may be seen in his voluminous literary productivity. Setting aside his important but not so well known biblical and devotional works, there are three major theological works that symbolize the synthesis he created.

The *Summa Contra Gentiles* was begun around 1260 and contains Thomas's treatment of Christian theology with special reference to issues raised by non-believers. It was an attempt to summarize the faith of Roman Catholicism for those "outside" the church, that is, the "gentiles," and as such is an apologetic work. In Book I there is an excellent account of the relation between reason and faith with their prerogatives properly designated.

The *Summa Theologiae*, or *The Sum of Theology* (more generally referred to as the *Summa Theologica*—a Theological Summary) was begun in 1256 and nearly but not quite finished at his death in 1274. It was and continues to be the theologian's theology, though it was originally written as a textbook of instruction for those who had already professed the faith and were members of the Christian community.

The *Summa*, divided into three parts (part two is subdivided in two), took as its subject matter everything about the Creator and the creation. John of Damascus, referred to by Thomas in this work as "Damascene," and Peter Lombard, author of the *Sentences*, helped provide the methodology for this massive work. The *Summa* repeats the device of questions and answers, quotations on one side and the other (reminiscent of Abelard), biblical references correlated with opinions from the theologians, doctrinal assertions, and philosophical speculations (mostly Aristotelian). Almost every conceivable philosophical or theological topic is treated in this work; all the pieces fit together harmoniously. If one takes even a brief look at the contents and outline of the work, one cannot but be impressed with its comprehensiveness.

Shortly before his death, Thomas prepared a brief summary of the Catholic faith for beginners and for laypeople. This work is known as the *Compendium Theologiae* and was structured on the theological virtues of "faith, hope, and love," a device used by Augustine in his famous *Enchiridion* (*Handbook*). Unfortunately, Thomas died before he could finish the discussion of the three parts, and the *Compendium* ends abruptly in the middle of the Lord's Prayer. Under the

Sumo Theologiae

treatment of faith, however, Thomas deals with the doctrine of the Trinity and the definition of the Person of Christ. In the latter, he states the Roman Catholic argument of the two natures in one person and reproduces exactly the argument of Anselm for understanding the death of Christ as atonement.

When we take these works together, we see a clear illustration of the all-embracing theological ability of Thomas Aquinas. Here the Catholic faith is presented and applied to the three great audiences of his time: the unbeliever, the believer, and the learner. That Thomas could speak so eloquently and so persuasively to all these groups is a clear indication of the stature and preeminence of this great "scholastic theologian."

Source: The Summa Theologiae, *English Dominican translation (New York: Benziger Bros., 1947), 11–14.*

▼ ▼ ▼

WHETHER, BESIDES PHILOSOPHY,
ANY FURTHER DOCTRINE IS REQUIRED?
We proceed thus to the First Article:

Objection 1: It seems that, besides philosophical science, we have no need of any further knowledge. For man should not seek to know what is above reason: "Seek not the things that are too high for thee" (Ecclus. iii. 22). But whatever is not above reason is fully treated of in philosophical science. Therefore any knowledge besides philosophical science is superfluous.

Objection 2: Further, knowledge can be concerned only with being, for nothing can be known, save what is true; and all that is, is true. But everything that is, is treated of in philosophical science—even God himself; so that there is a part of philosophy called theology, or the divine science, as Aristotle has proved (*Metaphysics* vi). Therefore, besides philosophi-

cal science, there is no need of any further knowledge.

On the contrary, It is written (2 Tim. 3: 16): "All scripture inspired of God is profitable to teach, to reprove, to correct, to instruct in justice." Now scripture, inspired of God, is no part of philosophical science, which has been built up by human reason. Therefore it is useful that besides philosophical science there should be other knowledge—i.e., inspired by God.

I answer that, it was necessary for man's salvation that there should be a knowledge revealed by God, besides philosophical science built up by human reason. Firstly, indeed, because man is directed to God, as to an end that surpasses the grasp of reason: "The eye hath not seen, O God, besides Thee, what things Thou hast prepared for them that wait for Thee" (Isa. 66:4). But the end must first be known by men who are to direct their thoughts and actions to the end. Hence it was necessary for the salvation of man that certain truths which exceed human reason should be made known to him by divine revelation. Even as regards those truths about God which human reason could have discovered, it was necessary that man should be taught by a divine revelation; because the truth about God such as reason could discover, would only be known by a few, and that after a long time, and with the admixture of many errors. Whereas man's whole salvation, which is in God, depends upon the knowledge of this truth. Therefore, in order that the salvation of men might be brought about more fitly and more surely, it was necessary that they should be taught divine truths by divine revelation. It was therefore necessary that, besides philosophical science built up by reason there should be a sacred science learned through revelation.

Reply to Objection 1: Although those things which are beyond man's knowledge may not be sought for by man through his reason, nevertheless, once they are revealed by

God they must be accepted by faith. Hence the sacred text continues, "For many things are shown to thee above the understanding of man" (Ecclus. 3:25). And in this sacred science consists.

Reply to Objection 2: Sciences are differentiated according to the various means through which knowledge is obtained. For the astronomer and the physicist may prove the same conclusion—that the earth, for instance, is round: the astronomer by means of mathematics (i.e., abstracting from matter), but the physicist by means of matter itself. Hence there is no reason why those things which may be learned from philosophical science, so far as they can be known by natural reason, may not also be taught us by another science so far as they fall within revelation. Hence theology included in sacred doctrine differs in kind from that theology which is part of philosophy.

WHETHER THE EXISTENCE OF GOD IS SELF-EVIDENT?

We proceed thus to the First Article:

Objection 1: It seems that the existence of God is self-evident. Now those things are said to be self-evident to us the knowledge of which is naturally implanted in us, as we can see in regard to first principles. But as Damascene (John of Damnascus) says (De Fide Orthodoxa, i. 1, 3), "the knowledge of God is naturally implanted in all." Therefore the existence of God is self-evident.

Objection 2: Further, those things are said to be self-evident which are known as soon as the terms are known, which the Philosopher (Aristotle) (Analytica Posteriora, 1, iii) says is true of the first principles of demonstration. Thus, when the nature of a whole and of a part is known, it is at once recognized that every whole is greater than its part. But as soon as the signification of the word "God" is understood, it is at once seen that God exists. For by this word is signified that thing than which nothing greater can be conceived. But that which

exists actually and mentally is greater than that which exists only mentally; it follows that it exists. There the proposition "God exists" is self-evident.

Objection 3: Further, the existence of truth is self-evident. For whoever denies the existence of truth grants that truth does not exist; and, if truth does not exist, then the proposition "Truth does not exist" is true; and if there is anything true, there must be truth. But God is truth itself: "I am the way, the truth, and the life" (John 14:6). Therefore "God exists" is self-evident.

On the contrary: No one can mentally admit the opposite of what is self-evident; as the Philosopher (De Metaphysica iv, lect. vi) states concerning the first principles of demonstration. But the opposite of the proposition "God is" can be mentally admitted: "The fool said in his heart, There is no God" (Ps. 52:1). Therefore, that God exists is not self-evident.

I answer that: A thing can be self-evident in either of two ways; on the one hand, self-evident in itself, though not to us; on the other, self-evident in itself, and to us. A proposition is included in the essence of the subject, as "Man is an animal," for animal is contained in the essence of man. If, therefore, the essence of the predicate and subject be known to all, the proposition will be self-evident to all; as is clear with regard to the first principles of demonstration, the terms of which are common things that no one is ignorant of, such as being and non-being, whole and part, and such like. If, however, there are some to whom the essence of the predicate and subject is unknown, the proposition will be self-evident in itself, but not those who do not know the meaning of the predicate and subject of the proposition. Therefore, it happens, as Boethius says (De Hebdomadibus, the title of which is "Whether all that is, is good"), "that there are some mental concepts self-evident only to the learned, as that incorporeal substances are not in space." Therefore I say that this proposition, "God exists," of itself is self-evident, for the predicate is the same as the subject; because God is his own existence as will be hereafter shown (Q.3, A.4). Now because we do not know the essence of God, the proposition is not self-evident to us; but needs to be demonstrated by things that are more known to us, though less known in their nature—namely, by effects.

Reply to Objection 1: To know that God exists in a general and confused way is implanted in us by nature, inasmuch as God is man's beatitude. For man naturally desires happiness, and what is naturally desired by man must be naturally known to him. This, however, is not to know absolutely that God exists; just as to know that someone is approaching is not the same as to know that Peter is approaching, even though it is Peter who is approaching; for many there are who imagine that man's perfect good which is happiness, consists in richness and others in pleasures, and others in something else.

Reply to Objection 2: Perhaps not everyone who hears this word "God" understands it to signify something than which nothing greater can be thought, seeing that some have believed God to be a body. Yet, granted that everyone understands that by this word "God" is signified something than which nothing greater can be thought, nevertheless, it does not therefore follow that he understands that what the word signified exists, but only that it exists mentally. Nor can it be argued that it actually exists, unless it be admitted that there actually exists something than which nothing greater can be thought; and this precisely is not admitted by those hold that God does not exist.

Reply to Objection 3: The existence of truth in general is self-evident but the existence of a Primal Truth is not self-evident to us.

WHETHER IT CAN BE DEMONSTRATED THAT GOD EXISTS?

We proceed thus to the Second Article:

Objection 1: It seems that the existence of God cannot be demonstrated. For it is an article of faith that God exists. But what is of faith cannot be demonstrated, because a demonstration produces scientific knowledge; whereas faith is of the unseen (Heb. 11:1). Therefore, it cannot be demonstrated that God exists.

Objection 2: Further, the essence is the middle term of demonstration. But we cannot know in what God's essence consists, but solely in what it does not consist; as Damascene says (*De Fide Orthodoxa,* i, 4). Therefore we cannot demonstrate that God exists.

Objection 3: Further, if the existence of God were demonstrated, this could only be from his effects. But his effects are not proportionate to him, since he is infinite and his effects are finite; and between the finite and infinite there is no proportion. Therefore, since a cause cannot be demonstrated by an effect not proportionate to it, it seems the existence of God cannot be demonstrated.

On the contrary, the apostle says: "The invisible things of him are clearly seen, being understood by the things that are made" (Rom. 1:20). But this would not be unless the existence of God could be demonstrated through the things that are made; for the first thing we must know of anything is, whether it exists.

I answer that, Demonstration can be made in two ways: One is through the cause, and is called *a priori,* and this is to argue from what is prior absolutely. The other is through the effect, and is called a demonstration *a posteriori;* this is to argue from what is prior only relatively to us. When an effect is better known that its cause, from the effect we proceed to the knowledge of the cause. And from every effect the existence of its proper cause can be demonstrated, so long as its effects are better known to us; because since every effect depends upon its cause, if the effect exists, the cause must pre-exist. Hence the existence of God, in so far as it is not self-evident to us, can be demonstrated from those of His effects which are known to us.

Reply to Objection 1: The existence of God and other like truths about God, which can be known by natural reason, are not articles of faith, but preambles to the articles; for faith presupposes natural knowledge, even as grace presupposes nature, and perfection supposes something that can be perfected. Nevertheless, there is nothing to prevent a man, who cannot grasp a proof, accepting, as a matter of faith, something which in itself is capable of being scientifically known and demonstrated.

Reply to Objection 2: When the existence of a cause is demonstrated from an effect, this effect takes the place of the definition of the cause in proof of the cause's existence. This is especially the case in regard to God, because, in order to prove the existence of anything, it is necessary to accept as a middle term the meaning of the word, and not its essence, for the question of its essence follows on the question of its existence. Now the names given to God are derived from his effects; consequently, in demonstrating the existence of God from his effects, we may take for the middle term the meaning of the word "God."

Reply to Objection 3: From effects not proportionate to the cause no perfect knowledge of that cause can be obtained. Yet from every effect the existence of the cause can be clearly demonstrated, and so we can demonstrate the existence of God from his effects; though from them we cannot perfectly know God as he is in his essence.

WHETHER GOD EXISTS?

We proceed thus to the Third Article:

Objection 1: It seems that God does not exist; because if one of two contraries be infinite, the other would be altogether destroyed. But the word "God" means that he is infinite goodness. If, therefore, God existed there would be no evil discoverable; but there is evil in the world. Therefore God does not exist.

Objection 2: Further, it is superfluous to suppose that what can be accounted for by a few principles has been produced by many. But it seems that everything we see in the world can be accounted for by other principles, supposing God did not exist. For all natural things can be reduced to one principle, which is nature; and all voluntary things can be reduced to one principle, which is human reason, or will. Therefore there is no need to suppose God's existence.

On the contrary, It is said in the person of God: "I am Who I am" (Exod. 3:14).

I answer that, The existence of God can be proved in five ways.

The first and more manifest way is the argument from motion. It is certain, and evident to our senses, that in the world some things are in motion. Now whatever is in motion is put in motion by another, for nothing can be in motion except it is in potentiality to that towards which it is in motion; whereas a things moves inasmuch as it is an act. For motion is nothing else than a reduction of something from potentiality to actuality. But nothing can be reduced from potentiality to actuality, except by something in a state of actuality. Thus that which is naturally hot, as fire, makes wood, which is potentially hot, to be actually hot, and thereby moves and changes it. Now it is not possible that the same thing should be at once in actuality and potentiality in the same respect, but only in different respects. For what is actually hot cannot be simultaneously potentially hot; but it is simultaneously cold. It is therefore impossible that in the same respect and in the same way a thing should be mover and moved, i.e. that it should move itself. Therefore, whatever is in motion must be put in motion by another. If that by which it is put in motion be itself put in motion, then this also must needs be put in motion by another, and that by another again. But this cannot go on to infinity, because then there would be no first mover, and, consequently, no other move; seeing that subsequent movers move only inasmuch as they are put in motion by the first mover; as the staff moves only because it is put in motion by the hand. Therefore it is necessary to arrive at a first mover, put in motion by no other; and this everyone understands to be God.

The second way is from the nature of efficient cause. In the world of sense we find there is an order of efficient causes. There is no case known (neither is it, indeed, impossible) in which a thing is found to be the efficient cause of itself; for so it would be prior to itself, which is impossible. Now in efficient cause it is not possible to go on to infinity, because in all efficient causes following in order, the first is the cause of the intermediate cause, and the intermediate is the cause of the ultimate cause, whether the intermediate be several, or one only. Now to take away the cause is to take away the effect. Therefore, if there be no first cause among efficient causes, there will be no ultimate, nor any intermediate cause. But if in efficient causes it is possible to go to infinity, there will be no first efficient cause, neither will there be an ultimate effect, nor any intermediate efficient causes; all of which is plainly false. Therefore it is necessary to admit a first effi-

cient cause, to which everyone gives the name of God.

The third way is taken from possibility and necessity and runs thus. We find in nature things that are possible to be and not to be, since they are found to be generated, and to be corrupted, and consequently, they are possible to be and not to be. But it is impossible for these to always exist, for that which is possible not to be at some time is not. Therefore, if everything is possible not to be, then at one time there could have been nothing in existence. Now if this were true, even now there would be nothing in existence, because that which does not exist only begins to exist by something already existing. Therefore, if at one time nothing was in existence, it would have been impossible for anything to have begun to exist; and thus even now nothing would be in existence—which is absurd. Therefore, not all beings are merely possible, but there must exist something the existence of which is necessary. But every necessary thing either has its necessity caused by another or not. Now it is impossible to go on to infinity in necessary things which have their necessity caused by

Going Somewhere?

another, as has been already proved in regard to efficient causes. Therefore we cannot but postulate the existence of some being having of itself its own necessity, and not receiving it from another, but rather causing in others their necessity. This all men speak of as God.

The fourth way is taken from the gradation to be found in things. Among beings there are some more and some less good, true, noble, and the like. But "more" and "less" are predicated of different things, according as they resemble in their different ways something which is the maximum, as a thing is said to be hotter according as it more nearly resembles that which is hottest; so that there is something which is truest, something best, something noblest, and, consequently, something which is uttermost being; for those things that are greatest in truth are greatest in being, as it is written in [Aristotle's] *De Metaphysica* ii. Now the maximum in any genus is the cause of all in that genus; as fire, which is the maximum of heat, is the cause of all hot things. Therefore there must also be something which is to all beings the cause of their being, goodness, and every other perfection; and this we call God.

The fifth way is taken from the governance of the world. We see that things which lack intelligence, such as natural bodies, act for an end, and this is evident from their acting always, or nearly always, in the same way, so as to obtain the best result. Hence it is plain that not fortuitously, but designedly, do they achieve their end. Now whatever lacks intelligence cannot move towards an end, unless it be directed by some being endowed with knowledge and intelligence, as the arrow is shot to its mark by the archer. Therefore some intelligent being exists by whom all natural things are directed toward their end; and this being we call God.

Reply to Objection 1: As Augustine says (*Enchiridion*, xi): "Since God is the highest good, he would not allow any evil to exist in his works, unless his omnipotence and good-ness were such as to bring good out of evil." This is part of the infinite goodness of God, that he should allow evil to exist, and out of it produce good.

Reply to Objection 2: Since nature works for a determinate end under the direction of a higher agent, whatever is done by nature must needs be traced back to God, as to its first cause. So also whatever is done voluntarily must also be traced back to some higher cause other than human reason or will, since these can change and fail; for all things that are changeable and capable of defect must be traced back to an immovable and self-necessary first principle, as was shown in the body of the Article.

▲ ▲ ▲

In the history of systematic theology, Thomas's *Summa Theologiae* is a landmark work if for no other reason than for the order it imposes on its material. Before the *Summa Theologiae*, the normative text for the study of theology was Peter Lombard's *Sentences* (ca. 1150). Thomas, for the first time, divides and orders subjects according to logical principles. Part One, Theology Proper, treats of the essence of God, the Trinity, creation, and providence. Part Two, Moral Theology, is comprised of two divisions; the first (*prima secunda*) deals with ethical foundations, and the second (*secunda secundae*) is an elaborate treatise on the virtues and vices. Part Three, Christology, deals with the nature and work of Jesus Christ, with the sacraments, and with the future life (eschatology). The last part of the discussions on the future life and the sacraments was completed by his disciples after the death of Thomas and is referred to as the Supplement.

The thirteenth century saw the rise of European universities, with their separate faculties of law, medicine, arts, and philosophy. It is not by chance that this departmentalization coincided with the rediscovery of Aristotle, whom Thomas calls "the philosopher" and who not only left masterful treatises on a wide variety of subjects, but also argued, at the same time, on principle that each deserved to be treated in its own way. Thus, Aristotle distinguished between the theoretical science of physics and the practical science of ethics; above both of these he placed philosophy. Thomas accepted this new way of thinking but believed that theology needed to set its own house in order, that the boundaries between philosophy and theology needed to be more clearly drawn with principles laid down to govern the relations between reason and faith.

Thomas was very much at home with Aristotle and contributed many volumes commenting on the work of the great Greek philosopher. *Summa Theologiae* is a theological work, however, and here philosophy is put at the service of theology. Thomas makes use of Aristotle's theory of knowledge (epistemology). According to Thomas, the Augustinian view, which had prevailed in earlier scholasticism, holds that the human intellect is able by divine illumination to possess immediate knowledge of supernatural reality. Using Aristotle, Thomas argues that human knowledge is mediated through the senses, and whatever knowledge we may have of divine realities must be made by inference from or by analogy with our knowledge of material things. Clearly, then, what humans can know about God by pure reason is strictly limited. Here we see his empiricism derived from Aristotle applied to what humans can know about God. It can be shown that a "First Cause" must exist over

nature, and it can be shown by the *via negativa* (the negative way)—abstracting from the imperfections of creatures, something of the perfection of the Creator. However, the internal life of God cannot be known, nor may God's purposes toward nature be known. Truths of this nature (such as the doctrine of the Trinity, the incarnation, and the doctrine of the resurrection) could not be known if God had not revealed them to us. Reason is employed, in connection with these revealed truths, to clarify and to make these truths intelligible.

God in Thomas's system resembles the "One" of Neoplatonism or the "Form of Forms" in Aristotle more than the God of Scripture. God is the Supremely Real who, in knowing God's self, knows all and in willing, wills all good. God's will is explained in typical Aristotelian fashion, namely, that it is the natural inclination of the intellect of God toward the Reality it contemplates.

Thomas's significant achievement was in effecting a synthesis of the Christian doctrine with a worldview that owed its origins to non-Christian thinkers. The legitimacy of this kind of undertaking has been questioned repeatedly in the history of the church—in the early church in the person of Tertullian, in modern times, by Karl Barth, and so forth. Is there continuity between Christ and the world? Yes, said Thomas! Christianity is continuous with Creation; revelation is a supplement to reason; redemption is a moment in the universal drama; Jesus Christ is the center of world history; and the church is not so much a challenge to civilization as it is its complement. Thomas was not uncomfortable with the secular and was favorably disposed toward civilization wherever he found it. Ancient thinkers with no other resources than those of their natural endowment did admirably well; so did the Jews and the Arabs with their partial revelation. If non-Christians were able to achieve so much, how much more should Christians achieve under the economy of God's grace? According to Thomas, there could and should be a Christian philosophy, a Christian art, a Christian morality, all built broadly on human foundations, but corrected at some points, extended at others in light of revelation.

15. JOHANNES MEISTER ECKHARDT (1260–1327)

A few facts concerning the life of Johannes Meister Eckhardt have been established. Born about 1260 in Hochheim, Germany, he was the son of a steward in the castle of a nobleman. As a young man he entered the Dominican Order and attended school in Cologne. He was made prior of his order at Erfurt and then provincial vicar of his order in Thuringia.

Being typical of the new kind of mystic that was developing, Eckhardt was not an emotional enthusiast, an ignorant firebrand, or a quietistic anchorite. Quite the contrary, he was a scholar who studied and preached at the University of Paris and maintained an active role in his Dominican Order.

From about 1321 until his death in 1327 he was embroiled in charges of heresy. Popular mystical movements were spreading in Germany at this time, much to the chagrin of Heinrich Von Virneberg, archbishop of Cologne. In 1325 a charge of heresy was brought against Eckhardt, but he was formally cleared, perhaps because his interrogator was also a Dominican. The archbishop, who was a Franciscan, persisted, however, and a second examination of Eckhardt's writings was made by Franciscans, who produced a formidable list of errors.

Eckhardt was accused of pantheism (God is all—all is God), and Pope John XXII declared some of his views to be heretical. These new mystics' practice of mutual confession of sins tended to undercut the sacrament of penance as established within the ecclesiastical organization. In addition, since Eckhardt and his followers claimed it was possible to attain direct communion with God, even apart from the visual sacramental aids, the entire sacramental system of the Roman Catholic Church was undermined. Indeed, sometimes, Eckhardt's critics claimed, this view obviated the mediating role of Jesus Christ. Thus, even though the avowed intent and purpose of scholars such as Eckhardt was to strengthen and renew the church, their own success in leading exemplary and often just lives in the midst of ecclesiastical corruption led many, according to their critics, to believe the church was not so important after all and that it was quite possible to live a good Christian life without the aid of a corrupt hierarchy. From this, it was only a step further to decide that in order to be faithful to the gospel, it was necessary to break with the corrupt practices and false doctrines of the established church. Meister Eckhardt appealed to Rome but was denied. He seems to have died shortly after being summoned by the archbishop of Cologne to defend himself.

It is simple to classify Eckhardt as a mystic; it is far less simple to give a precise definition to the term itself. Indeed, the term *mysticism* is notorious for its elasticity of usage. In the broad sense it refers to religious phenomena in which immediacy of knowledge is emphasized. *Intuition* is another term frequently used to describe such experiences.

Other interpretations add ideas to this minimal definition, such as the unity of human beings with God, experiences of ecstasy or rapture, the ascent of the soul to God, the idea of God as absolute or self-subsistent being, and the idea of emanation. The mystical tradition of the West includes such figures as Plato, Plotinus, Pseudo-Dionysius, and John Scotus Erigena. Eckhardt's writings show his familiarity with many of the figures and ideas. It should be noted, however, that the whole ethos of medieval Christianity was mystical in the primary sense noted above. Like any person, Johannes Meister Eckhardt was a child of his age.

Source: "Talks of Instruction 6" in Meister Eckhardt: A Modern Translation, *translated by R. G. Blakney (New York: Paulist Press, 1941), 7–10.*

▼ ▼ ▼

I was asked this question: "Some people withdraw from society and prefer to be alone; their peace of mind depends on it; wouldn't it be better for them to be in the church?" I replied, "No!" And you shall see why.

Those who do well do well wherever they are, and in whatever company, and those who do badly do badly wherever they are, and in whatever company. But if a man does well, God is really in him, and with him everywhere, on the streets and among people just as much as in church, or a desert place, or a cell. If he really has God, and only God, then nothing disturbs him. Why?

Because he has *only* God and thinks only God and everything is nothing but God to him. He discloses God in every act, in every place. The whole business of his person adds up to God. His actions are due only to him who is the author of them and not to himself, since he is merely the agent. If we mean God and only God, then it is God who does what we do and nothing can disturb him—neither company nor place. Thus, neither can any person disturb him, for he thinks nothing, is looking for nothing, and relishes nothing but God, who is one with him by perfect devotion. Furthermore, since God cannot be distracted by the number of things, neither can the person, for he is one in One, in which all divided things are gathered up to unity and there undifferentiated.

One ought to keep hold of God in everything and accustom his mind to retain God always among his feelings, thought, and loves. Take care how you think of God. As you think of him in church or closet, think of him everywhere. Take him with you among the crowds and turmoil of the alien world. As I have said so often, speaking of uniformity, we do not mean that one should regard all deeds, places, and people as interchangeable. That would be a great mistake, for it is better to pray than to spin and the church ranks above the street. You should, however, maintain the same mind, the same trust, and the same earnestness toward God in all your doings. Believe me, if you keep this kind of evenness, nothing can separate you from God-consciousness.

On the other hand, the person who is not conscious of God's presence, but who must always be going out to get him from this and that, who has to seek him by special methods, as by means of some activity, person, or place—such people have not attained God. It can easily happen that they are disturbed, for they have not God and they do not seek, think, and love only him, and therefore, not only will evil company be to them a stumbling block, but good company as well—not only the street, but the church; not only bad deeds and words, but good ones as well. The difficulty lies within the man, for whom God has not yet become everything. If God were everything, the man would get along well wherever he went and among whatever people, for he would possess God and no one could rob him or disturb his work.

Of what does this true possession of God consist, when one really has him? It depends on the heart and an inner, intellectual return to God and not on steady contemplation by a given method. It is impossible to keep such a method in mind, or at least difficult, and even then it is not best. We ought not to have or let ourselves be satisfied with the god we have thought of, for when the thought slips the mind, that god slips with it. What we want is rather the reality of God, exalted far above any human thought or creature. Then God will not vanish unless one turns away from him of his own accord.

When one takes God as his divine, having the reality of God within him, God sheds light on everything. Everything will taste like God and reflect him. God will shine in him all the time. He will have the disinterest, renunciation, and spiritual vision of his beloved, ever-present Lord. He will be like one athirst with a real thirst; he cannot help drinking even though he thinks of other things. Wherever he is, with whomsoever he may be, whatever his purpose of thoughts or occupation—the idea of the Drink will not depart as long as the thirst endures; and the greater the thirst the more lively, deep-seated, present, and steady the idea of the Drink will be. Or suppose one loves something with all that is in him, so that

Intercessory Prayer, Anyone?

nothing else can move him or give pleasure, and he cares for that alone, looking for nothing more; then wherever he is or with whomsoever he may be, whatever he tries or does, that Something he loves will not be extinguished from his mind. He will see it everywhere, and the stronger his love grows for it the more vivid it will be. A person like this never thinks of resting because he is never tired.

The more he regards everything as divine—more divine than it is of itself—the more God will be pleased with him. To be sure, this requires effort and love, a careful cultivation of the spiritual life, and a watchful, honest, active oversight of all one's mental attitudes toward things and people. It is not to be learned by world-flight, running away from things, turning solitary and going apart from the world. Rather, one must learn an inner solitude, wherever or with whomsoever he may be. He must learn to penetrate things and find God there, to get a strong impression of God firmly fixed in his mind.

It is like learning to write. To acquire this art, one must practice much, however disagreeable or difficult it may be, however impossible it may seem. Practicing earnestly and often, one learns to write, acquires the art. To be sure, each letter must first be considered separately, and accurately, reproduced over and over again; but once having acquired the skill, one need not pay any attention to the reproduction [of the letters] or even think of them. He will write fluently and freely whether it be penmanship of some bold work, in which his art appears. It is sufficient for the writer to know that he is using his skill and since he does not always have to think of it, he does his work by means of it.

So a man should shine with the divine Presence without having to work at it. He should get the essence of things and let the things themselves alone. That requires at first attentiveness and exact impressions, as with the stu-dent and his art. So one must be permeated with divine Presence, informed with the forms of beloved God who is within him, so that he may radiate that Presence without working at it.

▲ ▲ ▲

As we indicated in our introduction, Eckhardt was influenced by many classical personalities, including Plato, Plotinus, and Augustine. At the same time, however, he placed his own distinctive stamp upon these influences. Eckhardt's mysticism was as much the result of his intense personality and his deeply religious life as the result of these classic influences. So it is that much of the mysticism in the West has come to mean a form of inner individual experience that not only resists any rational or logical demonstration, but also stands in strong opposition to it.

According to Eckhardt, it really does not matter whether one begins one's journey into mystical theology by studying God or by studying the self, for human beings and God are ultimately aspects of a single seamless unity. Nevertheless, we should clearly understand that Eckhardt did not suggest a simple equation between humanity and deity, whether an actual, empirical human soul, or between deity and all human souls or all being. There is a special relationship, however, between God and humanity from the beginning: we are children of God, we have been created in God's own image, and it is our proper destiny to fulfill or realize our special destiny.

Humanity rises by degrees, according to Eckhardt, to a relationship characterized as intimate communion with God and often described as one in which all distinctions are left behind in the fullness of ontological union. In this experience we leave the world of things behind and enter the inner castle of the soul; we transcend time and space.

To achieve this inwardness, the fullness of this experience, one must have a pure heart, the total absence of ulterior motivation. One must desire God and do so for the sake of God. The mind as self so conceived is asserted to be free. By this freedom Eckhardt is suggesting precisely the capacity to shake oneself free of all attachment to finite things, without reservation. Perfection, as defined here by Eckhardt, is not perfect conformity to the will of God, but emancipation from all finitude.

One of the difficulties with Eckhardt's work was his view of God, who is the object of this search. Is it the deity of Christianity, or is it some extension of the views of classic writers such as Plato and Plotinus? "God," declared Eckhardt, "is being." This statement appears to be traditional, but, at the same time, it is luxuriant in its variety of meaning. Did not Plato and Plotinus declare deity to be self-subsistent reality? Did not the Lord in reply to the query of Moses in Exodus regarding the name of deity state the revealing words: "I AM THAT I AM?" And did not Thomas Aquinas, shortly before Eckhardt, bring both of these meanings together in his masterful synthesis? So it was that Christianity stated that God possesses Godself, the fullness and perfection of being that we, as human beings, only possess partially and imperfectly.

How did Eckhardt depart from all of this? Perhaps in this way: The deity of Christianity is a personal God, whereas the God of Eckhardt is an impersonal absolute unity that transcends all relations. As he expressed it in one of his sermons: "Distinctions are lost in God." Elsewhere he spoke of going beyond God to God, or beyond God to unity. For Eckhardt, God is truly the fullness of being that surpasses our human comprehension. God is like a blazing or dazzling light in whose brightness all human distinctions are lost.

Despite its impersonal nature, the deity of Eckhardt was nonetheless affirmative in tone. While he repeatedly recommended humility and self-negation, and while he charged his hearers to transcend the world of things, on balance he had an overwhelmingly positive view. There was relatively little asceticism and no outright negation of the world's reality and significance. In contrast to the negative character of much mysticism, the affirmative temper of Eckhardt must be seen as the result of his own personality.

Eckhardt's views were equally positive in terms of practicality. While the goal of mystical unity is beyond all action, there are many moral phases in this road to perfection. Eckhardt was hostile only to those works that were prompted by ulterior motives or that beget self-righteousness. The spirit of Eckhardt's thought was clearly one of respect for and affirmation of human personality.

Eckhardt blazed new paths, and his impact has been felt for centuries. His "God is Being" recurs from Baruch Spinoza to G. W. F. Hegel and Paul Tillich. His mysticism of individual subjectivity has been a lure and threat to religious thought ever since his time. His insights never allow us to place God in any type of box, either ecclesiastical or theological.

16. Women of the Middle Ages (1098–1423)

Hildegard of Bingen (1098–1179)

In medieval times the German Benedictine abbess Hildegard of Bingen seems to have been versed in logic as well as botany, biology, music, poetry, medicine, pharmacology, letters, biblical history, prayer, scriptural study, meditation, mysticism, epistemology, politics, alchemy, cosmology, the illumination arts, musical drama, singing, winemaking, financial administration, and other areas of the arts, sciences, crafts, and trades. Also a social activist, Hildegard was at times critic of pope, emperor, and bishop and regularly of patriarchal abuses. In her mid-seventies she apparently carried her writings to a growing University of Paris where she won faculty approval of her work. J. P. Migne included her writings in his *Patrologia Latina* many centuries later, but only recently have they been translated into English.

Hildegard was the tenth child born to a family of nobility. As was customary with the tenth child, she was dedicated at birth to the church. She started to have visions of luminous objects at an early age, and she soon realized that she was unique and hid this gift for many years.

At the age of eight she was sent to an anchoress named Jutta for religious education. The education she received was of the most rudimentary form, and Hildegard could never escape feelings of inadequacy. The proximity of the anchorage to the church of the Benedictine monastery at Disibodenberg exposed young Hildegard to musical religious services and were quite influential on her. After Jutta's death, she was elected at the age of thirty-eight the head of the budding convent living within the cramped walls of the anchorage. (Around 1150 Hildegard moved her convent from Disibodenberg to Bingen.)

The twelfth century was a time of schisms and religious ferment. Hildegard was critical of schismatics and preached against them, especially the Cathars. She desired to have her visions sanctioned (approved by the Catholic Church), although she never doubted the divine origins of her luminous visions. She wrote to St. Bernard seeking his blessing. While Bernard gave her only a perfunctory response, he did bring her to the attention of Pope Eugenius (1145–1153), an enlightened individual who exhorted Hildegard to finish her writings. With papal imprimatur, she was able to complete her first visionary work, *Scivas* ("Know the Ways of the Lord"), and her fame began to spread throughout Germany and beyond.

Hildegard was at home in the world of the sciences, deriving her views from the ancient Greek philosophers. Her writings are unique in that they give a generally positive and pleasurable view of human sexuality from a woman's perspective.

Sources: "Hildegard to the Prelates of Mainz," in The Letters of Hildegard of Bingen, *edited by Joseph L. Baird and Rodd K. Ehrman (New York: Oxford University Press, 1994), 76ff.;* Meditations, *translated by Gabriele Uhlein, OSF (Santa Fe, N.M.: Bear and Co., 1983), 28, 32, 54, 77, 104;* Scivias, *Book 2,* The Life and Visions of St. Hildegard of Bingen, *translated by F. M. Steele (London: Heath, Cranton and Ousely, 1914).*

▼ ▼ ▼

TO THE PRELATES OF MAINZ

By a vision, which was implanted in my soul by God the Great Artisan before I was born, I have been compelled to write these things because of the interdict by which our superiors have bound us, on account of a certain dead man buried at our monastery, a man buried without objection, with his own priest officiating. Yet only a few days after his burial, these men ordered us to remove him from our cemetery. Seized by no small terror, as a result, I looked as usual to the True Light, and, with wakeful eyes, I saw in my spirit that if this man were disinterred in accordance with their commands, a terrible and lamentable danger would come upon us like a dark cloud before a threatening thunderstorm.

Therefore, we have not presumed to remove the body of the deceased inasmuch as he had confessed his sins, had received extreme unction and communion, and had been buried without objection. Furthermore we have not yielded to those who advised or even commanded this course of action. Not, certainly, that we take the counsel of upright men or the orders of our superiors lightly, but we would not have it appear that, out of feminine harshness we did injustice to the sacraments of Christ, with which this man had been fortified while he was still alive. But so that we may not be totally disobedient we have, in accordance with their injunction, ceased from singing the divine praises and from participation in the Mass, as had been our regular monthly custom.

As a result, my sisters and I have been greatly distressed and saddened. Weighed down by this burden, therefore, I heard these words in a vision: It is of the Garment of the Word of God, Who, born virginally of the Virgin Mary, is your salvation. . . .

You and all prelates must exercise the greatest vigilance to clear the air by full and thorough discussion of the justification for such actions before your verdict closes the mouth of any church singing praises to God or suspends it from handling and receiving the divine sacraments. And you must be especially certain that you are drawn to this action out of zeal for God's justice rather than out of indignation, unjust emotions or a desire for revenge and you must always be on your guard not to be circumvented in your desires by Satan, who drove man from celestial harmony and the delights of paradise. . . .

Therefore, those who, without cause, impose silence on a church and prohibit the singing of God's praises and those who have on earth unjustly despoiled God of his honor and glory will lose their place among the chorus of angels, unless they have amended their lives through true penitence and humble restitution. Moreover, let those who hold the keys of heaven beware not to open those things which are to be kept closed nor to close those things with are to be kept open, for harsh judgment will fall upon those who rule, unless, as the apostle says, they rule with good judgment.

WHO IS THE TRINITY?

Who is the Trinity?

You are music.
You are life.

Source of everything,
creator of everything,
angelic hosts sing your praise.

Wonderfully radiant,
deep,
mysterious.

****

Invisible life that sustains ALL,
I awaken to life everything
in every waft of air.

The air is life,
greening and blossoming.
The waters flow with life.
The moon, when waning, is again
    rekindled by the sun,
    waxing with life once more.
The stars shine,
radiating with life-light.
    All creation is gifted with the
    ecstasy of God's light.

The earth,
at any point,
can be located by its relationship
    to the sun.

The earth has a scaffold of stones and
trees. In the same way is a person formed:
    flesh is the earth,
    the bones are the trees and stones.

The soul is the firmament of the organism,
then.
In the manner in which the soul permeates
the body with its energy, it causes and
consummates all human action.

This is how a person becomes a flowering
orchard.

The person that does good works is indeed
this orchard bearing good fruit. And this
is just like the earth with its ornamentation
of stone and blossoming trees.

****

Now in the people
that were meant to be green,
there is no more life of any kind.
There is only shriveled barrenness.

The winds are burdened
by the utterly awful stink of evil,
selfish goings-on.

Thunderstorms menace.

    The air belches out
    the filthy uncleanliness of the peoples.

There pours forth an unnatural,
a loathsome darkness,
that withers the green,
and wizens the fruit
that was to serve as food for the people.

Sometimes this layer of air
is full,
full of a fog that is the source
of many destructive and barren creatures,
that destroy and damage the earth,
rendering it incapable
of sustaining humanity.

****

In Nature, God established humankind
    in power.
We are dressed in the scaffold of
        creation:
    in seeing—to understand,
    in smelling—to discern,
    in tasting—to nurture,
    in touching—to govern.
In this way humankind comes to know God,
for God is the author of all creation.

VISIONS

Then I saw a most splendid light, and in that
light, the whole of which burnt in a most beautiful, shining fire, was the figure of a man of
sapphire color, and that most splendid light
poured over the whole of that shining fire, and
the shining fire over all that splendid light, and
that most splendid light and shining fire over
the whole figure of a man, appearing one light
in one virtue and power. And again I heard that
living Light saying to me: this is the meaning
of the mysteries of God, that it may be discerned and understood discreetly what that full-

ness may be, which is without beginning and to which nothing is wanting, who by the most powerful strength planted all the rivers of the strong [places]. For if the Lord is wanting in his own strength, what then would his work be?

Certainly vain, and so in a perfect work is seen who was its maker. On which account thou gavest this most splendid Light, which is without beginning and to whom nothing can be wanting: this means the Father, and in that figure of a man of a sapphire color, without any spot of the imperfection of envy and iniquity, is declared the Son, born of the Father, according to the divinity before all time, but afterwards incarnate according to the humanity, in the world, in time. The whole of which burns in a most beautiful, shining fire, which fire without a touch of any dark mortality shows the Holy Spirit, by whom the same only-begotten Son of God was conceived according to the flesh, and born in time of the Virgin, and poured forth the light of true brightness upon the world.

But that splendid Light pours forth all that shining fire, and that shining fire all that splendid Light, and the splendid shining light of the fire, the whole figure of the man, making one

Light existing in one strength and power: this is because the Father, who is the highest equity, but not without the Son nor the Holy Spirit who is the kinder of the hearts of the faithful, but not without the Father and the Son, and the Son who has the fullness of virtue, but not without the Father and the Holy Spirit, are inseparable in the majesty of the divinity; because the Father is not without the Son, neither the Son without the Father, nor the Father and the Son without the Holy Spirit, neither the Holy Spirit without them, and these three Persons exist one God in one whole divinity of majesty: and the unity of the divinity lives inseparable in three persons, because the Trinity is not able to be divided, but remains always inviolable without any without the word, nor the word without life. And where remains the word? In the man. Whence does it go out? From the man. In what way? From the living man.

Thus is the Son in the Father, whom son Father for the salvation of men sitting in darkness, sent to earth, conceived in the Virgin by the Holy Spirit. Which Son as he was only-begotten in his divinity, so he was only begotten in virginity, and as he is the only Son of the

If Hildegard Had Gone Camping . . .

Father, so he is the only Son of his mother, because as the Father begat him before all time, so his virgin mother bore him only in time, because she remained virgin after his birth. . . .

Thence, O man! thus embrace thy God in the courage of thy strength, before the Judge of thy works shall come, when all things shall be manifested, lest anything hidden should be left, when those times come which in their duration shall not fail. Concerning these things, but murmuring thou givest in thy human thought: "They do not please me, neither do I understand whether they are meritorious or not, because in this my human mind is always doubtful, for when a man does good works he is anxious whether they please God or not. And when he does evil he fears concerning the remission which is of salvation." But he who sees with watchful eyes, and hears with attentive ears, offers an embrace to these mystic words of mine which emanate from me, living. . . .

But as the shining fire illuminates darkness, burning those things upon which it had been lying, thus the Holy Spirit drives away infidelity, taking away all the foulness of iniquity. . . . As the flame in one fire has three powers, so the one God is in three Persons. In what manner? For in the flame abides splendid light, innate vigor, and fiery heat, but it has splendid light that it may shine, innate vigor that it may flourish, and fiery heat that it may burn. Thence consider in the splendid Light, the Father who in his paternal love sheds his light upon the faithful, and in that innate vigor of the splendid flame in which that same flame shows its power, understand the Son, who took flesh from the virgin, in which the divinity declared his wonders, and in the fiery heat, behold the Holy Spirit, who gently kindles the hearts and minds of the faithful.

▲ ▲ ▲

Julian of Norwich (1342–1423)

Very little is known of the life or the background of the medieval English mystic whose only name was Julian of Norwich. In spite of her protestations that she was ignorant, she was apparently well-versed in the Latin Vulgate and the spiritual literature of her time. Her writing was at its height during the latter part of the fourteenth century, when she would have been in her thirties. About the same time, Geoffrey Chaucer was translating Boethius's *Consolation of Philosophy*, a work she may well have known because of her mastery of the subtleties of rhetoric.

She lived as an anchoress (a religious contemplative living in seclusion) in a shed attached to the parish of St. Julian in Conisford at Norwich. Her revelations or showings were transcribed in both a short and a long form, the latter containing sixteen revelations in eighty-six chapters.

There are two special features of the mystical theology of Julian that should be mentioned. First, unlike many ascetics and contemplatives, Julian was unusually adept at translating her visions and reveries into sophisticated, conceptual language. Second, the most daring manifestation of her mystical-doctrinal idiom was her repeated insistence on "God as Mother," a concept she carefully factored into extended discussions of the Trinity. It is no surprise that Julian often thought in terms of threes—three graces, three parts, three degrees, three attitudes, and so forth. Her concept of God as Mother involved her and her translators in some confusion over gender pronouns.

Source: C. Jones, "The English Mystic: Julian of Norwich," in Katharina M. Wilson, ed., Medieval Women Writers *(Athens, Ga.: University of Georgia Press, 1984), 286ff.*

▼ ▼ ▼

REVELATIONS OF DIVINE LOVE

I saw the working of the blessed Trinity in this vision and I saw and understood three properties: the property of fatherhood, motherhood, and lordship in one God. In our Almighty Father we have our protection and our bliss as regards the nature of our substance, which belongs to us from our Creation for eternity; and in the second person through understanding and wisdom we have our protection regarding our sensuality [physical nature] and our restoration and our salvation, for he is our Mother, Brother, and Savior. . . . I saw and understood that the noble strength of the Trinity is our Father, and the depth of wisdom of the Trinity is our Mother, and the great love of the Trinity is our Lord. Furthermore, I saw that the second person, who is our Mother, substantially the same beloved person, is now our Mother sensual, for we have a double nature from God's making, that is to say substantial [spiritual] and sensual [physical]. Our substance is the higher part which we have in our Father, Almighty God; and the second person of the Trinity is our Mother in the nature of our substantial making, in Whom we are grounded and rooted, and he is our Mother of mercy concerning our physical needs. And so, our Mother works in various ways . . . in our Mother, Christ, we profit and grow, and in mercy he reforms and restores us.

▲ ▲ ▲

In the mystical theological work of Julian of Norwich the author emphasized the fullness of God's love in terms of God's motherhood. Although human beings see some things as good and others as evil, God sees all things as good. Human sin and the fall are part of the divine plan, and ultimately humans shall see why God ordained it. God does not blame Christians for their sins, but pities them for their sufferings. Yet more profound than the pit of God is the joy of God in the bliss that they shall have in heaven. In revealing these truths, Christ designs to teach Christians to rejoice in the great love that unites them with him. As Julian herself put it, "in our Mother Christ, we profit and grow, and in mercy he reforms and restores us."

Catherine of Siena (1347–1380)

The emotional rapture often identified with mysticism is well illustrated in Catherine of Siena. Born in the Italian hill town for which she is named, Catherine was the twenty-third child of a cloth merchant. At the age of sixteen she joined the Sisters of Penance of St. Dominic and spent her life in devotional exercises and a voluminous correspondence. (This was accomplished through secretaries, since she never learned to write.)

The sense of absolute devotion and ascetic mortifications by which Catherine ruled her life were commensurate with the vision in which she saw and conversed with Christ. She also reportedly received the stigmata, or signs of the wounds of Christ in her own body.

Catherine's *Dialogue* was composed in a mystical trance. Sometimes it reads like other spiritual devotional literature, and at other times it carries a distinct note of its own. The author, or perhaps better put, "the visionary," frequently struggles with the inadequacies of human language to express the ecstasy of the soul of the believer.

Source: S. Noffke, Catherine of Siena: The Dialogue *(Classics of Western Spirituality; New York: Paulist Press, 1980), 26–28.*

▼ ▼ ▼

DIALOGUE

Then God eternal, to stir up even more that soul's love for the salvation of souls, responded to her: Before I show you what I want to show you, and what you asked to see, I want to describe the bridge for you. I have told you that it stretches from heaven to earth by reason of my having joined myself with your humanity, which formed from the earth's clay.

This bridge, my only-begotten Son, has three stairs. Two of them he built on the wood of the most holy cross, and the third even as he tasted the great bitterness of the gall and vinegar they gave him to drink. You will recognize in these three stairs three spiritual stages.

The first stair is the feet, which symbolize the affections. For just as the feet carry the body, the affections carry the soul. My Son's nailed feet are a stair by which you can climb to his side, where you will see revealed his inmost heart. For when the soul has climbed up on the feet of affections and looked with her mind's eye into my Son's opened heart, she begins to feel the love of her own heart in his consummate and unspeakable love. (I say consummate because it is not for his own good that he loves you; you cannot do him any good, since he is one with me.) Then the soul, seeing how tremendously she is loved, is herself filled to overflowing with love. So, having climbed the second stair, she reaches the third. This is the mouth, where she finds peace from the terrible war she has had to wage because of her sins.

At the first stair, lifting the feet of her affections from the earth, she stripped herself of sin. At the second she dressed herself in love for virtue. And at the third she tasted peace. So the bridge has three stairs, and you can reach the last by climbing the first two. The last stair is so high that the flooding waters cannot strike it—for the venom of sin never touched my Son.

But though this bridge has been raised so high, it still is joined to the earth. Do you know when it was raised up? When my Son was lifted up on the wood of the most holy cross he did not cut off his divinity from the lowly earth of your humanity. So though he was raised so high he was not raised off the earth. In fact, his divinity is kneaded back into the clay of your humanity like one bread. Nor could anyone walk on that bridge until my Son was raised up. This is why he said, "If I am lifted up high I will draw everything to myself."

When my goodness saw that you could be drawn in no other way, I sent him to be lifted onto the wood of the cross. I made of that cross an anvil where this child of humankind could be hammered into an instrument to release humankind from death and restore it to the life of grace. In this way he drew everything to himself: for he proved his unspeakable love, and the human heart is always drawn by love. He could not have shown you greater love than by giving his life for you. You can hardly resist being drawn by love, then, unless you foolishly refuse to be drawn.

I said that, having been raised up, he would have drawn everything to himself. This is true in two ways: First, the human heart is drawn by love, as I said, and with all its powers: memory, understanding, and will. If these three powers are harmoniously united in my name, everything else you do, in fact or in intention, will be drawn to union with me in peace through the movement of love, because all will be lifted up in the pursuit of crucified love. So my Truth indeed spoke truly when he said, "If I am lifted up high, I will draw everything to myself." For everything you do will be drawn to him when he draws your heart and its powers.

What he said is true also in the sense that everything was created for your use, to serve your needs. But you who have the gift of reason were made not for yourselves but for me, to serve me with all your heart and all your love. So when you are drawn to me, everything is drawn with you, because everything was made for you.

It was necessary, then, that this bridge be raised high. And it had to have stairs so that you would be able to mount it more easily.

This bridge has walls of stone so that travelers will not be hindered when it rains. Do you know what stones these are? They are the stones of true solid virtue. These stones were not, however, built into walls before my Son's passion. So no one could get to the final destination, even though they walked along the pathway of virtue. For heaven had not yet been unlocked with the key of my Son's blood, and the rain of justice kept anyone from crossing over.

But after these stones were hewn on the body of the Word, my gentle Son (I have told you that he is the bridge), he built them into walls, tempering the mortar with his own blood. That is, his blood was mixed into the mortar of his divinity with the strong heat of burning love. By my power the stones of virtue were built into walls on no less a foundation than himself, for all virtue draws life from him, nor is there any virtue that has not been tested in him. So no one can have any life giving virtue but from him, that is, by following his example and his teaching. He perfected the virtues and planted them as living stones built into walls with his blood. So now all the faithful can walk without hindrance and with no cringing fear of the rain of divine justice, because they are sheltered by the mercy that came down from heaven through the incarnation of this Son of mine.

And how was heaven opened? With the keys of his blood. So, you see, the bridge has walls and a roof of mercy. And the hostelry of holy Church is there to serve the bread of life and the blood, lest the journeying pilgrims, my creatures, grow weary and faint on the way. So has my love ordained that the blood and body of my only-begotten Son, wholly God and wholly human, be administered.

At the end of the bridge is the gate (which is, in fact, one with the bridge), which is the only way you can enter. This is why he said, "I am the Way and Truth and Life; whoever walks with me walks not in darkness but in light." And in another place my Truth said that no one could come to me except through him, and such is the truth.

▲ ▲ ▲

For Catherine, through proper self-knowledge the soul learns of its complete dependence on God. True knowledge of God lies beyond human understanding and takes place in the mystical experience of the beatific vision, however. Suffering is integral to the religious life for it follows when the soul discerns its distance from God and it encourages the proper attitude of contrition. God made of Christ a bridge by which fallen human beings may travel the road to heaven.

* * *

The writings of Hildegard of Bingen, Julian of Norwich, and Catherine of Siena provide an alternative to the more traditional and more popular avenues of religious expression. They stress a direct, emotional connection with God.

17. Thomas à Kempis (1380–1471)

With the possible exception of the Christian Scriptures, no book has been translated into more languages than Thomas à Kempis's *Imitation of Christ (Imitatio Christi)*. At a time of general political unrest in Europe, this quiet, retiring monk in the Low Countries wrote an essay on the spiritual life. Ever since, it has spoken to every generation of those who seek communion with God through meditation on the life and example of Jesus of Nazareth, the Christ.

Thomas Hammerlein (little hammer), born at Kempen, north of Cologne, received his education at a school run by the Brethren of the Common Life, whose founder had been influenced by the mystic Jan van Ruysbroeck. Later he moved to the Augustinian monastery of Mount Saint Agnes near Zwolle in the Netherlands. He was ordained in 1413 and made superior of the monastery in 1429. His life was uneventful; he was practically a recluse.

The title of the devotional classic credited to him was taken from the first chapter, "Of the Imitation of Christ, and Contempt for All the Vanities of the World." Rigid in demand for spiritual sincerity, Thomas à Kempis nevertheless wrote as a wayfarer himself, urging the reader on from step to step in the pilgrimage of the inner life.

"We must make it our chief business," he wrote, "to train our thoughts upon the life of Jesus Christ." And he concluded, "What God wants of you is faith and a life of unalloyed goodness, not loftiness of understanding, not a probing of the deep mysteries of God." Revealing little of his own religious experiences and reacting strongly against abstract theological works, Thomas à Kempis spoke the universal language of mysticism.

Source: The Imitation of Christ (De Imitatione Christi), *edited by Johann Baptiste Weigl (Ratisbon, Bavaria: Fratreen de Seidel, 1887), 3, 7, 9, 11, 13, 15, 17. (Variations in English by W. P. Anderson.)*

▼ ▼ ▼

Chapter I:
On the Imitation of Christ and Contempt for All the Vanities of the World

1. The person who follows me does not walk in darkness, says the Lord. These are the words with which Christ admonishes us to imitate his life and manners if we wish truly to be enlightened and freed from all blindness of the heart. Let it be our chief study then to meditate on the life of Jesus Christ.

2. The doctrine of Christ surpasses all the doctrines of the saints, and whoever has the spirit will find there a hidden manna. But it happens that many people, from a too frequent hearing of the gospel, feel little desire because they do not have the Spirit of Christ. Whoever wants to understand full and wisely the words of Christ must study to conform all aspects of life to his.

3. What profit is there to make lofty analyses about the Trinity, if through lack of humility you are displeasing to the Trinity. Truly, lofty words do not make a person holy and just; only a virtuous life make a person dear to God. I had rather feel compunction than know its definition. If you knew the whole Bible by heart and the sayings of all the philosophers, what good would it be without the love of God and divine grace? Vanity of vanity and all is vanity except loving God and serving God alone. This is the highest wisdom: through contempt for the world to move towards the heavenly kingdom.

4. It is vanity therefore to seek perishable wealth and to trust in it. It is vanity also to be ambitious for honors and to raise oneself to high station. It is vanity to follow after desires of the flesh, and to want something for which eventually you must be punished. It is vanity to hope for a long life and to care too little about living a good life. It is vanity to pay attention only to this life and not provide for what is to come.

CHAPTER II:

AGAINST USELESS KNOWLEDGE, AND ON TAKING A LOW VIEW OF OURSELF

1. Everyone naturally desires knowledge [said Aristotle]. But what value is there in knowledge without the fear of God? A humble farmer who serves God is much more acceptable to God than is a proud philosopher who analyzes the movement of the stars. He who knows himself well is lowly in his own sight, and takes no delight in the vain praise of others. If I knew all the things that exist in this world, but live not in charity, what would it avail me before God, who will judge me according to my deeds?

2. Cut off yourself from an excessive desire for knowledge; because in this there is great distraction and deceit. Those who have great knowledge usually want to be held as special in the world. But there are many things the knowledge of which bring but little profit to the soul, and a person is very unwise to take heed of any other thing, than that which serves for salvation. Words do not satisfy the soul; but a good life refreshes the mind and a clean conscience brings a person to a great trust in God.

3. The more knowledge you have, the more seriously you will be judged, unless you have also lived a more holy life. So do not puff yourself up about your skills or knowledge, but have all the more fear in your heart. If you think that you know many things and understand them quite well, know that there are many more things that you do not know. Do not spout wisdom from on high, but confess your ignorance. Why should you prefer yourself to anyone else since there are many more learned than you to be found and more experienced in the law?

If you want to know and learn something really useful, love to be unknown and obscure.

Before the Sears Catalog

This is the highest and most useful lesson: true knowledge of self is to look down on one's own self. It is a great wisdom and high perfection to think nothing of ourselves but always to have a good and high opinion of others.

If you see another person openly sinning or committing some serious wrong, do not think the more of yourself for that, because you have no idea how long you will persevere in goodness. We are all frail, but hold no one more frail than yourself.

CHAPTER III:

OF THE TEACHING OF THE TRUTH

Happy is the person whom truth itself teaches and informs, not by direct calculations and logic, but just as it is in itself. Our thoughts and our senses often deceive us, so that we see little. What profit is there in solemn argumentations about complex and obscure matters, when ignorance of these things will not be held against us at the day of judgment? It is thus great folly to be negligent in those things that are profitable and necessary to us, and to busy ourselves with things that are just harmful pedantry. Truly if we do so, we have eyes but see not.

2. Of what concern is it to us [to know about] genera and species [as the scholastics do], when the person to whom the Word speaks is set free from conflicting opinions? From one Word all things proceed, and all things speak of this one thing. And this Word is the basis of everything else, which speaks to us also. No one can understand things rightly without it, or judge correctly.

The person to whom all things are one, and who draws all things into unity, and sees the unity in everything, is a person of steady heart and rests peacefully in God. O truth, my God, make me one with you in everlasting love. It tires me to read and listen to many things; in you is all that I desire or seek. Let all the teach-

ers be quiet; let all creatures be silent in your sight. May you alone speak to me. . . .

4. Tell me, where now are all the great clerics and famous teachers? When they lived they flourished through their learning. But now others occupy their places and I cannot tell what thought anyone has for them. In their life they seemed to be something, and now few mention them. . . .

6. O how quickly the glory of this world passes away and all its false and deceptive pleasures. Would to God the pattern of their daily life had fit well with their learning, for then their learning would have been worthwhile. How many perish in this world by vain knowledge, those that care little about the service of God. Because they desire to be great rather than lowly, they lose themselves in their own mental manipulations.

Truly great is the person with great love; great the one who is little in her or his own sight, and that treats world honors as nothing. That person is very wise who accounts all worldly pleasures as excrement, in order to win Christ. That person is truly learned who sacrifices personal choices and follows the will of God.

▲ ▲ ▲

Augustine's famous dictum that our hearts are restless until they find their rest in God was given full expression in the life and work of this fifteenth-century monk. As can be seen from these brief excerpts, Thomas believed that the primary focus in the life of any Christian is to imitate, insofar as humanly possible, the life modeled to us in Jesus of Nazareth. To achieve this goal one must turn away from the affairs of this world completely as well as from our own outwardly directed desires. To become interior and devout is our aim and purpose, and the model life is a life of contemplation. We are to withdraw our hearts from the love of visible things and to direct our affections to things invisible.

Knowledge also is of very little value. We not only forget our thoughts very quickly, but also are frequently deceived by our thoughts and senses. We are only able to understand things properly when we are "right" with God, according to Thomas. The key in all of this is Love—our greatest asset, which must be teamed with humility. Thomas scorned all worldly accomplishments, including the accomplishments of the intellect. Fear and love of God as the *All*, despising oneself as almost nothing—these were the bases upon which to build life, and these were the basic rules of Thomas's own life. He is certainly not the person one would be quoting in the chapels of great universities. Nevertheless, the correctives that Thomas offered to Christians preoccupied with their self-importance are in startling contrast to earlier, scholastic theologies and anticipate a more direct theology and piety characteristic of the Reformation.

Part Three

The Reformation

Moving out of the Middle Ages into the age of the Reformation and its developments over a period of two hundred years is to leave behind the unity of medievalism for the vitality and variety of Protestantism in its earliest forms. The so-called medieval synthesis, as described by John Dillenberger and Claude Welch in their *Protestant Christianity: Interpreted through Its Development,* was of less importance to the Reformers than were biblical purity and apostolic witness. For Roman Catholics, the Reformation appeared the consequence of unhappy zealots who broke away from mainstream Christianity. But for the Reformers it was never this way. For them it was simply a reformation of the church and its faith.

Although united in the Archimedean insight of Martin Luther that humans, confronted by the Word of God, are saved by faith alone, the Reformation also presents almost endless variety. From a theoretical point of view this was almost inevitable as the Reformation leaders advocated the right of private interpretation of Scripture and the priesthood of all believers. The dissolution of the medieval synthesis is not due totally to the Reformation movement, however. Society was in flux. The face of Europe, Britain, and even America was being transformed, albeit gradually, but also radically. The fact that the Reformation arose simultaneously in many widely scattered regions suggests that there was something in the air.

Nevertheless, the Reformation was, and remains, primarily a religious movement. The Christian tradition was subjected to fresh, critical scrutiny. The church and her authority were not simply taken for granted. Scripture was newly translated and interpreted. Learning in Greek and Hebrew led a revival in the field of exegesis and began to replace learning in Latin. Education expanded in the interests of an emerging, intelligent laity, and the winds of freedom began to blow. As the name itself suggests, Protestantism involved a "principle of protest." Frequently this was a negative reaction to abuses in the church or a challenge to church doctrine. Underlying this tumult was the Reformers' conviction that the truth of God as revealed in Scripture is the authority on which everything else must be judged.

Protestantism distinguished itself early on because it dared to turn the principle of critical, creative protest upon even itself. Therefore it was possible for the Reformers to speak as if further reflection or later examination might prove them wrong. In other words, their work was "open-ended." Typical of this is a remark made by Martin Luther that "if anyone should come who knew the sense of the Word better than I, then I should close my mouth and keep still, and receive knowledge from him." Even the seventeenth century's Westminster Confession of Faith, speaking of church authority, presumably including itself, stated: "All synods or councils since the Apostles' times, whether general or particular, may err, and may have erred; therefore, they are not to be made the rule of faith or practice, but to be used as a help in both."

The Reformers did not merely mean to initiate a crash program to clean up the mess. To be reformed did not mean attaining a fixed state requiring no further self-criticism.

Being reformed meant being in the continual process of being reformed (*reformata sed semper reformanda*). All the reforming activity of this period and conceivably of every period, has an element of tentativeness about it. The task of reforming is never-ending.

In light of these discoveries, or better put, rediscoveries, there was a new demand to rewrite theological textbooks and a need to draft new creeds, confessions of faith, and catechisms. The Reformers were aided in this process by the arrival of the printing press. Many of these creeds, such as "The Augsburg Confession of 1530," were destined to become authoritative doctrinal standards of faith. Others were more limited in appeal and scope. Reformers who took part in this creedal reconstruction included Luther, Philipp Melanchthon, Huldrych Zwingli, John Calvin, Johann Heinrich Bullinger, Thomas Cranmer, John Knox, John Wesley, and many others less well-known.

As one might expect, not all this creedal activity was creative. History has a way of cooling Reformers' enthusiastic fires. Nevertheless, the post-Reformation theological activity often ran in the direction of technical refinements, a type of "Protestant Scholasticism." Doctrinal issues were drawn more stringently; disputes arose within groups that were otherwise harmonious; creeds and movements like Pietism in Germany, the so-called radical Reformers in Switzerland and the Netherlands, the Quakers in England, the Wesleyan revival in Anglicanism, and the Great Awakening in the United States—all these movements "protested" against doctrinal sterility in the more established churches.

As a unified medieval world began to break up at the beginning of the Reformation, churches and people were required to learn how to live with one another even as they disagreed on many matters of faith and life. Thus began the centuries-long movement in the West toward religious tolerance.

18. Martin Luther (1483–1546)

The life of Martin Luther was punctuated with continual controversy. Looking forward to a quiet life of scholarship and study, Luther was plunged against his will into an ecclesiastical and political whirlpool. Not since Augustine had a church theologian been forced by circumstances to address himself so directly, and often so polemically, to the divisive issues of the day. As with Augustine, with whom he has much in common, troubled events only served to spark a ceaseless, voluminous literary output. Like Thomas Aquinas, with whom he had so little in common, Luther fathered a theological tradition that is still normative for a large segment of the Christian community. More of a prophet than a systematic theologian, more at home in the world of Scripture than in papal vestment, Luther has always been acknowledged by his admirers and his detractors as the foremost representative of the Protestant Reformation. Indeed his name is almost synonymous with the movement.

Ordained to the priesthood in 1507 and a highly respected monk and teacher, Luther had no idea that ten years hence a modest proposal for theological discussion would explode into his own excommunication and the schism dividing Roman Catholicism and Protestant evangelicalism. The nailing of the Ninety-Five Theses on the church door at Wittenberg in 1517 precipitated the long papal litigation against Luther, resulting in his repeated denunciation as a heretic, and marking at the same time on the calendar the birthday of the Protestant Reformation.

It was Luther's good fortune to have his local political ruler, the Saxon Elector Frederick III, also known as "the Wise," on his side. Consequently, he was physically protected against his enemies and allowed freedom to preach, to write, and to lead the growing reform movement in Germany.

Luther's theology was as simple and straightforward as it was unsystematic and uncomplicated; it derived in part from personal anxiety about his own redemption, the impossibility of complete confession of sin, and a questioning of the validity of the medieval sacramental system. He found little or no help for his religious dilemmas in the textbooks of the scholastic theologians. It was only when he retraced his steps back to Augustine, and by way of Augustine to Paul, and through Paul to the whole biblical tradition, that Martin Luther learned his first evangelical lesson about faith, righteousness, and justification.

Justification or salvation, Luther came to understand, depends on a new relationship to God through faith in Jesus Christ rather than on any work one could do to merit God's favor. The righteousness of God is not so much divine requirement as forgiving grace. To have

Hitting the Nail on the Head

faith is not to assent intellectually to propositions about God and the world, but to venture upon a radically new kind of trustful life. To be justified is not to be made righteous so that one may stand without blemish before the bar of God's justice; to be justified is to be forgiven and accepted as righteous for the sake of Jesus Christ.

These related theological themes were proclaimed repeatedly by Luther in treatises, pamphlets, and commentaries that spanned his entire life. In the midst of all this activity he was constantly preaching, carrying on an extensive correspondence, and, during his Wartburg confinement, translating the Bible into German from the Hebrew and Greek rather than from the Latin Vulgate.

In his voluminous literary output certain themes are of obvious significance. The early *Lectures on Romans* (1515–1516) indicates how Luther learned from Paul the meaning of justification by faith. As one of a series of notable biblical commentaries, these lectures were not published during Luther's life and curiously attracted almost no attention until modern times. Yet it was in his exposition of Romans that the Reformer enunciated his crucial theological principle that in Christ we are both justified and sinner at the same time *(simul iustus et peccator).*

During the year 1520 Luther prepared three major treatises summing up the issues that divided Rome and Wittenberg. In *An Open Letter to the Christian Nobility,* he called for church reform and the breaching of the medieval walls built to protect the papal prerogatives. In the *Babylonian Captivity of the Church,* the Roman sacramental system was placed under merciless scrutiny, resulting in Luther's rejection of the Mass in the

scholastic terms of transubstantiation. The treatise *On Christian Liberty* delineates the evangelical paradox that a Christian is free, subject to none, yet the dutiful servant of all. Thus a Christian is not only to enjoy the freedom that is in Christ but to be a Christ to one's neighbor (cf. Rom. 1:1ff.).

Source: Luther's Primary Works, *edited by Henry Wace and C. A. Buchheim (London: Hadden and Stoughton, 1896).*

AN OPEN LETTER TO THE
CHRISTIAN NOBILITY

The Romanists have very cleverly surrounded themselves with three walls, which have protected them till now in such a way that no one could reform them. As a result, the whole of Christendom has suffered woeful corruption. In the first place, when under the threat of secular force, they have stood firm and declared that secular force had no jurisdiction over them; rather the opposite was the case, and the spiritual was superior to the secular. In the second place, when the Holy Scriptures have been used to reprove them, they have responded that no one except the pope was competent to expound Scripture. In the third place, when threatened with a council, they have pretended that no one but the pope could summon a council. In this way, they have adroitly nullified these three means of correction, and avoided punishment. Thus they still remain in secure possession of these three walls, and practice all the villainy and wickedness we see today. . . .

May God now help us, and give us one of those trumpets with which the walls of Jericho were overthrown; that we may blow away these walls of paper and straw, and set free the Christian, corrective measures to punish sin, and to bring the devil's deceits and wiles to the light of day. In this way, may we be reformed through suffering and again receive God's blessing.

The First Wall

Let us begin by attacking the first wall. To call popes, bishops, priests, monks and nuns, the religious class, but princes, lords, artisans, and farm workers the secular class, is a specious device invented by certain time-servers; but no one ought to be frightened by it, and for good reason. For all Christians whatsoever really and truly belong to the religious class, and there is no difference among them except in so far as they do different work. That is St. Paul's meaning, in 1 Corinthians 12:12f., when he says, "We are all one body, yet each member hath his own work for serving others." This applies to us all, because we have one baptism, one gospel, one faith, and are all equally Christian. For baptism, gospel, and faith alone make men religious, and create a Christian people. When a pope or bishop anoints, grants, tonsures, ordains, consecrates, dresses differently from laymen, he may make a hypocrite of a man, or an anointed image, but never a Christian or a spiritually minded man. The fact is that our baptism consecrates us all without exception, and makes us all priests. As St. Peter says, 1 Peter 2:9, "You are a royal priesthood and a realm of priests," and Revelation, "Thou hast made us priests and kings by thy blood" (Rev. 5:9f.). If we ourselves as Christians did not receive a higher consecration than that given by pope or bishop, then no one would be made priest even by consecration at the hands of pope or bishop; nor would anyone be authorized to celebrate Eucharist, or preach, or pronounce absolution.

When a bishop consecrates, he simply acts on behalf of the entire congregation, all of whom have the same authority. They may select one of their number and command him to exercise this authority on behalf of the others. It would be similar if ten brothers, king's sons and equal heirs, were to choose one of themselves to rule the kingdom for them. All would be kings and of equal authority, although one would be appointed to rule. To put it more plainly, suppose a small group of earnest Christian laymen were taken prisoner and settled in the middle of a desert without any episcopally ordained priests among them; and they then agreed to choose one of themselves, whether married or not, and endow him with the office of baptizing, administering the sacrament, pronouncing absolution, and preaching; that man would be as truly a priest as if he had been ordained by all the bishops and popes. It follows that, if needs be, anyone may baptize or pronounce absolution, an impossible situation if we were not all priests. . . .

Hence we deduce that there is, at bottom, really no other difference between laymen, priests, princes, bishops, or, in Romanist terminology, between religious and secular, then that of office or occupation, and not that of Christian status. All have spiritual status, and all are truly priests, bishops, and popes. But Christians do not all follow the same occupation. Similarly, priests and monks, do not all work at the same task. . . .

The Second Wall

The second wall is more loosely built and less defensible. The Romanists profess to be the only interpreters of Scripture, even though they never learn anything contained in it their lives long. They claim authority for themselves alone, juggle with words shamelessly before our eyes, saying that the pope cannot err as to the faith, whether he be bad or good; although they cannot quote a single letter of Scripture to support their claim. Thus it comes about that so many heretical, unchristian, and even unnatural laws are contained in canon law—matters of which there is no need for discussion at the present juncture. Just because Romanists profess to believe that the Holy Spirit has not abandoned them, no matter if they are as ignorant and bad as they could be, they presume to assert whatever they please. In such a case, what is the need or the value of Holy Scripture? Let it be burned, and let us be content with the ignorant gentlemen at Rome who "possess the Holy Spirit within," who, however, in fact, dwells in pious souls only. Had I not read it, I should have thought it incredible that the devil should have produced such ineptitudes at Rome, and have gained adherents to them. But lest we fight them with mere words, let us adduce Scripture. St. Paul says, 1 Corinthians 14:30, "If something superior be revealed to any one sitting there and listening to another speaking God's word, the first speaker must be silent and give place." What would be the virtue of this commandment if only the speaker or the person in the highest position, were to be believed? Christ himself says, John 6:45, "that all Christians shall be taught by God." Then if the pope and his adherents were bad men, and not true Christians, i.e., not taught by God to have a true understanding; and if, on the other hand, a humble person should have the true understanding, why ever should we not follow him? Has not the pope made many errors? Who could enlighten Christian people if the pope erred, unless someone else, who had the support of Scripture, were more to be believed than he? . . .

The Third Wall
The third wall falls without more ado when the first two are demolished; for, even if the pope acts contrary to Scripture, we ourselves are bound to abide by Scripture. We must punish him and constrain him, according to the passage, "If thy brother sin against thee, go and tell it him between thee and him alone; but if he hear thee not, take with thee one or two more; and if he hear them not, tell it to the church; and if he hear not the church, let him be unto thee as a gentile" (Matt. 18:15-17).

This passage commands each member to exercise concern for his fellow; much more is it our duty when the wrongdoer is one who rules over us all alike, and who causes much harm and offense to the rest of us by his conduct. And if I am to lay a charge against him before the church, then I must call it together.

Romanists have no Scriptural basis for their contention that the pope alone has the right to summon or sanction a council. This is their own ruling, and only valid as long as it is not harmful to Christian well-being or contrary to God's laws. If, however, the pope is in the wrong, this ruling becomes invalid, because it is harmful to Christian well-being not to punish him through a council. . . .

It is empty talk when the Romanists boast of possessing an authority such as cannot be properly contested. No one in Christendom has authority to do evil, or to forbid evil from being resisted. The church has no authority except to promote the greater good. Hence, if the pope should exercise his authority to prevent a free council, and so hinder the reform in the church, we ought to pay no regard to him and his authority. If he should excommunicate and fulminate, that ought to be despised as the proceedings of a foolish man. Trusting in God's protection, we ought to excommunicate him in return and manage as best we can; for this authority of his be presumptuous and empty.

THE BABYLONIAN CAPTIVITY
OF THE CHURCH
It gives a new and foolish twist to the words to hold that "bread" means the form, or the "accidents," of the bread; and "wine" the form, or the accidents of the wine, when they do not take everything else to consist of forms and accidents. Even if all else were consistent with that idea, nevertheless the word of God ought not to be taken so lightly, nor deprived of its original meaning, with so little justification.

For over 1,200 years the church remained orthodox. On no occasion, and in no place, do the Fathers mention the word transubstantiation—monstrous whether as a locution or as an idea—until the specious philosophy of Aristotle took root in the church, and attained a rank growth in the last 300 years. During this time, many other perverse conclusions were arrived at. Examples are: "That the divine Being is not begotten, nor does it beget"; "That the soul is the form to which the human body corresponds as the substance"; and the like. . . .

The Romanists may perhaps object that the danger of idolatry forbids that the bread and wine should be real. This is a very ridiculous objection, because the laity have never understood the hair-splitting philosophy of substance and its accidents; nor, if they were taught it, could they grasp it. Thus the danger remains the same whether it is the visible accidents that are retained or the invisible substance. For they do not worship the accidents, but the Christ which they conceal, why should they worship the bread which they do not see?

Why could not Christ maintain His body within the substance of the bread as truly as within its accidents? Iron and fire are two substances which mingle together in red-hot iron in such a way that every part contains both iron and fire. Why cannot the glorified body of Christ be similarly found in every part of the substance of the bread?

What will they reply? Christ is believed to have been born from his mother's virgin womb. Let them aver, here also, that the flesh of the virgin was temporarily deprived of being, or, as they would more aptly have put it, "transubstantiated," in order that Christ, having been enfolded in the accidents, might come forth through the accidents. The same thing will have to be said of the shut door of the upper room and the closed mouth of the sepulchre, through which He went in and out without doing them injury. Out of this theory has arisen that Babel of philosophy of a constant quantity distinct from substance, till the stage is reached when they themselves do not know which are the accidents and which the substance. No one has given a certain proof that heat, color, cold, luminosity, weight, and shape, are accidents. Further, they have been forced to pretend that a new substance is created on the altar. This has been required because Aristotle said: "The nature of accidents is to be in something." They have been led to an infinite number of monstrous ideas, from all of which they would be free if they would simply grant that the bread was truly there. And I rejoice to think that, at least among the ordinary people, simple faith in this sacrament still abides. Because they do not understand the dispute, they do not argue whether the accidents are there without the substance; rather they believe, in simple faith, that the body and blood of Christ are truly contained there, and they leave the business of arguing what contains them to those who have time to spare.

Perhaps the Romanists will say: "Aristotle teaches that, in an affirmative sentence, the subject and the predicate ought to mean the same thing"; or, to quote this beast's own words in the Metaphysics VI, "An affirmative proposition requires the agreement of the extremes." It would then follow that when Christ said, "This is my body," the subject cannot stand for the bread, but for the body of Christ. What is our response when Aristotle, and the doctrines of men, are made arbiters of these very sublime and divine things? Why not hiss these ingenious inquiries off the stage, and hold to the words of Christ in simple faith, satisfied not to understand what takes place, and content to know that true body of Christ is there by virtue of the words of institution? We do not need to understand completely the mode of the divine operation.

But what do the Romanists say when Aristotle attributes a subject to all the categories of accidents, although he grants that the substance is the prime subject? According to him "this white," "this great," "this something," are all subjects because something is predicated of them. If this is true, then, since transubstantiation has to be propounded in order to avoid declaring the bread to be the body of Christ, I ask: Why not propound a transaccidentation and so avoid affirming that an accident is the body of Christ? The danger remains the same if one were to understand the "subject" to be "this white or this round object," and to be the body of Christ. On whatever grounds transubstantiation is taught, on the same grounds transaccidentation might be taught, the principle being that the two terms of a proposition refer to the same thing.

But if, by a tour de force, you rise above this accident, and do not wish to regard it as signified by the subject when you say, "This is my body," why not, with equal ease, transcend the substance of the bread when you do not wish to regard it as the subject? Then to say, "This is my body," will be as true in the substance as the accident, especially as this would be a miracle performed by God's almighty power, which can operate to the same degree, and in the same way, in the substance as in the accident. . . .

Thus what is true in regard to Christ is also true in regard to the sacrament. It is not necessary for human nature to be transubstantiated before it can be the corporeal habitation of the divine, and before the divine can be contained under the accidents of human nature. Both natures are present in their entirety, and one can appropriately say: "This man is God"; or, "This God is man." Though philosophy cannot grasp it, yet faith can. The authority of the word of God goes beyond the capacity of our mind. Thus, in order that the true body and the true blood should be in the sacrament, the bread and the wine have no need to be transubstantiated, and Christ contained under the

accidents; but while both remain the same, it would be true to say; "This bread is my body, this wine is my blood," and conversely. That is how I would construe the words of divine Scripture and, at the same time, maintain due reverence for them. I cannot bear their being forced by human quibbles, and twisted into other meanings.

CONCERNING CHRISTIAN LIBERTY

Christian faith has appeared to many an easy thing; nay not a few even reckon it among the social virtues, as it were; and this they do because they have not made proof of it experimentally, and have never tasted of what efficacy it is. For it is not possible for any man to write well about it, or to understand well what is rightly written, who has not at some time tasted of its spirit, under the pressure of tribulation; while he who has tasted of it, even to a very small extent, can never write, think, speak, think, or hear about it sufficiently. For it is a living fountain, springing up unto eternal life, as Christ calls it in John 4.

Now, though I cannot boast of my abundance, and though I know how poorly I am furnished, yet I hope that, after having been vexed by various temptations, I have attained some little drop of faith, and that I can speak of this matter, if not with more elegance, certainly with more solidity, than those literal and too subtle disputants who have hitherto discoursed upon it without understanding their own words. That I may open then an easier way for the ignorant—for these alone I try to serve—I first lay down two propositions, concerning spiritual liberty and servitude.

A Christian man is the most free lord of all, and subject to none; a Christian man is the most dutiful servant of all and subject to everyone.

Although these statements appear contradictory, yet, when they are found to agree together, they will do excellently for my purpose. They are both the statements of Paul himself, who says, "Though I be free from all men, yet have I made myself a servant unto all" (1 Cor. 9:19), and "Owe no man anything but to love one another" (Rom. 8:8). Now love is by its own nature dutiful and obedient to the beloved object. Thus even Christ, though Lord of all things, was yet made of a woman; made under the law; at once free and a servant; at once in the form of God and in the form of a servant.

Let us examine the subject on a deeper and less simple principle. Man is composed of a twofold nature, a spiritual and a bodily. As regards the spiritual nature, which they call the soul, he is called the spiritual, inward, new man; as regards the bodily nature, which they name the flesh, he is called fleshly, outward, old man. The Apostle speaks of this: "Though our outward man perish, yet the inward man is renewed day by day" (2 Cor. 4:16). The result of this diversity is that in the Scriptures opposing statements are made concerning the same man, the fact being that in the same man these two men are opposed to one another; the flesh lusting against the spirit, and the spirit against the flesh (Gal. 5:17).

We first approach the subject of the inward man, that we may see by what means a man becomes justified, free, and a true Christian; that is: spiritual, new, and inward man. It is certain that absolutely none among outward things, under whatever name they may be reckoned, has any influence in producing Christian righteousness or liberty, nor, on the other hand unrighteousness or slavery. This can be shown by an easy argument.

What can it profit the soul that the body should be in good condition, free, and full of life; that it should eat, drink, and act according to its pleasure; when even the most impious of slaves of every kind of vice are prosperous in these matters? Again, what harm can ill-health, bondage, hunger, thirst, or any other outward evil, do to the soul, when even the most pious of men, and the freest in the purity of their conscience, are harassed by these things? Neither of these states of things has to do with the liberty or the slavery of the soul.

And so it will profit nothing that the body should be adorned with sacred vestments, or dwell in holy places, or be occupied in sacred offices, or pray, fast, and abstain from certain meats, or do whatever works can be done through the body and in the body. Something widely different will be necessary for the justification and liberty of the soul, since the things I have spoken of can be done by an impious person, and only hypocrites are produced by devotion to these things. On the other hand, it will not injure the soul that the body should be clothed in profane raiment, should dwell in profane places, should eat and drink in the ordinary fashion, should not pray aloud, and should leave undone all the things mentioned, which may be done by hypocrites.

And—to cast everything aside—even speculations, meditations, and whatever things can be performed by the exertions of the soul itself, are of no profit. One thing, and one alone is necessary for life, justification, and Christian liberty; and that is the most holy word of God, the Gospel of Christ, as He says, "I am the resurrection and the life; he that believes in Me shall not die eternally" (John 11:25), and also, "If the Son shall make you free, ye shall be free indeed" (John 8:36), and, "Man shall not live by bread alone, but by every word that proceedeth out of the mouth of God" (Matt. 4:4).

Let us therefore hold it for certain and firmly established that the soul can do without everything except the word of God, without which none at all of its wants are provided for. But, having the word, it is rich and wants for nothing, since that is the word of life, of truth, of light, of peace, of justification, of salvation, of joy, of liberty, of wisdom, of virtue, of grace, of glory, and of every good thing. It is on this account that the prophet in a whole Psalm (Ps. 119), and in many other places, sighs for and calls upon the word of God with so many groanings and words. . . .

But you will ask, what is this word, and by what means is it to be used, since there are so many words of God? I answer, the Apostle Paul (Rom. 1) explains what it is, namely, the Gospel of God, concerning his Son, incarnate, suffering, risen, and glorified through the Spirit, the Sanctifier. To preach Christ is to feed the soul, to justify it, to set it free, and to save it, if it believes the preaching. For faith alone, and the efficacious use of the word of God, bring salvation. "If thou shalt confess with thy mouth the Lord Jesus, and shalt believe in thine heart that God hath raised him from the dead, thou shalt be saved" (Rom. 9:9); and again, "Christ is the end of the law for righteousness to every one that believes" (Rom. 12:4), and "The just shall live by faith" (Rom. 1:17). For the word of God cannot be received and honored by any works but by faith alone. Hence it is clear that as the soul needs the word alone for life and justification, so it is justified by faith alone, and not by any works. For if it could be justified by any other means, it would have no need for the word, nor consequently of faith.

But this faith cannot consist at all with works; that is, if you imagine that you can be justified by those works, whatever they are, along with it. For this would be to halt between two opinions, to worship Baal, and to kiss the hand to him, which is a very great iniquity, as Job says. Therefore, when you begin to believe, you learn at the same time that all that is in you is utterly guilty, sinful, and damnable, according to the saying, "all have sinned, and come short of the glory of God" (Rom. 3:23), and also, "There is none righteous, no not one; they are all gone out of the way; they are together become unprofitable: there is none that doeth good, no, not

one" (Rom. 3:1-12). When you have learnt this, you will know that Christ is necessary for you, since he has suffered and risen again for you, that, believing in him, you might by this faith become another man, all your sins being remitted, and you being justified by the merits of another, namely Christ alone.

Since then this faith can reign only in the inward man, as it is said, "With the heart man believeth unto righteousness" (Rom. 10:10); and since it alone justifies, it is evident that by no outward work or labor can the inward man be at all justified, made free, and saved; and that no works whatever have any relation to him. And so, on the other hand, it is solely by impiety and incredulity of heart that he becomes guilty and a slave of sin, deserving condemnation, not by any outward sin or work. Therefore, the first care of every Christian ought to be to lay aside all reliance on works, and strengthen his faith alone more and more, and by it grow in knowledge, not of works, but of Christ Jesus, who has suffered and risen again for him, as Peter teaches (1 Pet. 5) when he makes no other work to be a Christian one. Thus Christ, when the Jews asked Him what they should do that they might work the works of God, rejected the multitude of works, with which He saw that they were puffed up, and commanded them one thing only, saying, "This is the work of God: that ye believe on him whom he hath sent, for him hath the Father sealed" (John 6:27, 29).

Hence all we who believe on Christ are kings and priests in Christ, as it is said, "Ye are a chosen generation, a royal priesthood, a holy nation, a peculiar people, that ye should show forth the praises of him who hath called you out of darkness into his marvelous light" (1 Pet. 2:9).

▲ ▲ ▲

Martin Luther's name is almost automatically identified with the Reformation because of the courageous stand he took against what was the most powerful institution of his day in order to declare what he perceived to be the truth of the gospel. Luther was a prolific writer; here we have dealt only with his tracts published early in his "Reformed" career. They are of great importance in the life of the Reformation. Historically, many of his ideas had been raised by others, but for Luther, the time for their emergence was right. The printing press and the rise of the middle class, among other things, made it possible for his ideas to take root and grow where they had not been able to before.

Luther's opposition to the medieval church increased at a steady pace after his dramatic posting of the now-famous Ninety-Five Theses to the door of the Church of All Saints in Wittenberg, but these theses on indulgences would pale in comparison to what would follow—his challenge to papal authority.

In 1519, shortly before the writing of the tracts, Luther was challenged to debate with the clever and brilliant theologian Johannes Eck who taught at the University of Leipzig. Eck was successful in maneuvering Martin Luther into a position of agreeing with the condemned reformer John Hus. In doing so Eck pointed out that Luther not only rejected papal authority but also seemed to reserve for himself the right to agree or to disagree with church councils.

After an initial melancholy reaction to the debate with Eck, Luther rallied and articulated his views in several now-famous treatises. *An Open Letter to the Christian Nobility* shows Luther writing as an outraged German, outraged at the exploitation and greed of the papacy that was living off the German people. Appeal-

ing to Charles V, the newly elected emperor, he challenged Charles and the German princes to reform the church. In this challenge Luther lays out his famous "three walls": (1) the false distinction that exists between the "spiritual estate" and the "temporal" estate; (2) the papal claim to absolute and sole authority in scriptural interpretation; (3) and the idea that only the pope has the authority to call a church council.

Luther argues that in the Christian church, baptism confers upon "all" members of the community the same basic states and responsibilities, so that the right to interpret Scripture and to call reforming councils extends to all Christian believers. The Christian princes and nobles of Germany must, according to Luther, take the initiative in wresting German political and religious life out of corrupt papal control and in reforming German practices and institutions.

In *The Babylonian Captivity of the Church*, Luther critiqued the elaborate sacramental system by which the Roman Catholic Church enslaved its members and which could not be justified by appeal to Scripture. A true sacrament, for Luther, must have dominical institution; that is, it must be instituted by Jesus of Nazareth, the Christ, include a promise of a specific spiritual benefit or grace and an outer sign or symbolic act, and require faith on the part of the recipient. In this sense, argued Luther, only baptism and the Lord's Supper qualified as sacraments. Furthermore, the Roman Catholic Church corrupted the Lord's Supper by the doctrine of Transubstantiation—holding the laity in captivity to the power of the church through the priesthood—and by the teaching that the Mass is a sacrifice offered by human beings to God. It can be seen here that the sacrament of "Holy Orders" in the Roman Catholic Church was the most powerful of the sacraments, since it was necessary for performing all the remaining ones.

The treatise *On Christian Liberty* was the last of Luther's trilogy. Published in November of 1520, it reflected more strictly the religious aspects of Luther's many-sided personality. Luther believed that, through faith (or trust) in God as revealed in Jesus the Christ, the Christian achieved complete freedom from all adversities that may affect the body. The gift of grace, or divine justification, made the Christian free of any necessity of a type of "works righteousness"—that is, making oneself worthy of redemption through ceremonial, legal, and moral works. Anyone who considered it neces-sary to earn salvation through meritori-ous works demonstrated distrust of the absolute sufficiency of the grace and goodness of God revealed in Jesus Christ. Although totally free of any necessity to do anything for one's own redemption, the Christian would subject her/himself to whatever discipline was necessary to express faith in God and concern for others. The justified Christian would love his/her neighbor without any thought or hope of reciproca-tion, just as the Christian was the beneficiary of God's grace, God's free unconditional love. This freedom engendered by faith would not cause the Christian to disregard ceremonies or routines, but the Christian would despise only the ceremonialism that expressed a lack of faith in God and that became idolatrous.

19. JOHN CALVIN (1509–1564)

The task of putting together the main doctrinal emphases of the Reformation into a structure of theology occupied a major portion of the life of John Calvin. As the Reformation took root and spread throughout Germany, France, and Switzerland, the next step beyond the prophetic utterances of Martin Luther was organization. The times called for a systematizer who could clearly and persuasively structure ideas, theological issues, biblical exegesis, and all the potentially divisive matters relating to church government and administration. In addition to having this skill, John Calvin was an original thinker whose principal work on doctrinal theology is comparable to Thomas Aquinas's *Summa Theologiae*.

Calvin was born in Noyon, France, a cathedral town midway between two more famous centers, Amiens and Reims. At first he studied for the priesthood at Paris and in law in Orleans and Bourges. Although he was never ordained, he became along with Luther one of the greatest reformers of the day; he helped the City of Geneva rewrite their civil statutes, but he never actually practiced law (although licensed to do so). The Protestant tradition, that is, the Reformed tradition, which he helped to establish, has always been involved in political as well as religious matters.

When Calvin was about twenty-five, he experienced what he himself referred to as a sudden conversion. Essentially he turned from Roman Catholicism toward the Reformation way of thinking. A short time later, in 1536, he published the first edition of *The Institutes of the Christian Religion*. (The Latin *institutio* means instruction.) This volume was only a hint of the magnum opus that developed over the years until it reached its final edition in 1559. Calvin's work in this volume was modeled on the sequence of the Apostles' Creed as his way of indicating an allegiance to apostolic Christianity. Calvin took liberties with the ancient formula, however, and inserted long, closely knit discussions on a variety of theological topics.

Calvin also busied himself by engaging in the publication of tracts and essays on particular problems, preaching constantly, preparing commentaries on almost every book in the Bible, and carrying on an extensive correspondence. His main headquarters for this was Geneva, which had become a haven for English, Scottish, French, and German refugees. For a brief period of time, from 1538–1541, he was run out of Geneva and retreated to Strasbourg, where he worked with another famous reformer, Martin Bucer.

While Luther and Calvin were both Augustinians, following the thought of the great North African architect of Western theology, their ideas gave rise to two different Protestant traditions. Lutheranism spread through Germany and the countries to the North—Sweden, Denmark, and Norway. The Reformed faith of Calvin moved from Switzerland into the Rhine valley, providing the theological impulse of the French Hugenots, the Protestants in Holland, the Puritans of England and New England, and the Presbyterians of Scotland and America.

People are rarely neutral about John Calvin. His detractors see him as a stubborn, intolerant, coldly rational authority figure. On the other hand, his admirers, while not pretending that he was the most lovable person in the world, note his wide circle of friends and colleagues who looked to him for advice, and they point to his unflinching loyalty to the truth as he understood it in the Word of God (the Scriptures). Calvin was convinced from Scripture and from his own experience that God is sovereign in the process of salvation, that it is God in Christ who takes the initiative, and that we have nothing in us whatever deserving of God's favor. It was because he was so sure of the divine glory that he could speak of total depravity and predestination.

Excerpts have been selected from *The Necessity of Reforming the Church*, his biblical commentaries, and *The Institutes of the Christian Religion*. These texts show several aspects of Calvin and his life's work: (1) his link in the cause of Reformation to Martin Luther; (2) the Bible, the Word of God, as foundational for everything he wrote or said; (3) and finally, passages from the *Institutes* indicating not only the scope of the whole, but something of John Calvin's principal interests as he articulated his understanding of the sequence of the Christian faith.

Source: "The Necessity of Reforming the Church," Tracts Relating to the Reformation, *vol. 1, translated by Henry Beveridge (Edinburgh: Calvin Translation Society, 1844), 183–84, 211, 215–16, 233–34.*

▼ ▼ ▼

THE NECESSITY OF REFORMING THE CHURCH

When Luther at first appeared, he merely touched, with a gentle hand, a few abuses of the grossest description, now grown intolerable. And he did it with a modesty which intimated that he had more desire to see them corrected, than determination to correct them himself. The opposite party forthwith sounded to arms; and when the contention was more and more inflamed, our enemies deemed it the best and shortest method to suppress the truth by cruelty and violence. Accordingly, when our people challenged them to friendly discussion, and desired to settle disputes by calm arguments, they were cruelly persecuted with sanguinary edicts, until matters have been brought to the present miserable pass. . . .

The last and principle charge which they bring against us is, that we have made a schism in the church. And here they boldly maintain against us, that in no case is it lawful to break the unity of the church. How far they do us injustice, the books of our authors bear witness. Now, however, let them take this brief reply— that we neither dissent from the church, nor are aliens from her communion. . . .

Let our opponents, then, in the first instance, draw near to Christ, and then let them convict us of schism, in daring to dissent from them in doctrine. But, since I have made it plain, that Christ is banished from their society, and the doctrine of his gospel exterminated, their charge against us simply amounts to this, that we adhere to Christ in preference to them. For what man, pray, will believe that those who refuse to be led away from Christ and his truth, in order to deliver themselves into the power of men, are thereby schismatics, and deserters from the communion of the church? . . .

In regard to ourselves, whatever be the event, we will always be supported, in the sight of God, by the consciousness that we have desired both to promote his glory and do good to his church; that we have labored faithfully for that end; that, in short, we have done what we could. Our conscience tells us, that in all our wishes, and all our endeavors, we have had no other aim. And we have essayed, by clear proof, to testify the fact. And, certainly, while we feel assured that we both care for and do the work of the Lord, we are also confident, that he will by no means be wanting, either to himself or to it. . . .

But be the issue what it may, we will never repent of having begun, and of having proceeded thus far. The Holy Spirit is a faithful and unerring witness to our doctrine. We know, I say, that it is the eternal truth of God that we preach. We are, indeed, desirous, as we ought to be, that our ministry may prove salutary to the world; but to give it this effect belongs to God, not to us. If, to punish, partly the ingratitude, and partly the stubbornness of those to whom we desire to do good, success must prove desperate, and all things go to worse, I will say what it befits a Christian man to say, and what all who are true to this holy profession will subscribe: We will die, but in death even be conquerors, not only because through it we shall have a sure passage to a better life, but because we know that our blood will be as seed to propagate the Divine truth which men now despise.

The Bible and the Word of God

"All scripture is given by the inspiration of God, and is profitable for doctrine, for reproof, for correction, for instruction in righteousness; that the man of God may be perfect, thoroughly furnished unto all good works" (2 Tim. 3:16-17).

All Scripture, or the whole of it; both phrases mean the same. He (Paul) now continues with his praise of Scripture which had been much too brief. He commends first its authority, and then the usefulness which proceeds from it. He asserts its authority by teaching that it is inspired by God. If this is the case, men should receive it reverently and without further argument. Our religion is distinguished from all others in that the prophets have spoken not of themselves, but as instruments of the Holy Spirit; and what they have brought to us, they received by heavenly commission. Any man then who would profit by the Scriptures, must hold first of all and firmly that the teaching of the law and the prophets came to us not by the will of man, but as dictated by the Holy Spirit.

Somebody may object: But how do we know all this? I answer, the selfsame Spirit revealed both to the disciples and to the teacher (*doctorem*) that the author of the Scriptures is God. Neither Moses nor the prophets brought to us by chance the things we have received at their hands; they spoke as moved by God, and testified with confidence and courage that God's very mouth had spoken. The same Spirit who made Moses and the prophets certain of their calling, has now testified to our own hearts that he used them as his servants for our instruction. It is not surprising that many have doubts as to the author of Scripture. For, even though the majesty of God is displayed in it, only those illumined by the Spirit have the eyes to see what should be evident to all men, but in fact is seen only by the elect. So, the first point is that we treat Scripture with the same reverence that we do God, because it is from God alone, and unmixed with anything human.

And is profitable. The second part of this praise of Scripture follows from the first; that is, it contains the perfect rule of a good and happy life. He means that Scripture is useful because it is free from the kind of corruption which comes from the abuse of God's Word by sinful men. Thus he indirectly rebukes those woolly-headed men who feed the people with empty speculations as with wind. For this reason, today, we ought to condemn all those who make it their business not to build up the people but to

arouse them with questions which are as childish as they are clever. Whenever men come to us with such clever trifles, we must repel them with the principle that the Scripture is for upbuilding. Consequently, it is unlawful to handle it as a useless thing. God gave us Scripture for our good, and not to satisfy our curiosity, or to indulge our desire for showing off, or to give us material for babble and fable. Therefore, to use Scripture rightly is at times to profit by it. . . .

That the man of God may be whole. Whole means perfect, in the sense of unmutilated. He asserts that Scripture is adequate and sufficient for our perfecting. Therefore, anyone who is not satisfied with Scripture, hopes to know more than he needs or than is good for him. But now comes a serious objection. Since Paul means by Scripture the Old Testament, how are we to believe that it makes us perfect? If the Old Testament makes us perfect, then the apostolic additions are superfluous. I answer that, as to substance, the apostles add nothing. The writings of the apostles contain nothing that is not simply a natural explanation of the law and the prophets, together with a straightforward presentation of what they contain. Therefore, Paul's praise of the Old Testament was not wrong. And since its teaching is understood more fully and shines more brightly now that the gospel has been added to it, must we not hope that the value of Scripture, of which Paul speaks, shall be all the more displayed, if only we will try living by it and take hold of it?

The Knowledge of God

Experience teaches that the seed of religion has been divinely planted in all men. But barely one man in a hundred can be found who nourishes in his own heart what he has conceived; and not even one in whom it matures, much less bears fruit in its season (cf. Ps. 1:3). Now some lose themselves in their own superstition, while others of their own evil intention revolt from God, yet all fall away from the true knowledge of him. As a result, no real piety remains in the world. . . . Accordingly, we see that many, after they have become hardened in insolent and habitual sinning, furiously repel all remembrance of God, although this is freely suggested to them inwardly from the feeling of nature. . . . Yet that seed remains which can in no wise be uprooted: that there is some sort of divinity; but this seed is so corrupted that by itself it produces only the worst fruits. . . . There are innumerable evidences both in heaven and on earth that declare his wonderful wisdom; not only those more recondite matters for the closer observation of which astronomy, medicine, and all natural science are intended, but also those which thrust themselves upon the sight of even the most untutored and ignorant persons, so that they cannot open their eyes without being compelled to witness them. Indeed, men who have either quaffed or even tasted the liberal arts penetrate with their aids far more deeply into the secrets of divine wisdom. Yet ignorance of them prevents no one from seeing more than enough of God's workmanship in his creation to lead him to break forth in admiration of the Artificer. . . . It is, accordingly, clear that there is no one to whom the Lord does not abundantly show his wisdom. . . .

But although the Lord presents both himself and his everlasting Kingdom in the mirror of his works with very great clarity, such is our stupidity that we grow increasingly dull toward so manifest testimonies, and they flow away without profiting us. . . . That brightness which is borne in upon the eyes of all men both in heaven and on earth is more than enough to withdraw all support from men's ingratitude—just as God, to involve the human race in the same guilt, sets forth to all without exception his presence portrayed in his creatures. Despite this, it is needful that another and better help be added to direct us aright to the very Creator of the universe. It was not in vain, then, that he added the light of his Word by which to become known unto salvation; and he regarded as worthy of this privilege those whom he pleased to gather more closely and intimately to himself. . . . Just as old or bleary-eyed men

Apostles Are So Sensitive!

and those with weak vision, if you thrust before them a most beautiful volume, even if they recognize it to be some sort of writing, yet can scarcely construe two words, but with the aid of spectacles will begin to read distinctly; so Scripture, gathering up otherwise confused knowledge of God in our minds, having dispersed our dullness, clearly shows us the true God. This, therefore, is a special gift, where God, to instruct the church, not merely uses mute teachers but also opens his own most hallowed lips. Not only does he teach the elect to look upon a god, but also shows himself as the God upon whom they are to look. . . .

Sin and Depravity

As it was the spiritual life of Adam to remain united and bound to his Maker, so estrangement from him was the death of his soul. Nor is it any wonder that he consigned his race to ruin by his rebellion when he perverted the whole order of nature in heaven and on earth. . . . Therefore, after the heavenly image was obliterated in him, he was not the only one to suffer this punishment—that, in place of wisdom, virtue, holiness, truth, and justice, with which adornments he had been clad, there came forth the most filthy plagues, blindness, impotence, impurity, vanity, and injustice—but he also entangled and immersed his offspring in the same miseries.

This is the inherited corruption, which the church fathers termed "original sin," meaning by the word "sin" the depravation of a nature previously good and pure. . . .

Therefore all of us, who have descended from impure seed, are born infected with the contagion of sin. In fact, before we saw the light of this life we were soiled and spotted in God's sight. . . . Hence, rotten branches came forth from a rotten root, which transmitted their rottenness to the other twigs sprouting from them. For thus were the children corrupted in the parent, so that they brought disease upon their children's children. That is, the beginning of corruption in Adam was such that it was conveyed in a perpetual stream from the ancestors into the descendants. . . .

So that these remarks may not be made concerning an uncertain and unknown matter, let us define original sin. It is not my intention to investigate the several definitions proposed by various writers, but simply to bring forward the one that appears to me most in accordance with truth. Original sin, therefore, seems to be a hereditary depravity and corruption of our nature, diffused into all parts of the soul, which first makes us liable to God's wrath, that also brings forth in us those works which Scripture calls the "works of the flesh" (Gal. 5:19). . . . For, since it is said that we became subject to God's judgment through Adam's sin, we are to understand it not as if we, guiltless and undeserving, bore the guilt of his offense, but in the sense that, since we through his transgression have become entangled in the curse, he is said to have made us guilty. . . .

In every age there have been persons who, guided by nature, have striven toward virtue throughout life. I have nothing to say against them even if many lapses can be noted in their moral conduct, for they have by the very zeal of their honesty given proof that there was some purity in their nature. . . . These examples, accordingly, seem to warn us against adjudging man's nature wholly corrupted, because some men have by its prompting not only excelled in remarkable deeds, but conducted themselves most honorably throughout life. But here it ought to occur to us that amid their corruption of nature there is some place for God's grace; not such grace as to cleanse it, but to restrain it inwardly. For if the Lord gave loose rein to the mind of each man to run riot in his lusts, there would doubtless be no one who would not show that, in fact, every evil thing for which Paul condemns all nature is most truly to be met in himself (Ps. 14:3; Rom. 3:12).

What then? Do you count yourself exempt from the number of those whose "feet are swift to shed blood" (Rom. 3:15); whose hands are fouled with robberies and murders; "whose throats are like open graves, whose tongues deceive, whose lips are envenomed" (Rom. 3:13); "whose works are useless, wicked, rotten, deadly; whose hearts are without God; whose inmost parts, depravities; whose eyes are set upon stratagems; whose minds are eager to revile—to sum up, whose every part stands ready to commit infinite wickedness" (Rom. 3:10-18)? . . .

Therefore let us hold this as an undoubted truth which no siege engines can shake: the mind of man has been so completely estranged from God's righteousness that it conceives, desires, and undertakes, only that which is impious, perverted, foul, impure, and infamous. The heart is so steeped in the poison of sin, that it can breathe out nothing but a loathsome stench. But if some men occasionally make a show of good, their minds nevertheless ever remain enveloped in hypocrisy and deceitful craft and their hearts bound by inner perversity.

Election and Predestination

If it is plain that it comes to pass by God's bidding that salvation is freely offered to some while others are barred from access to it, at once great and difficult questions spring up, explicable only when reverent minds regard as settled what they may suitably hold concerning election and predestination. A baffling question this seems to many. For they think nothing more inconsistent than that out of the common multitude of men some should be predestined to salvation, others to destruction. . . .

But before I enter into the matter itself, I need to mention by way of preface two kinds of men. Human curiosity renders the discussion of predestination, already somewhat difficult of itself, very confusing and even dangerous. No restraints can hold it back from wandering into forbidden bypaths and thrusting upward to the heights. If allowed, it will leave no secret to God that it will not search out and unravel. . . . Let this, therefore, first of all be before our eyes: to seek any other knowledge of predestination than what the Word of God discloses is not less sane than if one should purpose to walk in a pathless waste (cf. Job 12:24), or to see in darkness. And let us not be ashamed to be ignorant of something in this matter, wherein there is a certain learned ignorance. . . .

There are others who, wishing to cure this evil, all but require that every mention of predestination be buried; indeed, they teach us to avoid any question of it as we would a reef. . . . Therefore, to hold a proper limit in this regard also, we shall have to turn back to the Word of the Lord, in which we have a sure rule for the understanding. For Scripture is the school of the Holy Spirit, in which, as nothing is omitted that is both necessary and useful to know, so nothing is taught but what is expedient to know. Therefore we must guard against depriving believers of anything disclosed about predestination in Scripture, lest we seem either wickedly to defraud them of the blessing of their God, or to accuse and scoff at the Holy Spirit for having published what it is in any way profitable to suppress. . . .

As Scripture, then, clearly shows, we say that God once established by his eternal and unchangeable plan those whom he long before determined once for all to receive into salvation, and those whom, on the other hand, he would devote to destruction. We assert that, with respect to the elect, this plan was founded upon his freely given mercy, without regard to human worth; but by his just and irreprehensible but incomprehensible judgment he has barred the door of life to those whom he has given over to damnation. Now among the elect we regard the call as a testimony of election. . . .

Now a word concerning the reprobate. . . . If, then, we cannot determine a reason why he vouchsafes mercy to his own, except that it so pleases him, neither shall we have any reason for rejecting others, other than his will. For when it is said that God hardens or shows mercy to whom he wills, men are warned by this to seek no cause outside his will. . . .

If we seek God's favor by mercy and kindly heart, we should turn our eyes to Christ, on whom alone God's Spirit rests (cf. Matt. 3:17). If we seek salvation, life, and the immortality of the Heavenly Kingdom, then there is no other to whom we may flee, seeing that he alone is the fountain of life, the anchor of salvation, and the heir of the Kingdom of Heaven. Now what is the purpose of election but that we, adopted as sons by our Heavenly Father, may obtain salvation and immortality by his favor? . . . Christ, then, is the mirror where we must, and without self-deception may, contemplate our own election. . . .

Therefore, if we desire to know whether God cares for our salvation, let us inquire whether he has entrusted us to Christ, whom he has established as the sole Savior of all his people. If we still doubt whether we have been received by Christ into his care and protection, he meets that doubt when he willingly offers himself as shepherd, and declares that we shall be numbered among his flock if we hear his voice (John 10:3). Let us therefore embrace Christ, who is graciously offered to us, and comes to meet us. He will reckon us in his flock and enclose us within his fold.

▲ ▲ ▲

From the first publication of the *Institutes of the Christian Religion* in 1536, John Calvin was recognized as an authoritative and effective spokesperson for the Protestant Reformation. Laboring for harmony and a common front on the part of the Reformation churches, Calvin

noted the debt the churches owed to the pioneering work of Luther, even though his own views proved to be more congenial to non-Lutheran or Reformed churches.

It was the intention of Calvin to advance the Reformation by supporting Luther's views and by establishing continuity with the writers of the early church. One can see Calvin's skillful mind reflecting on passages from Augustine, Cyprian, Gregory the Great, and other early writers, while providing support for the advancement of the ideas of Luther.

The Necessity of Reforming the Church is a supplicatory remonstrance presented to Charles V, the holy Roman emperor who reigned from 1519 to 1555, and the estates of the Empire gathered at the Diet of Spires in 1544. Calvin wrote this treatise at the urging of his friend Martin Bucer, with whom he spent time during his exile from Geneva from 1538 to 1541. The work is apologetic, defending what has been accomplished by the Reformation up to that point, as well as a challenge to Charles V, the princes assembled, and the free cities to extend these accomplishments. Calvin's appeal to the secular power for reform tended to discount such interferences, while reform-minded Catholics looked to a general council or existing ecclesiastical institutions for change.

Calvin's coolness toward the idea of a general council as the proper way of reform reflected a new stage, a new phase in the evolutionary developments of Protestantism. Enthusiasm for the way of conciliar reform had been seriously dampened by years of delay, political complexities, the intransigence of the papacy, and second thoughts on the likelihood of the authority of Scripture or the presence of the Spirit at such councils.

Several issues were articulated by Calvin. Basic to his argument was his understanding of Christianity as the knowledge of proper worship of God together with the knowledge of the source of salvation. Church government and sacraments, while significant, were given a secondary status by Calvin as being not ends in themselves but means for the preservation of this twofold knowledge. This knowledge was precisely what Calvin contended was lost in the swirl of corruption in the pre-Reformation church.

Proper worship for Calvin was the recognition of God as "the only source of all virtue, justice, holiness, wisdom, truth, power, goodness, mercy, life, and salvation; in accordance with this to ascribe to him the glory of all that is good, to seek all things in him alone, and in every want have recourse to him alone." God abominates all impure worship, such as prayer, adoration of the saints, ceremonialism, or "will-worship," which proceeds from the imagination of humans rather than from the will of God. This, Calvin argued, was rebuked by the Reformation. The Reformation restored the proper worship of God, the true

knowledge of salvation, and the conviction that human beings cannot save themselves, in any way. Good works are praiseworthy, but they have no value in the restoration of a human being; rather, human acceptance before God is totally the gratuitous work of grace.

In all that they were doing, the Protestants had not separated from the church; in Calvin's view they had restored it. The pastoral office had fallen into disrepute, and the episcopal succession had long been interrupted. In the pre-Reformation church, according to Calvin, the people were deprived of their rights, and the rights of the clergy were usurped by the bishops and the rights of the episcopate by the papacy.

In prosecuting his case, Calvin uses strong language: "I deny that See [Rome] to be Apostolical, wherein nought is seen but a shocking apostasy—I deny him to be vicar of Christ, who, in furiously persecuting the gospel, demonstrates by his conduct that he is Antichrist—I deny him to be the successor of Peter, who is doing his utmost to demolish every edifice that Peter built—I deny him to be head of the church, who by his tyranny lacerates and dismembers the church, after dissevering her from Christ, her true and only head" (from *The Necessity of Reforming the Church*).

PART FOUR

THE MODERN PERIOD

It is not without reason that historian Kenneth Scott Latourette devoted three volumes of his massive seven-volume work, *A History of the Expansion of Christianity*, to the nineteenth century, for it was, he insisted, "a great century." This judgment by Latourette has been confirmed many times by scholars and historians in later decades.

To some degree the nineteenth century is a continuation of the original passion of the Reformation, coupled with the critical thinking of the Enlightenment. Much of the unfinished business of the reformed thinkers such as Martin Luther and John Calvin was moved forward on the agenda after a post-Reformation scholasticism that tended to close the doors on creative theological thought. New developments in science and philosophy as well as the political and economic development of peoples and cultures were forward looking and not mere reproductions of patterns already laid down. It was a creative, dynamic time.

For Christian thought, the modern age up to the close of the First World War provided the presuppositions on which later developments can be evaluated. The breakup of traditional theological axioms—whether in doctrine, biblical studies, or the interpretation of church history—required a radical reconsideration of both the heritage and the destiny of Christianity.

To select just one representative of each of the major new theological developments of the modern age would in itself make an impressive roll call. In philosophy: Immanuel Kant; dogmatics: Friedrich Schleiermacher; biblical criticism: David F. Strauss; psychology of religion: William James; the social gospel: Walter Rauschenbusch, to mention only a few of the obvious—these were the fermenting spirits of an exhilarating era.

It would be a mistake of course to claim too much for this age, for later reflection has often denounced the heady experimentation in the nineteenth century. The limitations of the period became a dirge played in criticisms following both World War I and World War II. On balance, however, it is difficult to avoid the cumulative effect of the progressive and futuristic direction of the "great century" from Kant to Rauschenbusch. Among other things, this was the age of the great modern dictionaries and encyclopedias, the standard texts and reference works that gave a basic foundation for scholarly research, and the age in which what has come to be known as "higher criticism" of Scripture was given birth.

If revolutions were precipitated by the times, the inspiration of creative ideas and creative spirits could not be denied. Enlightenment ideals of freedom and equality led not only to nationalistic rebellion but also to great moral contests over the rights of slaves, women, and colonized peoples. Christian institutions were inevitably caught up in this stormy reassessment.

20. Immanuel Kant (1724–1804)

The dialogue between philosophy and theology finds perfect illustration in the influence of Immanuel Kant (sometimes referred to as the Copernicus of philosophy) upon the nineteenth century. Born in Koenigsberg, East Prussia, this famous German philosopher, whose works were to become standard textbooks of generations of thinkers in many fields, lived out a peculiarly uneventful existence. Philosophical thought totally and constantly monopolized his attention; unmarried, untraveled, unattached to his time and community, he nevertheless gave uncommon distinction to his university and to the scholarly integrity of his subject. With all the good and bad qualities of the stereotype, Kant was the German professor without equal.

For Kant philosophy involved two major issues: epistemology (what do we know and how do we know it?) and ethics (what is the good and how do we do it?). Asking such basic questions became the trademark of Kantian critical philosophy, which sought to go beyond both the rationalism and the empiricism of his predecessors.

In his *Critique of Pure Reason* (1781) Kant addressed the epistemological question. He argued that reason provides the categories and forms of "intuition" (knowledge) and is therefore an indispensable instrument for fashioning both the content and method of knowledge in such areas as mathematics and pure science. On the other hand, reason is worthless in such areas of thought as proofs for the existence of God. Just as the transcendental ego cannot be made an object of investigation (since the "I" is always involved in the process), so God cannot be rationally demonstrated to exist without the arguments becoming hopelessly entangled in logical antinomies.

In 1788 Kant addressed the ethical question in his *Critique of Practical Reason*. The nature of the good is posited on freedom, he argued (I can; therefore, I must), and this issues in a categorical imperative such as the rigorous assertion: "I must act in such a way that I can at the same time will that my maxim should become a universal law." An important corollary of Kant's ethics was related to theology, for, since goodness and justice are required and yet seldom prevail in human society, there must be a God who, as moral arbitrator and divine judge, undergirds and authenticates the categorical imperative, if not now, then hereafter.

Kant's last significant work was published in 1793 under the title *Religion within the Limits of Reason Alone*. In this work Kant was once again drawn into the philosophy of religion dialogue. Of no great importance for subsequent philosophy, this little book was nonetheless substantially influential in shaping the direction that nineteenth-century theology was to take. Here both the rational and ethical concerns of Kant merge in an interpretation of religion, and of Christianity in particular, which was as ingenious as it was controversial.

Religion for Kant was his ethic writ large. Though human beings are created with a radical evil that tends to warp their progress toward the good life, there is also in human nature a good disposition or divine inclination that constantly battles with the radical evil, eventually overcoming it and setting one's course in the right direction. The supreme historical illustration of this divine-human struggle for us is Jesus the Christ. Jesus is the personification of the victory of the principle of good over radical evil, and he is therefore our model and archetype of ideal humanity.

Source: Religion within the Limits of Reason Alone, *translated by T. H. Groehe and H. H. Hudson (LaSalle, Ill.: Court Publishing Co., 1960), 17, 40, 50, 54–55, 57, 79, 100.*

▼ ▼ ▼

We shall say . . . of the character (good or evil) distinguishing a man from other possible rational beings, that it is innate in him. Yet in so doing we shall ever take the position that nature is not to bear the blame (if it is evil) or take the credit (if it is good), but that man himself is its author. . . .

Man himself must make or have made himself into whatever, in a moral sense, whether good or evil, he is or is to become. Either condition must be an effect of his free choice; for otherwise he could not be held responsible for it and could therefore be morally neither good nor evil. When it is said, Man is created good, this can mean nothing more than: He is created for good and the original predisposition in man is good; not that, thereby, he is already actually good, but rather that he brings it about that he becomes good or evil, according to whether he adopts or does not adopt into his maxim the incentives which this predisposition carries with it ([an act] which must be left wholly to his own free choice). Granted that some supernatural cooperation may be necessary to his becoming good, better, yet, whether this cooperation consists merely in the abatement of hindrances or indeed in positive assistance, man must first make himself worthy to receive

it, and must lay hold of this aid (which is no small matter)—that is, he must adopt this positive increase of power into his maxim, for only thus can good be imputed to him and he be known as a good man. . . .

To become morally good it is not enough merely to allow the seed of goodness implanted in our species to develop without hindrance; there is also present in us an active and opposing cause of evil to be combated. Among the ancient moralists it was preeminently the Stoics who called attention to this fact by their watchword "virtue," which (in Greek as well as Latin) signifies courage and valor and thus presupposes the presence of an enemy. . . .

Yet those valiant men (the Stoics) mistook their enemy: for he is not to be sought in the merely undisciplined natural inclinations which present themselves so openly to everyone's consciousness; rather is he, as it were, an invisible foe who screens himself behind reason and is therefore all the more dangerous. They called out wisdom against this folly, which allows itself to be deceived by the inclinations through mere carelessness, instead of summoning here against wickedness (the wickedness of the human heart), which secretly undermines the disposition with soul-destroying principles. . . .

Mankind (rational earthly existence in general) in its complete moral perfection is that which alone can render a world the object of a divine decree and the end of creation. . . .

Now it is our universal duty as men to elevate ourselves to this ideal of moral perfection, that is, to this archetype of the moral disposition in all its purity—and for this the idea itself, which reason presents to us for our zealous emulation, can give us power. But just because we are not the authors of this idea, and because it has established itself in man without our comprehending how human nature could have been capable of receiving it, it is more appropriate to say that this archetype has come down to us from heaven and has assumed our humanity (for it is less possible to conceive how man, by nature evil, should of himself lay aside evil and raise himself to the ideal of holiness, than that the latter should descend to man and assume a humanity which is, in itself, not evil). Such union with us may therefore be regarded as a state of humiliation of the Son of God if we represent to ourselves this godly-minded person, regarded as our archetype, as assuming sorrows in fullest measure in order to further the world's good, though he himself is holy and therefore is bound to endure no sufferings whatsoever. Man, on the contrary, who is never free from guilt even though he has taken on the very same disposition, can regard as truly merited the sufferings that may overtake him, by whatever road they come; consequently he must consider himself unworthy of the union of his disposition with such an idea, even though this idea serves him as an archetype.

This ideal of a humanity pleasing to God (hence of such moral perfection as is possible to an earthly being who is subject to wants and inclinations) we can represent to ourselves only

as the idea of a person who would be willing not merely to discharge all human duties himself and to spread about him goodness as widely as possible by precept and example, but even, though tempted by the greatest allurements, to take upon himself every affliction, up to the most ignominious death, for the good of the world and even for his enemies. For man can frame to himself no concept of the degree and strength of a force like that of moral disposition except by picturing it as encompassed by obstacles, and yet, in the face of the fiercest onslaughts victorious.

Man may then hope to become acceptable to God (and so be saved) through a practical faith in this Son of God (so far as he is represented as having taken upon himself man's nature). In other words, he, and he alone, is entitled to look upon himself as an object not unworthy of divine approval who is conscious of such a moral disposition as enables him to have a well-grounded confidence in himself and to believe that, under like temptations and afflictions (so far as these are made the touchstone of that idea), he would be loyal unswervingly to

The Effects of Free Choice

the archetype of humanity and, by faithful imitation, remain true to his exemplar. . . .

Now if it were indeed a fact that such a truly godly-minded man at some particular time had descended, as it were, from heaven to earth and have given men in his own person, through his teachings, his conduct, and his sufferings, as perfect an example of a man well-pleasing to God as one can expect to find in external experience (for be it remembered that the archetype of such a person is to be sought nowhere but in our own reason), and if he had, through all this, produced immeasurably great moral good upon earth by effecting a revolution in the human race—even then we should have no cause for supposing him other than a man naturally begotten. (Indeed, the naturally begotten man feels himself under obligation to furnish just such an example in himself.) This is not, to be sure, absolutely to deny that he might be a man supernaturally begotten. But to suppose the latter can in no way benefit us practically, inasmuch as the archetype which we find embodied in this manifestation must, after all, be sought in ourselves (even though we are but natural men). And the presence of this archetype in the human soul is in itself sufficiently incomprehensible without our adding to its supernatural origin the assumption that it is hypostatized in a particular individual. The elevation of such a holy person above all the frailties of human nature would rather, so far as we can see, hinder the adoption of the idea of such a person for our imitation. For let the nature of this individual pleasing to God be regarded as human in the sense of being encumbered with the very same needs as ourselves, hence the same sorrows, with the very same inclinations, hence with the same temptations to transgress; let it, however, be regarded as superhuman to the degree that his unchanging purity of will, not achieved with effort but innate, makes all transgression on his part utterly impossible: his distance from the natural man would then be so infinitely great that such a divine person could no longer be held up as an example to him. . . .

If a moral religion (which must consist not in dogmas and rites but in the heart's disposition to fulfill all human duties as divine commands) is to be established, all miracles which history concocts with its inauguration must themselves in the end render superfluous the belief in miracles in general; for it bespeaks a culpable degree of moral unbelief not to acknowledge as completely authoritative the command of duty—command primordially engraved upon the heart of men through reason—unless they are in addition accredited through miracles: "Except ye see signs and wonders, ye will not believe." Yet, when a religion of mere rites and observances has run its course, and when one based on the spirit and the truth (on the moral disposition) is to be established in its stead, it is wholly conformable to man's ordinary ways of thought, though not strictly necessary, for the historical introduction of the latter to be accompanied and, as it were, adorned by miracles, in order to announce the termination of the earlier religion, which without miracles would never have any authority. Indeed, in order to win over the adherents of the older religion, the new order is interpreted as the fulfillment, at last, of what was only prefigured in the older religion and has all along been the design of Providence. If this be so it is quite useless to debate those narratives or interpretations; the true religion, which in its time needed to be introduced through such expedients, is now here, and from now on is able to maintain itself on rational grounds. Otherwise one would have to assume that mere faith in, and repetition of, things incomprehensible (which anyone can do without thereby being or ever becoming a better man) is a way, and indeed the only way, of pleasing God—an assertion to be combated with might and main. The person of the teacher of the one and only religion, valid for all worlds, may indeed be a mystery; his appearance on earth, his translation thence, and his eventful life and his suffering may all be nothing but miracles; nay, the historical record, which is to authenticate the account of all these miracles, may itself be a miracle (a supersensible revelation). We need not call in question any of these miracles and indeed may honor the trappings which have served to bring into public currency a doctrine whose authenticity rests upon a record indelibly registered in every soul and which stands in need of no miracle. But it is essential that, in the use of these historical accounts, we do not make it a tenet of religion that the knowing, believing, and professing of them are themselves means whereby we can render ourselves well-pleasing to God. . . .

A church dispenses with the most important mark of truth, namely, a rightful claim to universality, when it bases itself upon a revealed faith. For such a faith, being historical (even though it be far more widely disseminated and more completely secured for remotest posterity through the agency of scripture) can never be universally communicated so as to produce conviction. Yet, because of the natural seed and desire of all men for something sensibly tenable, and for a confirmation of some sort from experience of the highest concepts and grounds of reason (a need which really must be taken into account when the universal dissemination of a faith is contemplated), some historical ecclesiastical faith or other, usually to be found at hand, must be utilized.

If such an empirical faith, which chance, it would seem, has tossed into our hands, is to be united with the basis of a moral faith (be the first end or merely a means), an exposition of the revelation which has come into our possession is required, that is, a thoroughgoing interpretation of it in a sense agreeing with the universal practical rules of a religion of pure

reason. For the theoretical part of ecclesiastical faith cannot interest us morally if it does not conduce to the performance of all human duties as divine commands (that which constitutes the essence of all religion).

▲ ▲ ▲

For Kant, religion is founded on moral concepts, especially on that of human beings as free moral agents. As a free moral agent a human being is bound to unconditional love through the use of reason, and without this moral ability, religion would be impossible. Although guilt and reward depend upon the notion of human freedom, it is not necessary to add to morality the idea of a Being over humanity so that human beings might be provided with a basis for duty other than the moral law. Morality is quite capable of ignoring all ends when it comes to a question of duty.

The central issue for religion, according to Kant, is the opposition of good and evil. Since an essentially good moral disposition can yet perform evil acts, explanation for a human being's possibility for self-destruction is necessary. Human nature then is only the subjective ground for the exercise of the freedom with which humans are endowed. In human beings there exists the ultimate ground for the selection of either good or evil maxims, and the ultimate adoption of either maxim must itself lie in human freedom, even though such a fact cannot be revealed in experience. Good or evil is innate in humans only in the sense that the ground for the use of freedom is present in humans at birth. A person must decide, however; he or she must exercise this freedom. A person's disposition with respect to the moral law can never be indifferent, neither good nor evil. Indeed the will must always be specific, always either good or evil.

Kant was convinced human beings are created for good and the original predisposition is good. Thus, humans must have made themselves into whatever they have morally become, whether good or evil. A command to become better persons continually resounds within human beings, and so it must be within their power to do so. We may have reversed the proper moral order of incentive (in other words, we are evil when we place self-love over moral law), but we have never lost our greatest incentive—respect for the moral law.

In Kant's view, religion is the acknowledgment that all duties are divine commands. God is the moral lawgiver, and the highest goal of moral perfection in finite creatures is love of the law. Thus, Jesus of Nazareth was the divinely given moral example. Through his teachings, actions, and personal commitment shown in his suffering, Jesus provided a model of what it means to be a person well-pleasing to God. His example was as close to perfect as anyone could possibly expect in the external world, since the archetype is really to be found in our own reason and not outside it.

21. FRIEDRICH SCHLEIERMACHER (1768–1834)

As Immanuel Kant may be said to have begun the modern philosophical movement, so Friedrich Schleiermacher is often regarded as the initiator of modern theology. Combining in his person many of the emerging elements of his day, Schleiermacher influenced all sorts of developments. Yet he never founded a school of thought later known by his name, and his contribution can be measured as much in terms of mood and spirit as substance or content.

Like Kant, Schleiermacher was born in eastern Germany, in Breslau, but his professional life centered in Berlin for the most part. He was an ordained minister in the Reformed or Calvinist church, a classical scholar whose translations of Plato were well received, an early member of the Romantic movement in Germany, an advocate of church

union between Lutherans and the Calvinists in 1817, a hospital chaplain, a popular preacher, and a distinguished professor of theology at the University of Berlin.

Reared in the simple piety of the Moravian tradition, Schleiermacher retained throughout his entire life the subjective dimension in all his interpretations of theological truth. Later he was to add to this pietistic background an eager acceptance of the newer developments in biblical criticism that left him restless in the presence of unreflective orthodoxy and theological scholasticism. Nevertheless, in looking forward, Schleiermacher did not abandon his roots, either classical or evangelical.

The fame of Schleiermacher is usually attributed to two major theological works written some twenty years apart and in many ways quite different. The first work bore the descriptive, if somewhat cumbersome, title *On Religion: Speeches to Its Cultured Despisers* (1799). It was a series of rambling essays growing out of his association with the Romantic movement, which prided itself on cultural sophistication and intellectual humanism. Schleiermacher had much in common with this spirit, but it pained him sorely that religion, for no good reason, was largely disdained by his friends, even as a topic of conversation.

Arguing firmly and politely, Schleiermacher sought to make a place for religious discussion. He was not the least concerned to defend dogma or even to put the Christian religion above other religions. He felt instinctively, however, that religious emotion at the sublime level manifested its own integrity, based on an innate sense or feeling of absolute dependence on God.

Twenty years later Schleiermacher published a substantial work on systematic theology known simply as *The Christian Faith* (1820–1821; 2nd edition 1830–1831). It was the first creatively original structure of doctrine since John Calvin's *Institutes* three hundred years earlier. Drawing upon biblical criticism and the classic Christian tradition enshrined in the evangelical Reformation creeds, Schleiermacher sought to represent the Christian faith in such a way as to retain the living tradition and at the same time to move ahead into the new day.

Carefully distinguishing his position from both rationalism and moralism, the two dominant sensibilities of the day, Schleiermacher maintained that religion was not a knowing or a doing, but a feeling of absolute dependence.

Picking up the thread of his concern in *Speeches* to give religion integrity and respectability for its own sake, the doctrinal volume abandoned the earlier discussion of religion-in-general for a very specific definition of Christianity as located in the redemption accomplished by Jesus Christ.

Moving out from a self-conscious feeling of absolute dependence on God, Schleiermacher constructed his system so that the doctrines of faith became formal dogmatic descriptions of the subjective states of faith. This meant a more concentrated attention upon the doctrines of sin and grace, and a less important status within the system for such a traditional doctrine as the Trinity (which is relegated to an appendix).

The continuing controversial features of Schleiermacher's theology revolved around differing interpretations of what he meant by the subjectivity of faith, on the one hand, and the centrality of Christ and his unique God-consciousness, on the other. The ups and downs of later reactions by theologians to Schleiermacher, together with the vehemence of the debate, constitute in many ways the story of modern theology and an index to the vitality of his theological construction.

Sources: On Religion: Speeches to Its Cultured Despisers, *translated by John Oman (London: K. Paul, Trubner & Co., 1896), 1–2, 12–13, 14–16, 18–19, 21;* The Christian Faith, *translated by H. R. MacIntosh and J. J. Stewart (Edinburgh: T & T Clark, 1928), 374–76, 385–89, 425–28.*

It may be an unexpected and even a marvelous undertaking, that any one should still venture to demand from the very class that have raised themselves above the vulgar, and are saturated with the wisdom of the centuries, attention for a subject so entirely neglected by them. I confess that I am aware of nothing that promises any easy success, whether it be in winning for my efforts your approval, or in the more difficult and more desirable task of instilling into you my thought and inspiring you for my subject. Faith has never been every man's affair. At all times but few have discerned religion itself, while millions, in various ways, have been satisfied to juggle with its trappings. Now especially the life of the cultivated people is far from anything that might have even a resemblance to religion. Just as little, I know, do you worship the Deity in sacred retirement, as you visit forsaken temples. In your ornamented dwellings, the only sacred things to be met with are the sage maxims of our wise men, and the splendid compositions of our poets. Suavity and sociability, art and science have so fully taken possession of your minds, that no room remains for the eternal and holy Being that lies beyond the world. I know how well you have succeeded in making your earthly life so rich and varied, that you no longer stand in need of an eternity. Having made a universe for yourselves, you are above the need of thinking of the Universe that made you. You are agreed, I know, that nothing new, nothing convincing can any more be said on this matter, which on every side by sages and seers, and I might add by scoffers and priests, has been abundantly discussed. To priests, least of all, are you inclined to listen. . . . All this I know, and yet, divinely swayed by an irresistible necessity within me, I feel myself compelled to speak, and cannot take back my invitation that you and none else should listen to me. . . .

Let us then, I ask you, examine whence exactly religion has its rise. Is it from some clear intuition, or from some vague thought? Is it from the different kinds and sects of religion found in history, or from some general idea which you have perhaps conceived arbitrarily? . . .

You are doubtless acquainted with the histories of human follies, and have reviewed the various structures of religious doctrine from the senseless fables of wanton peoples to the most refined Deism, from the rude superstition of human sacrifice to the ill-put together fragments of metaphysics and ethics now called purified Christianity, and you have found them all without rhyme or reason. I am far from wishing to contradict you. Rather, if you really mean that the most cultured religious system is no better than the rudest, if you only perceive that the divine cannot lie in a series that ends on both sides in something ordinary and despicable, I will gladly spare you the trouble of estimating further all that lies between. Possibly they may all appear to you transitions and stages towards the final form. Out of the hand of its age each comes better polished and carved, till at length art has grown equal to that perfect plaything with which our century has presented history. . . . What are all these [theological] systems, considered in themselves, but the handiwork of the calculating understanding, wherein only by mutual limitation each part holds its place? What else can they be, these systems of theology, these theories of the origin and the end of the world, these analyses of the nature of an incomprehensible Being, wherein everything runs to cold arguing, and the highest can be treated in the tone of a common controversy? And this is certainly—let me appeal to your own feeling—not the character of religion. . . .

In order to take possession of its own domain, religion renounces herewith all claims to whatever belongs to those others and gives back everything that has been forced upon it. It does not wish to determine and explain the universe according to its nature as does metaphysics; it does not desire to continue the universe's development and perfect it by the power of freedom and the divine free choice of a human being as does morals. *Religion's essence is neither thinking nor acting, but intuition and feeling.* It wishes to intuit the universe, wishes devoutly to overhear the universe's own manifestations and actions, longs to be grasped and filled by the universe's immediate influences in childlike passivity. Thus, religion is opposed to these two in everything that makes up its essence and in everything that wishes its effects. Metaphysics and morals see in the whole universe only humanity as the center of all relatedness, as the condition of all being and the cause of all becoming; religion wishes to see the infinite, its imprint and its manifestation, in humanity no less than in all other individual and finite forms. Metaphysics proceeds from finite human nature and wants to define consciously, from its simplest concept, the extent of its powers, and its receptivity, what the universe can be for us and how we necessarily must view it. Religion also lives its whole life in nature, but in the infinite nature of totality, the one and all; what holds in nature for everything individual also holds for the human being; and wherever everything, including man, may press on or tarry within this eternal ferment of individual forms and beings, religion wishes to intuit and to divine this in detail in quiet submissiveness. Morality proceeds from the consciousness of freedom; it wishes to extend freedom's realm to infinity and to make everything subservient to it. Religion breathes there where freedom itself has once more become nature; it apprehends man beyond the play of his particular powers and his personality, and views him from the vantage point where he must be what he is, whether he likes it or not.

Thus religion maintains its own sphere and its own character only by completely removing itself from the sphere and character of speculation as well as from that of praxis. Only when it places itself next to both of them is the common ground perfectly filled out and human

nature completed from this dimension. Religion shows itself to you as the necessary and indispensable third next to those two, as their natural counterpart, not slighter in worth and splendor than what you wish of them. To want to have speculation and praxis without religion is rash arrogance. It is insolent enmity against the gods; it is the unholy sense of Prometheus, who cowardly stole what in calm certainty he would have been able to ask for and to expect. Man has merely stolen the feeling of his infinity and godlikeness, and as an unjust possession it cannot thrive for him if he is not also conscious of his limitedness, the contingency of his whole form, the silent disappearance of his whole existence in the immeasurable. The gods have also punished this crime from the very beginning. Praxis is an art, speculation is a science, religion is the sensibility and taste for the infinite. Without religion, how can praxis rise above the common circle of adventurous and customary forms? How can speculation become anything better than a stiff and barren skeleton? Or why, in all its action directed outwardly and toward the universe, does your praxis actually always forget to cultivate humanity itself? It is because you place humanity in opposition to the universe and do not receive it from the hand of religion as a part of the universe and as something holy. How does praxis arrive at an impoverished uniformity that knows only a single ideal and lays this as the basis everywhere? It is because you lack the basic feeling for the infinite, whose symbol is multiplicity and individuality. Everything finite exists only through the determination of its limits, which must, as it were, "be cut out of" the infinite. Only thus can a thing be infinite and yet be self-formed within these limits; otherwise you lose everything in the uniformity of a universal concept. Why, for so long, did speculation give you deceptions instead of a system, and words instead of real thoughts? Why was it nothing but an empty game with formulas that always reappeared changed and to which nothing would ever correspond? Because it lacked religion, because the feeling for the infinite did not animate it, and because longing for it and reverence for it did not compel its fine, airy thoughts to assume more rigorous consistency in order to preserve itself against this powerful pressure. Everything must proceed from intuition, and those who lack the desire to intuit the infinite have no touchstone and indeed need none in order to know whether they have given any respectable thought to the matter.

But concerning immortality, I cannot conceal that the way in which most people take it and their longing after it is completely irreligious, exactly contrary to the spirit of religion. Their wish has no other basis than their aversion to that which is the goal of religion. Recall how in religion everything strives to expand the sharply delineated outlines of our personality and gradually to lose them in the infinite in order that we, by intuiting the universe, will become one with it as much as possible. But they resist the infinite and do not wish to get beyond themselves; they wish to be nothing other than themselves and they are anxiously concerned about their individuality. Recall how it was the highest goal of religion to discover a universe beyond and above humanity, and its only complaint was that this goal would not properly succeed in this world. But they do not want to seize the sole opportunity death affords them to transcend humanity; they are anxious about how they will take it with them beyond this world, and their highest endeavor is for further sight and better limbs. But the universe speaks to them, as it stands written: "Whoever loses his life for my sake, will find it, and whoever would save it will lose it." The life they would keep is lamentable, for if it is the eternity of their persons that concerns them, why do they not attend just as anxiously to what they have been as to what they will be?

How does going forward help them if they cannot go backward? In search of an immortality that they could have, which is none, and over which they are not masters, they lose the immortality that they could have, and in addition their mortal life with thoughts that vainly distress and torment them. But try to yield up your life out of love for the universe. Strive here already to annihilate your individuality and to live in the one and all; and if you have fused with as much of the universe as you find here and a greater and holier longing has arisen in you, then we will want to speak further about the hopes death gives to us and concerning the infinity to which we unerringly soar through it. . . .

THE PERSON OF JESUS

92. On the Person of Jesus Christ: The peculiar activity and the exclusive dignity of the Redeemer imply each other, and are inseparably one in the self-consciousness of believers.

Whether we prefer to call Christ the Redeemer, or to regard him as the one in whom the creation of nature, which up to the point had existed only in a provisional state, was perfected, each of these points of view means only that we ascribe to him a peculiar activity, and that in connection with a peculiar spiritual content of his person. For if his influence is only of the same kind as others, even if it is ever so much more complete and inclusive, then its result also, that is, the salvation of mankind, would be a work common to him and the others, although his share might be greater; and there would be, not one Redeemer over against the redeemed, but many, of whom one would only be the first among those like him. Nor would the human creation then be completed through him, but through all of those redeemers together, who, in so far as their work implies in them a peculiar quality of nature, are all alike distinguished from the rest of mankind. It would be just the same, if his activity were indeed peculiar to himself, but this less in virtue of an inner quality belonging to him than of a peculiar position in which he had been put. The second form of expression, that the human creation had been completed in him, would then be altogether without content, since it would be more natural to suppose that there are many like him, only they did not happen to occupy the same position. In that case he would not even be properly Redeemer, even though it could be said that mankind had been redeemed through his act of his suffering, as the case might be. For the result, namely, salvation, could not be something communicated from him (since he had nothing peculiar to himself); it could only have been occasioned or released by him.

Just as little could the approximation to the condition of blessedness be traced to him, if he had indeed an exclusive dignity, but had remained passive in it, and had exercised no influence corresponding to it. For (apart from the fact that it is incomprehensible how his contemporaries, and we after them, should ever have come to attribute such an influence to him, especially when the manner of his appearance was what it was), supposing that the blessedness could have been communicated merely through men's observing this dignity, although there were united with it no influence acting on others, then in the observers there must have been something more than receptivity; his appearance would have to be regarded rather as merely the occasion for this idea, spontaneously produced by themselves.

Thus the approximation to blessedness, out of the state of misery, cannot be explained as a fact mediated through Jesus, by reference to either of these elements without the other. It follows, therefore, that they must be most intimately related and mutually determined. . . .

This division falls accordingly into two doctrines—that of the Person of Christ, and that of his work. These two are quite different so far as

the individual propositions are concerned, but their total content is the same. . . .

94. The Redeemer, then, is like all men in virtue of the identity of human nature, but distinguished from them all by the constant potency of his God-consciousness, which was a veritable existence of God in him.

That the Redeemer should be entirely free from all sinfulness is no objection at all to the complete identity of human nature in him and others, for . . . sin is so little an essential part of the being of man that we can never regard it as anything else than a disturbance of nature. It follows that the possibility of a sinless development is in itself not incongruous with the idea of human nature; indeed, this possibility is involved, and recognized, in the consciousness of sin as guilt, as that is universally understood. This likeness, however is to be understood in such a general sense that even the first man before the first sin stood no nearer the Redeemer, and was like him in no higher sense, than all other men. For if even in the life of the first man we must assume a time when sin had not yet appeared, yet every first appearance of sin leads back to a sinful preparation. But the Redeemer too shared in the same vicissitudes of life, without which we can hardly imagine the entrance of sin at a definite moment even in Adam, for they are essential to human nature. Furthermore, the first man was originally free from all the contagious influences of a sinful society, while the Redeemer had to enter into the corporate life when it had already advanced far in deterioration, so that it would hardly be possible to attribute his sinlessness to external protection—which we certainly must somehow admit in the case of the first man, if we would not involve ourselves in contradictions. Of the Redeemer, on the contrary, we must hold that the ground of his sinlessness was not external to himself, but that it was a sinlessness essentially grounded in himself, if he was to take away, through what he was in himself, the sinfulness of the corporate life. Therefore, so far as sin is concerned, Christ differs no less from the first man than from all others. . . .

Working backwards we must now say, if it is only through him that the human God-consciousness becomes an existence of God in human nature, and only through the rational nature that the totality of finite powers can become an existence of God in the world, in so far as he bears within himself the whole new creation which contains and develops the potency of the God-consciousness. . . .

The origin of every human life may be regarded in a twofold manner, as issuing from the narrow circle of descent and society to which it belongs, and as a fact of human nature in general. The more definitely the weaknesses of that narrow circle repeat themselves in an individual, the more valid becomes the first point of view. The more the individual by the kind and degree of his gifts transcends that circle, and the more he exhibits what is new within it, the more we are thrown back upon the other explanation. This means that the beginning of Jesus' life cannot in any way be explained by the first factor, but only and exclusively by the second; so that from the beginning he must have been free from every influence from earlier generations which disseminated sin and disturbed the inner God-consciousness, and he can only be understood as an original act of human nature, i.e. as an act of human nature as not affected by sin. The beginning of his life was also a new implanting of the God-consciousness which creates receptivity in human nature; hence this content and that manner of origin are in such a close relation that they mutually condition and explain each other. That new implanting came to be through the beginning of his life, and therefore that beginning must have transcended every detrimental influence of his immediate circle; and because it was such an original and sin-free act of nature, a filling of his nature with God-

consciousness became possible as its result. So that upon this relation too the fullest light is thrown if we regard the beginning of the life of Jesus as the completed creation of human nature. The appearance of the first man constituted at the same time the physical life of the human race; the appearance of the Second Adam constituted for this nature a new spiritual life, which communicates and develops itself by spiritual fecundation. And as in the former its originality (which is the condition of the appearance of human nature) and its having emerged from creative divine activity are the same thing, so also in the Redeemer both are the same—his spiritual originality, set free from every prejudicial influence of natural descent, and that existence of God in him which also proves itself creative. If the impartation of the Spirit to human nature which was made in the first Adam was insufficient, in that the Spirit remained sunk in sensuousness and barely glanced forth clearly at moments as a presentiment of something better, and if the work of creation has only been completed through the second and equally original impartation to the second Adam, yet both events go back to one undivided eternal divine decree and form, even in a higher sense, only one and the same natural system, though one unattainable by us. . . .

100. The Redeemer assumes believers into the power of his God-consciousness, and this is his redemptive activity. . . .

The activity by which he assumes us into fellowship with him is, therefore, a creative production in us of the will to assume him into ourselves, or rather—since it is only receptiveness for his activity as involved in the impartation—only our assent to the influence of his activity. But it is a condition of that activity of the Redeemer that the individuals should enter the sphere of his historical influence, where they become aware of him in his self-revelation. Now this assent can only be conceived as conditioned by the consciousness of sin; yet it is not necessary that this should precede entrance into the sphere of the Redeemer. Rather it may just as well arise within that sphere as the effect of the Redeemer's self-revelation, as indeed it certainly does come to full clarity as we contemplate his sinless perfection. Accordingly, the original activity of the Redeemer is best conceived as a pervasive influence which is received by its object in virtue of the free movement with which he turns himself to its attraction, just as we ascribe an attractive power to everyone to whose educative intellectual influence we gladly submit ourselves. Now, if every activity of the Redeemer proceeds from the being of God in him, and if in the formation of the Redeemer's Person the only active power was the creative divine activity which established itself as the being of God in him, then also his every activity may be regarded as a continuation of that person-forming divine influence upon human nature. For the pervasive activity of Christ cannot establish itself in an individual without becoming person-forming in him too, for now all his activities are differ-

ently determined through the working of Christ in him, and even all impressions are differently received—which means that the personal self-consciousness too becomes altogether different. And just as creation is not concerned simply with individuals (as if each creation of an individual had been a special act), but it is the world that was created, and every individual as such was created only in and with the whole, for the rest not less than for itself, in the same way the activity of the Redeemer too is world-forming, and its object is human nature, in the totality of which the powerful God-consciousness is to be implanted as a new vital principle. He takes possession of the individuals relative to the whole, wherever he finds those in whom his activity does not merely remain, but from whom, moving on, it can work upon others through the revelation of his life. And thus the total effective influence of Christ is only the continuation of the creative divine activity out of which the person of Christ arose. For this, too, was directed towards human nature as a whole, in which that being of God was to exist, but in such a

Touchdown

way that its effects are mediated through the life of Christ, as its most original organ, for all human nature that has already become personal in the natural sense, in proportion as it allows itself to be brought into spiritual touch with that life and its self-perpetuating organism. And this in order that the former personality may be slain and human nature, in vital fellowship with Christ, be formed into persons in the totality of that higher life. . . .

▲ ▲ ▲

Schleiermacher's Speeches

Romanticism's greatest contribution to modern religious thought was the attempt to establish the nature and warrants of religious belief on new grounds. A prime example of this attempt at reconstruction is Schleiermacher's *On Religion: Speeches to Its Cultured Despisers.*

The educated or so-called cultured despisers of Schleiermacher's time considered religion to be of very little real value especially when viewed through its externalities. Thus religion was basically rejected, or at least ignored, by them. In the *Speeches* (which were not actually delivered orally), Schleiermacher's purpose was to demonstrate that they had misunderstood religion in its essence and that what they were rejecting was not really the essence of religion at all. Schleiermacher even saw that their complaints against religion were justifiable when directed against the external representatives of religion. In this sense, then, the "cultured despisers" are actually seen to be allies of what religion truly is. To grasp religion, however, they must go beyond these outward appearances and penetrate the incorruptible inner essence of religion.

To vindicate religion, Schleiermacher spoke to its foundational origins. These origins are not historical but rather in human nature itself. Customarily we think of religion as a way of thinking faith, a peculiar way of contemplating the world, or a way of acting, a special conduct or character. In other words, religion is viewed either from a theoretical (metaphysical) point of view or from a practical (ethical) point of view. The orthodox rationalists and G. W. F. Hegel identified religion with theoretical knowledge, Kant and the Deists with morality. But this is to reduce religion to something else and therefore to make religion itself unnecessary. Religion, according to Schleiermacher, is neither a "knowing" nor a "doing," nor a combination of the two. it is an abuse of religion to defend it as a prop for some spiritual or cultural function. Science, metaphysics, act, and morality all have their autonomous scope in which religion, correctly understood, has neither the right nor the need to interfere. Religion has its own domain in a person's true being. "True science is complete vision; true practice is culture and act self-produced; true religion is a sense and taste for the infinite."

For Schleiermacher feeling is the unique element of the religious life; religion is essentially feeling. This is a difficult, somewhat ambiguous concept, but it is clear Schleiermacher was not simply referring to emotion. It was for him an immediate self-consciousness. The feeling, or intuition, of immediate self-consciousness that issues in the uniquely religious feeling is, as Schleiermacher put it, "the immediate consciousness of the universal existence of all finite things in and through the infinite, and of all temporal things in and through the eternal. . . . It is to have life in immediate feeling, only as such an existence in the infinite and eternal."

Not all feeling is religious *per se*. It is the intuition of the self "in and through the infinite." The *infinite,* as Schleiermacher used the term, simply means feeling the infinity of existence in the concrete world upon us and in relation to us. This feeling for the infinite through our experience of the world is the primordial means of God's operation upon us—whether or not this feeling issues in thought or action. In his later work, *The Christian Faith*, Schleiermacher elaborated on this concept and was able to give it greater clarity by speaking of religion as the "feeling of absolute dependence," a phrase for which he is well-known. If Kant had rendered arguments for God's existence problematic, Schleiermacher could still point to a universal "intuition" or sense of the divine.

If this is the essence of religion, then what of those dogmas and doctrines that are so widely considered to be the essence of religion? For Schleiermacher they are the result of contemplation or reflection on feeling. They are not even necessary for religion itself, scarcely even for communicating religion, Schleiermacher suggested. But when feeling is made the subject of reflection and comparison, they are unavoidable. Doctrines are the product of reflection on feelings, but just because a person holds certain religious ideas does not necessarily make that person religious.

Schleiermacher's Christology

It is not really possible to discuss all of Schleiermacher's systematic treatment of the doctrine of God, including Christology. Suffice it to say that each divine attribute is related to a feeling that is integral to the Christian experience of dependence so central to his thought. As a result, Schleiermacher does not give consideration to such a traditional doctrine as the Trinity because he did not consider that the Trinity was given immediately in the Christian consciousness. This does not mean that he necessarily considered the Trinity to be an unimportant doctrine, even though he treated it only in an appendix to *Christian Faith*. Behind this "metaphysical" abstraction lay a profound truth: the whole of Christianity is dependent upon the reality of the vision of the divine with the human, both in the person of Jesus of Nazareth and in the vision of the Spirit with the church.

Central to Schleiermacher's understanding of the Christian faith was his understanding of sin and the redemptive work of Jesus of Nazareth, the Christ. Sin is the experience of our innate "God-consciousness" being hindered by the conflict between our fleshly sensuous nature and our higher spiritual nature. Like Augustine of Hippo before him, Schleiermacher saw sin as a disorder and a confusion of humanity's loves, whereby humans place their love in that which is worldly or temporal rather than in God and the Eternal.

The redemptive work comes only from outside of humanity, from the person of Jesus Christ, by means of his self-communication to human beings of his "unique" God consciousness. Schleiermacher argued that Christ is known through his work, his benefits, and that his effect upon us is the impress of the special dignity of his person, that is, his God-consciousness. Along with the growth of his natural powers, his God-consciousness gained perfect control of his entire person. In this sense, according to Schleiermacher, we can say that Jesus had perfection and sinlessness, and we can do so without reference to the metaphysical distinctions and obstacles of the past. Jesus is best understood as the full historical realization of archetypal humanity, the second Adam, the true Adam. He embodies concretely the new race of humans and thus becomes the exemplar of God's will for us. He is the mirror in which we see our true image and measure.

22. DAVID F. STRAUSS (1808–1874)

In the nineteenth century the most dramatic shift of theological emphasis occurred in the area of critical biblical studies. The centrality of the Scriptures in the Reformation, which hardened in the seventeenth and eighteenth centuries into Protestant scholasticism, was rediscovered in the nineteenth century and given fresh scholarly impetus.

Research in the texts and versions of the Old and New Testaments (usually referred to as "lower criticism") led to radical reinterpretation of the historical and theological background of the documents (usually referred to as "higher criticism"). Such studies cast suspicion on many older, traditional doctrines about the Scriptures, the life and teachings of Jesus, and the creeds of the church. An early precursor of this trend was David F. Strauss.

Strauss was born in Stuttgart and spent most of his life in and around his birthplace. For a few years he was a professor at the University of Tübingen. There is a strain of tragedy and bitter frustration in Strauss: He went to Berlin to study with the philosopher G. W. F. Hegel, who died shortly thereafter; he listened to Schleiermacher lecture but thought him not to be radical enough. He returned to Tübingen to lecture on the Gospels and in 1835 published his most famous work, *The Life of Jesus, Critically Examined* (translated into English in 1846 by Marian Evans, known by her literary pseudonym, George Eliot). The book provoked such a storm of protest that Strauss was removed from his post, and henceforth he became more and more of a religious skeptic, alienated from and without sympathy from his associates.

Strauss's great conviction about the Gospel accounts of the life of Jesus was tied to the hypothesis that the four evangelists ascribed to Jesus the miraculous acts and aphoristic statements that the Hebrew prophets had predicted for the coming Messiah. Certain other events and sayings of Jesus filled out the messianic prophecy with the result that the Gospels provide, on critical examination, very little historical substance but a great deal of theological interpretation. For Strauss the key word and concept in the research was *myth* or *mythus*, which was used as a technical term to designate what was nonhistorical in the biblical record though not necessarily untrue religiously or theologically.

Deeply influenced by the philosophical development that moved from Kant to Fichte to Hegel, Strauss saw the life of Jesus as a dialectical formula whereby creature and Creator, humanity and divinity, finite and infinite, were wonderfully conjoined. The Jesus of the Gospels was thus taken more as a principle than as a person, illustrating in a historical incident the eternal truth of the essential unity of divine and human.

Casting himself in the role of reformer, Strauss was bitterly disappointed by the negative response to the publication of his *Life of Jesus*. He rewrote the argument on a more popular level in 1864 (a year after Ernst Renan's *Life of Jesus* had appeared in France). Moving from hypotheses to assertion in his second effort, Strauss now contended that the four evangelists had actually fabricated what they wrote and that Jesus was a deceiver and an imposter. The final break came with a little book, *The Old and New Faith* (1872), in which he completely cut himself off from any form of Christianity.

The positive contribution in Strauss's otherwise tragic career came as a by-product to his *Life of Jesus,* namely, the strong impulse to do deeper and more scholarly research into the biblical records. Many of Strauss's points were brilliantly posited but clearly unsupported by textual data. So radical was his interpretation of the biblical texts that other scholars, more patient and less revolutionary, were forced to take up the challenge and pursue the painstaking research that so greatly enriched biblical criticism in the decades thereafter.

Source: The Life of Jesus, Critically Examined, *translated by George Eliot (New York: Blanchard Press, 1900), 69–70, 892–96.*

▼ ▼ ▼

We distinguish by the name evangelical mythus a narrative relating directly or indirectly to Jesus, which may be considered not as the expression of a fact, but as the product of an idea of his earliest followers; such a narrative being mythical in proportion as it exhibits this character. . . .

The pure mythus in the Gospel will be found to have two sources, which in most cases contributed simultaneously, though in different proportions, to form the mythus. The one source is, . . . the messianic ideas and expectations existing according to their several forms in the Jewish mind before Jesus, and independently of him; the other is that particular impression which was left by the personal character, actions, and fate of Jesus, and which served to modify the messianic idea in the minds of his people. The account of the transfiguration, for example, is derived almost exclusively from the former source; the only amplification taken from the latter source being—that they who appeared with Jesus on the Mount spake of his decease. On the other hand, the narrative of the rending of the veil of the temple at the death of Jesus seems to have had its origin in the hostile position which Jesus, and his church after him, sustained in relation to the Jewish temple worship. Here already we have something historical, though consisting merely of certain general features of character, position, etc.; we are thus at once brought upon the ground of the historical mythus.

The historical mythus has for its ground work a definite individual fact which has been seized upon by religious enthusiasm, and twined around with mythical conceptions culled from the idea of the Christ. This fact is perhaps a saying of Jesus such as that concerning "fishers of men" or the barren fig tree, which now appears in the Gospels transmitted into marvelous histories; or, it is perhaps a real transaction or event taken from his life; for instance, the mythical traits in the account of the baptism were built upon such a reality. Certain of the miraculous histories may likewise have had some foundation in natural occurrences, which the narrative has either exhibited in a supernatural light, or enriched with miraculous incidents. . . .

As man, considered as a finite spirit, limited to his finite nature, has not truth; so God, considered exclusively as an infinite spirit, shut up in his infinitude, has not reality. The infinite spirit is real only when it discloses itself in finite spirits; as the finite spirit is true only when it merges itself in the infinite. The true and real existence of spirit, therefore, is neither in God by himself, nor in man by himself, but in the God-man; neither in the infinite alone, nor in the finite alone, but in the interchange of impartation and withdrawal between the two, which on the part of God is revelation, on the part of man religion.

If God and man are in themselves one, and if religion is the human side of this unity: then must this unity be made evident to man in religion, and become in him consciousness and reality. Certainly, so long as man knows not that he is a spirit, he cannot know that God is man: while he is under the guidance of nature only, he will deify nature; when he has learned to submit himself to law, and thus to regulate his natural tendencies by external means, he will set God before him as a lawgiver. But when, in the vicissitudes of the world's history, the natural state discloses its corruption, the legal its misery; the former will experience the need of a God who elevates it above itself, the latter, of a God who descends to its level. Man being once mature enough to receive as his religion the truth that God is man, and man of a divine race; it necessarily follows, since religion is the form in which the truth presents itself to the popular mind, that this truth must appear, in a guise intelligible to all, as a fact obvious to the senses: in other words, there must appear a human individual who is recognized as the visible God. This God-man uniting in a single being the divine essence and the human personality, it may be said of him that he has the Divine Spirit for a father and a woman for his mother. . . .

The God-man, who during his life stood before his contemporaries as an individual distinct from themselves, and perceptible by the senses, is by death taken out of their sight; he enters into their imagination and memory; the unity of the divine and human in him, becomes

Myth Interpretation?

part of the general consciousness; and the church must repeat spiritually, in the souls of its members, those events of his life which he experienced externally. The believer, finding himself environed with the conditions of nature, must, like Christ, die to nature—but only inwardly, as Christ did outwardly—must spiritually crucify himself and be buried with Christ, that by the virtual suppression of his sensible existence, he may become, in so far as he is a spirit, identical with himself, and participate in the bliss and glory of Christ. . . .

If reality is ascribed to the idea of the unity of the divine and human natures, is this equivalent to the admission that this unity must actually have been once manifested, as it never had been, and never more will be, in one individual? This is indeed not the mode in which the idea realizes itself; it is not wont to lavish all its fullness on one exemplar, and be niggardly towards all others—to express itself perfectly in that one individual, and imperfectly in all the rest; it rather loves to distribute its riches among a multiplicity of exemplars which reciprocally complete each other—in the alternate appearance and suppression of a series of individuals. And is this no true realization of the idea? Is not the idea of the unity of the divine and human natures a real one in a far higher sense, when I regard the whole human race of mankind as its realization, than when I single out one man as such a realization? Is not an incarnation of God from eternity, a truer one than an incarnation limited to a particular point of time?

This is the key to the whole subject of Christology, that, as subject of the predicate which the church assigns to Christ, we place, instead of an individual, an idea; but an idea which has an existence in reality, not in the mind only, like that of Kant. In an individual, a God-man, the properties and functions which the church ascribes to Christ contradict themselves; in the idea of the race, they perfectly

agree. Humanity is the union of two natures—God become man, the infinite manifesting itself in the finite, and the finite spirit remembering its infinitude; it is the child of the visible Mother and the invisible Father, Nature and Spirit; it is the worker of miracles, in so far as in the course of human history the spirit more and more completely subjugates nature, both within and around man, until it lies before him as the inert matter on which he exercises his active power; it is the sinless existence, for the course of its development is a blameless one, pollution cleaves to the individual only, and does not touch the race or its history. It is humanity that dies, rises, and ascends to heaven, for from the negation of its phenomenal life there ever proceeds a higher spiritual life; from the suppression of its mortality as a personal, national, and terrestrial spirit, arises its union with the infinite spirit of the heavens. By faith in this Christ, especially in his death and resurrection, man is justified before God: that is, by the kindling within him of the idea of humanity, the individual man participates in the divinely human life of the species.

▲ ▲ ▲

For Strauss a rigorous critical understanding of the Scriptures requires a mythical approach, in light of which two common ideas must give way: (1) rationalism, that is, the idea that the face value of those stories out of keeping with natural law can be used as a point of departure for the interpreter to offer her or his own plausible explanation of the original event, and (2) supernaturalism, that is, the notion that Scripture contains a literary history correct in detail (including miraculous events). In this venue Scripture stories are viewed not as "eyewitness" efforts to record data, but as representations of religious ideas. Strauss employed this technique comprehensively in his analyses of Scripture. Thus, in his work we have the initiation of a total, mythical approach to the accounts of Jesus of Nazareth in the four Gospels more than a century before Rudolf Bultmann's famous 1941 essay on demythologizing.

For Strauss, determining that an event is mythical, not factual, can be done using one of two methods. The "negative" method is to find that the event conflicts with modern views or contemporary understandings of the world, such as if the representation of the divine or of demonic beings intervenes miraculously in the cause-effect process. The "positive" method is to find that the event demonstrates pre-existing tendencies at work in the religious community that has produced the questionable account.

How do we identify myth? It is clear, first, that we cannot sustain anything that is irreconcilable with the known and universal laws that govern the course of events. This categorically rejects the miraculous, for philosophy and science teach us that "the absolute never disturbs the chain of secondary causes by single, arbitrary acts of interposition." In a similar fashion, whatever is contrary to "habitual" human behavior, such as the long speeches in the Gospel of John, or whatever is morally or psychologically implausible, such as the Sanhedrin bribing the watchmen at the tomb, is decidedly suspect. Furthermore, a historical account must be consistent with itself and with other accounts.

In handling the material of the Gospels, Strauss was extremely critical but not undiscriminating. He carefully pondered the evidence and inferred that myth-forming faith has been at work everywhere. Even if there are no remaining islands of pure untouched fact, however, Strauss often detected an influence of the original Jesus of Nazareth in and through the myth. For example, the question of Jesus' formal education is conditioned by the undoubted fact of his unique genius. Likewise, that there is a historical core beneath the mythicized narratives of the baptism by John, the teachings, and the ministry in general, Strauss was far from denying.

Although Strauss acknowledged that on appearance he seemed to have destroyed the heart of the Christian faith, he insisted that was not the case. Hence he concluded by trying to re-establish dogmatically what had been destroyed critically. He looked at the orthodox christological dogma no longer acceptable to the critical modern mind. Against this arose rationalism's distinguished person, intellectually inoffensive, but religiously empty. Schleiermacher's reconstruction was a noble effort, but his eclecticism could not satisfy either science or faith. Immanuel Kant's symbolic interpretation had proved to be more promising, but it remained yet an "ideal," not a reality. A really adequate position emerged in G. W. F. Hegel.

According to Hegel, religious ideas are symbolic expressions of philosophical truth—not merely of the ideal, as with Kant, but of the real. This insight supplied the basis for affirming the supreme truth of the whole complex of Christian symbols and dogmas. Thus faith can be satisfied. But so also is the critical intellect appeased for the symbols are true mythically, poetically, pictorially, but not literally.

In the incarnation speculative Christology perceives the truth that absolute spirit becomes finite and concrete over against itself. Strauss argued that the divine essence is the power that subdues nature, a worker of miracles, but as God in a human manifestation, Christ is dependent upon nature, subject to its necessities and sufferings. The abasement of God extends even to the lowest depths of the finite. The resurrection, however, symbolizes the eternal return of God to God, and as the divine has come down to humanity, so humanity's spirit shares in the divine eternity.

The followers of Hegel disagreed as to how or rather where the idea of reconciliation has been realized. Some argued that it has occurred in the individual person of Jesus of Nazareth. Strauss rejected this theory as an abortive effort still at odds with science. For him, the proper subject of the Christ myth is not an individual but the human race as a whole. Humanity, for Strauss, is the union of the two natures. And by faith in this Christ, especially in his death and resurrection, humanity is justified before God; that is, by the kindling within him or her of the idea of humanity, the individual person participates in the divinely human life of the species. Strauss has been much attacked and vilified, but as a catalyst of modern Christian reflection he has really had few equals.

23. SØREN KIERKEGAARD (1813–1855)

Standing with both feet in the nineteenth century and speaking to his own time, Søren Kierkegaard was not heeded until a hundred years later. He seems, in retrospect, to have been born prematurely; most of his contemporaries ignored him or put him down as a crank, a fanatic. He wrote in Danish, a minor European language, adopted cryptic literary devices such as pseudonyms, scorned and ridiculed all accepted conventions of his day—little wonder that recognition was late in coming. Yet the influence of this eccentric thinker became so pervasive in later philosophy and theology that without him the current status of either is unintelligible.

Kierkegaard was born in Copenhagen in 1813 and died in his birthplace at the early age of forty-two. His life was a riddle: his relationship with his stern, moralistic father disturbed him deeply; his broken marriage engagement haunted him; his critical diatribes against church and state isolated him. Turning to writing as a career and an outlet for his views, he became a prolific author of a series of books, monographs, and articles in an almost endless variety of literary forms. On the basis of his authorship, Kierkegaard could easily qualify as a novelist, essayist, satirist, philosopher, humorist, theologian, psychologist, journalist, sociologist, and poet.

We may single out three of many facets pertaining to Kierkegaard for special attention. First, of significance was Kierkegaard's bold rejection of the prevalent Hegelian philosophy. The solemn, speculative cast of Hegel's way of thinking, coupled with assumptions about rational reality, the synthesis of opposites, and the progressive path of truth—these and other features of the

German philosopher's work were subjected to pitiless scrutiny and ridicule by Kierkegaard. What emerged was a new regard for actual existence over against abstract essence, and thus existentialism was born. The trademark of existence is ambiguity; to exist is to be in the middle between finite and infinite, meaning and meaningless, time and eternity, hope and despair. The present moment, the individual, subjectivity, the contextual situation—all become more significant for the existentialist than eternal truths, absolute values, humanity in general, objective reality.

Second, another enduring feature of the insight of Kierkegaard was his radical redefinition of what it means to be a Christian. He often remarked that this was his consuming concern in all his writings. He freely admitted that he himself was not a Christian, or that he did not claim to be, but he knew what it meant to be one. To be a Christian, he said, is not simply to be born in a Christian country and grow up with Christian virtues of decency, tolerance, and graciousness. To be a Christian is to become contemporary with the Christ who suffered and was persecuted, who castigated the Pharisees and was crucified. For this person was not merely a very, very, very good man but God in person, though not obviously recognizable as such.

Third, the influence of Kierkegaard followed from his stringent view of the nature of the true Christian. Real Christianity—that is, New Testament Christianity—did not exist any longer in Christendom. The perfunctory but effete Christianity of Denmark in the early nineteenth century filled Kierkegaard with disgust. This, he preached, was not really Christianity at all but a socially acceptable national pseudo-religion. Where everyone is a Christian in this sense, he noted, no one is a Christian, and Christianity has ceased to exist. Disdainful of polite practitioners of such conventional Christianity and also of the clergy who make a business out of their profession, Kierkegaard angered his contemporaries but sounded a prophetic note for every age.

Source: Attack upon Christendom, *translated by Walter Lawrie (Princeton: Princeton University Press, 1948), 29–32, 121–22.*

▼ ▼ ▼

The religious situation in our country is: Christianity (that is, the Christianity of the New Testament—and everything else is not Christianity, least of all by calling itself such), Christianity does not exist—as almost anyone must be able to see as well as I.

We have, if you will, a complete crew of bishops, deans, and priests; learned men, eminently learned, talented, gifted, humanly well-meaning; they all declaim—doing it well, very well, eminently well, or tolerably well, or badly—but not one of them is in the character of the Christianity of the New Testament. But if such is the case, the existence of this Christian crew is so far from being, Christianly considered, advantageous to Christianity that it is far rather a peril, because it is so infinitely likely to give rise to a false inference that when we have such a complete crew we must of course have Christianity, too. A geographer, for example, when he has assured himself of the existence of this crew, would think that he was thoroughly justified in putting into his geography the statement that the Christian religion prevails in the land.

We have what one might call a complete inventory of churches, bells, organs, benches, alms-boxes, foot-warmers, tables, hearses, etc. But when Christianity does not exist, the existence of this inventory, so far from being, Christianly considered, an advantage, is far rather a peril, because it is so infinitely likely to give rise to a false impression and the false inference that when we have such a complete Christian inventory we must of course have Christianity, too. A statistician, for example, when he had assured himself of the existence of the Christian inventory, would think that he was thoroughly justified in putting into his statistics the statement that the Christian religion is the prevailing one in the land.

We are what is called a "Christian nation"—but in such a sense that not a single one of us is in the character of the Christianity of the New Testament, any more than I am, who again and again have repeated, and do now repeat, that I am only a poet. The illusion of a Christian nation is due doubtless to the power which number exercises over the imagination. I have not the least doubt that every single individual in the nation will be honest enough with God and with himself to say in solitary conversation, "If I must be candid, I do not deny that I am not a Christian in the New Testament sense; if I must be honest, I do not deny that my life cannot be called an effort in the direction of what the New Testament calls Christianity, in the direction of denying myself, renouncing the world, dying from it, etc.; rather the earthly and the temporal become more and more important to me with every year I live." I have not the least doubt that everyone will, with respect to ten of his acquaintances, let us say, be able to hold fast to the view that they are not Christians in the New Testament sense, and that their lives are not even an effort in the direction of becoming such. But when there are 100,000, one becomes confused.

They tell a ludicrous story about an innkeeper, a story moreover which is related incidentally by one of my pseudonyms, but I would use it again because it has always seemed to me to have a profound meaning. It is said that he sold his beer by the bottle for a cent less than he paid for it; and when a certain man said to him: "How does that balance the account? That means to spend money," he replied, "No, my friend, it's the big number that does it"—

Kierkegaard as Poet

big number, that also in our time is the almighty power. When one has laughed at this story, one would do well to take to heart the lesson which warns against the power which number exercises over imagination. For there can be no doubt that this innkeeper knew very well that one bottle of beer which he sold for three cents meant a loss of one cent when it cost him four cents. Also with regard to ten bottles the innkeeper will be able to hold fast that it is a loss. But 100,000 bottles! Here the big number stirs the imagination, the round number runs away with it, and the innkeeper becomes dazed—it's a profit says he, for the big number does it. So along with the calculation which arrives at a Christian nation by adding up units which are not Christian, getting the result by means of the notion that the big number does it. For true Christianity this is the most dangerous of all illusions, and at the same time it is of all illusions precisely the one to which every man is prone; for number (the higher number, when it gets up to 100,000, into the millions) tallies precisely with the imagination. But Christianly of course the calculation is wrong, and a Christian nation composed of units which honestly admit that they are not Christians, *item,* honestly admit that their life cannot in any sense be called an effort in the direction of what the New Testament understands by Christianity—such a Christian nation is an impossibility. On the other hand, a knave could not wish to find a better hiding place than behind such phrases as "the nation is Christian," "the people are making a Christian endeavor," since it is almost as difficult to come to close quarters with such phrases as it would be if one were to say, "N. N. is a Christian, N. N. is engaged in Christian endeavor."

But inasmuch as Christianity is spirit, the sobriety of spirit, the honesty of eternity, there is of course nothing which to its detective eye is so suspicious as are all fantastic entities: Christian states, Christian lands, a Christian people, and (how marvelous!) a Christian world. And

even if there were something true in this talk about Christian peoples and states—but, mind you, only when all mediating definitions, all divergences from the Christianity of the New Testament, are honestly and honorably pointed out and kept in evidence—yet it is certain that at this point a monstrous criminal offense has been perpetrated, yea everything this world has hitherto seen in the way of criminal affairs is a mere bagatelle in comparison with this crime, which has been carried on from generation to generation throughout long ages, eluding human justice, but has not yet got beyond the arm of divine justice.

This is the religious situation. And to obviate if possible a waste of time I will at once anticipate a turn which one will perhaps give the matter. Let me explain by means of another case. If there were living in the land a poet who in view of the ideal of what it is to love talked in this fashion: "Alas, I must myself admit that I cannot truly be said to be in love; neither will I play the hypocrite and say that I am endeavoring more and more in this direction, for the truth unfortunately is that things are rather going backward with me. Moreover, my observation convinces me that in the whole land there is not a single person who can be said to be truly in love"—then the inhabitants of the land could reply to him, and in a certain degree with justice: "Yes, my good poet, that may be true enough with your ideals; but we are content, we find ourselves happy with what we call being in love, and that settles it." But such can never be the case with Christianity. The New Testament indeed settles what Christianity is, leaving it to eternity to pass judgment upon us. In fact the priest is bound by an oath upon the New Testament—so it is not possible to regard that as Christianity which men like best and prefer to call Christianity. As soon as we assume that we may venture to give the matter this turn, Christianity is *eo ipso* done away with, and the priest's oath . . . but here I break off, I do not wish to draw the inference before they constrain me further to do so, and even then I do not wish to do it. But if we do not dare to give the matter this turn, there are only two ways open to us: either (as I propose) honestly and honorably to make an admission as to how we are related to the Christianity of the New Testament; or to perform artful tricks to conceal the true situation, tricks to conjure up the vain semblance that Christianity is the prevailing religion in the land. . . .

But what then is "Christendom"? Is not "Christendom" the most colossal attempt at serving God, not by following Christ, as he required, and suffering for the doctrine, but instead of that, by "building the sepulchers of the prophets and garnishing the tombs of the righteous" and saying, "If we had been in the days of our fathers, we should not have been partakers with them in the blood of the prophets" (Matt. 23:29-33; Luke 11:47-48)?

It is of this sort of divine service I used the expression that, in comparison with the Christianity of the New Testament, it is playing Christianity. The expression is essentially true and characterizes the thing perfectly. For what does it mean to play, when one reflects how the word must be understood in this connection? It means to imitate, to counterfeit, a danger when there is no danger, and to do it in such a way that the more art is applied to it, the more delusive the pretense is that the danger is present. So it is that soldiers play war on the parade grounds; there is no danger, one only pretends that there is, and the art essentially consists in making everything deceptive, just as if it were a matter of life and death. And thus Christianity is played in "Christendom." Artists in dramatic costumes make their appearance in artistic buildings—there really is no danger at all, anything but that: the teacher is a royal functionary, steadily promoted making a career— and now he dramatically plays Christianity, in short, he plays comedy. He lectures about renunciation, but he himself is being steadily

promoted; he teaches all that about despising worldly titles and rank, but he himself is making a career; he describes the glorious ones ("the prophets") who were killed, and the constant refrain is: If we had been in the days of our fathers, we should not have been partakers with them in the blood of the prophets—we who build their sepulchers and garnish their tombs. So they will not go so far even as to do what I have constantly, insistently and imploringly proposed, that they should at least be so truthful as to admit that they are not a bit better than those who killed the prophets. No, they take advantage of the circumstance that they are not in fact contemporary with them to assert mendaciously of themselves that they are far, far better than those who killed the prophets, entirely different beings from those monsters—they in fact build the sepulchers of the men so unjustly killed and garnish their tombs.

However, this expression, "to play Christianity," could not be used by the authoritative teacher; he has a different way of talking about it.

Christ calls it (O give heed!), he calls it "hypocrisy." And not only that, but he says (now shudder!), he says that this guilt of hypocrisy is as great, precisely as great a crime as that of killing the prophets, so it is blood-guilt. Yea, if one could question him, he would perhaps make answer that this guilt of hypocrisy, precisely because it is adroitly hidden and deliberately carried on through a whole lifetime, is a greater crime than theirs who in an outburst of rage killed the prophets.

This then is the judgment, Christ's judgment upon "Christendom." Shudder, for if you do not, you are implicated in it. It is so deceptive: must not we be nice people, true Christians, we who build the sepulchers of the prophets and garnish the tombs of the righteous, must not we be nice people, especially in comparison with those monsters who killed them? And besides, what else shall we do? We surely cannot do more than be willing to give our money to build churches, etc., not be stingy with the priest, and go ourselves to hear him. The New Testament answers: What thou shalt do is to follow Christ, to suffer, suffer for the doctrine; the divine service thou wouldst like to carry on is hypocrisy; what the priests, with family, live on is that thou art a hypocrite, or they live by making thee a hypocrite, by keeping thee a hypocrite.

"Your fathers killed them, and ye build their tombs: so ye are witnesses and consent unto the works of your fathers." (Luke 11:48)

Yes, Sunday Christianity and the huge gang of tradesmen-priests may indeed become furious at such a speech, which with one single word closes all their shops, quashes all this royally authorized trade, and not only that, but warns against their divine worship as against blood-guilt. However, it is Christ who speaks. So profoundly does hypocrisy inhere in human nature that just when the natural man feels at his best, has got a divine worship fixed up entirely to his own liking, Christ's judgment is heard: This is hypocrisy, it is blood-guilt. It is not true that while on weekdays thy life is worldliness, the good thing about thee is that after all on Sundays thou goest to church, the church of official Christianity. No, no, official Christianity is much worse than all thy weekday worldliness, it is hypocrisy, it is blood-guilt.

At the bottom of "Christendom" there is this truth, that man is a born hypocrite. The Christianity of the New Testament was truth. But man shrewdly and knavishly invented a new kind of Christianity which builds the sepulchers of the prophets and garnishes the tombs of the righteous and says, "If we had been in the days of our fathers." And this is what Christ calls blood-guilt.

▲ ▲ ▲

Søren Kierkegaard was a brilliant and enigmatic philosopher-theologian who is widely regarded as the forerunner of the existential school of philosophy. While he was little known beyond his native borders and thus had minimal impact on the nineteenth century, and while he did not really establish any so-called Kierkegaardian School, he nevertheless caught the attention of many philosophers and theologians in the twentieth century.

Kierkegaard's varied theological writings, which, like his philosophical works, attacked German Idealism and in particular the philosophy of G. W. F. Hegel, stressed the "total otherness" of God and the necessity for complete personal commitment in faith. Sometimes he has been called the "philosopher of faith." We have chosen a brief selection from an English translation of some of his pamphlets of 1854 and 1855 published under the title *Attack upon Christendom.* In these direct and unsparing works, Kierkegaard bitterly and sarcastically attacked the formal, conformist Christianity into which he claimed Protestantism had fallen.

It was during the last decade of his life that Kierkegaard came to a profound awareness of the Christian faith and felt that he was called to witness to this truth as he saw and understood it. He realized that the consequences would be severe and would entail his personal suffering at the hands of the majority. But then, true Christianity is often unpopular, and in a way Kierkegaard's work was prophetic preaching of the highest order. Furthermore, it was clear to him that this was the vocation of Christian discipleship. The prophetic writings during this time frame point to the difficulty of becoming a Christian and the hypocrisy of the institutional church and conventional Christianity.

What provoked Kierkegaard to an unsparing, scathing attack was the funeral oration of Bishop Hans Lassen Martensen for Bishop Jakob Mynster, in which Mynster was referred to as a true witness to the truth, a man of humility, suffering, and poverty. To Kierkegaard this was not only outrageous but ludicrous. Bishop Mynster was a clever man, very much at home in the secular world, a man who, in Kierkegaard's mind, had nothing at all in common with the martyrs of early Christianity.

The national Church of Denmark was itself apostate, the clergy self-satisfied functionaries of the government who spent their time baptizing, marrying, and burying people who otherwise considered the church to be irrelevant. In Kierkegaard's view, where everyone is considered Christian by the perfunctory, conventional act of baptism, Christianity *eo ipso* does not exist. A true Christian, Kierkegaard held, is rarer than a genius, yet the preachers of the Danish Christian Church won thousands of converts in a short time. Whereas Christ won a dozen followers in three years, the popular evangelists of the nineteenth century "won" as many as three thousand in an

hour! He blasted the Sunday orators who made a popular success of preaching a facile Christianity. These silken and velvet orators created tears and put them in a bottle. It was this dangerous and even dishonest destruction of Christianity undertaken in pretense of its support and defense that elicited Kierkegaard's most profound disgust. New Testament Christianity was so alien to the comfortable congregations of Denmark that they were not even capable of seeing the ludicrous disparity between the early Christian message and the elegant orations of the bishops.

Kierkegaard's scathing polemic continued until, at the pinnacle of his passionate attack, he was stricken with paralysis. Hospitalized for several weeks, he refused to retract his polemical statements about the church and to receive communion from the clergy. He died strong in his religious convictions and seemingly in a state of great spiritual peace. As we read his words, excessive to many, on target to others, one is reminded of the words of Dietrich Bonhoeffer speaking a little less than a century later, "cheap grace—costly grace," and more recently, Pierre Berton's book, *The Comfortable Pew.* For Christians, Kierkegaard still poses the nettling question of religious integrity.

24. ALBRECHT RITSCHL (1822–1889)

Often linked with Friedrich Schleiermacher, with whom he had much in common, Ritschl moved in a different theological world. While Schleiermacher emphasized feeling as paramount in religion, Ritschl emphasized the will. For Schleiermacher it was the person of Jesus Christ, whereas for Ritschl it was the work of Jesus Christ. Schleiermacher sought to reconstruct theology; Ritschl was more interested in the ethical implications of the kingdom of God.

Albrecht Ritschl was born in Berlin and studied at Halle, Heidelberg, Tübingen, and Bonn, where he was professor of theology for thirteen years. In 1864 he was called to the University of Göttingen, where he lectured until his death in 1889. He was a popular teacher and gathered a large circle of students from many countries, who later continued and extended his views. His theology was characterized by an abiding interest in the biblical records, an avoidance of metaphysical abstractions, an insistence on the ethical rather than the mystical side of faith, and a methodological distinction between judgments of fact and judgments of value.

Ritschl's major work was a three-volume study on the *Christian Doctrine of Justification and Reconciliation* (1870–1874). The first volume was historical, the second biblical, the third theological; the title is not precise, and Ritschl wrote on a variety of topics. He was disinclined toward speculative attempts to define the ultimate mysteries of belief, partly because he considered the effort futile, and partly because he imagined that the thoughtful people of his day were more drawn to the religious-ethical side of Christianity.

In the New Testament context of justification and reconciliation, according to Ritschl, the religious experience of redemption is related on the one hand to the work of Jesus Christ and on the other to the kind of life—individually and collectively—that is appropriate to the kingdom of God. To speculate about the person of Jesus Christ or the relation of the divine and human natures is to try to make scientific, factual judgments in an area in which value judgments alone make sense. Ritschl believed that we know Christ is the Son of God because he has the worth or value of God for us. And we know this because he accomplishes a religious and ethical work in us which only God could do.

Source: The Christian Doctrine of Justification and Reconciliation, *translated by H. R. Mackintosh and A. B. Macauley (Edinburgh: T. & T. Clark, 1900), 272–73, 281–82, 480–82, 591–92.*

▼ ▼ ▼

Theology, in delineating the moral order of the world must take as its starting-point that conception of God in which the relation of God to his Son our Lord is expressed, a relation which, by Christ's mediation, is extended likewise to his community. . . .

As this conception of God is recognized as coming from the source of knowledge which is authoritative for the Christian community, it likewise follows that the goodness of God to all men, in bestowing on them the good things of nature (Matt. 5:45; Acts 14:17), is an inference which Christ drew from the knowledge he possessed of the love of God to him and to his community. Thus the goodness of God, as the general presupposition of everything, is embraced in the specific attribute of the divine fatherhood; or, in other words, the truth that he has revealed himself to the Christian community as love. There is no other conception of equal worth beside this which need be taken into account. . . .

The idea of the kingdom of God, therefore, gives a supramundane character to humanity as bound to him, i.e., it both transcends and completes all the nature and particular motives which unite men together. Consequently, the unity of the human race thus reached is so far akin to the unity of the divine will that it may be seen the object of the divine love. But the community, which is called on to form itself by union into the kingdom of God, and whose activity consists in carrying out this assigned task, depends entirely for its origin on the fact that the Son of God is its Lord, to whom it renders obedience. The community, as the object to which God's love extends, cannot even be conceived apart from the presupposition that it is governed continually by its founder as its Lord, and that its members go through the experience of being transformed into that peculiar character of which their Lord is the original, and which, through him, is communicated to them (2 Cor. 3:18; Rom. 8:29). The community of Christ, therefore, is the correlative of the love of God, only because the love in which God embraces his Son and assures to him his unique position (Mark 1:11; 9:7; John 15:9; 17:24; Col. 1:13; Eph. 1:6), comes through him to act upon those likewise who belong to him as his disciples or his community. . . .

If, now, the creation and government of the world are accordingly to be conceived as the means whereby created spiritual beings—men—are formed into the kingdom of God in the community of Christ, then the view of the world given in Christianity is the key to solve the problem of the world in general. The fact that this religion, in its origin, wears a particular historical guise, is no hindrance to its being destined to become the universal faith of humanity. . . .

The religious estimate of Christ must not be set over against the ethical, but added to it, as that without which it would not be complete. The question arises as to what is implied in this view. If the life-work of Christ is the work of God, this involves the assumption that the personal self-end of Christ has the same content as is contained in the self-end of God, which content Christ knew and adopted as such, in accordance with the fact that he was already known and loved by God himself as the bearer of the divine self-end. This statement, which essentially coincides with Matt. 11:27 (". . . no one knows the Son except the Father. . . ."), is inevitable, if we hold to the position that a universal ethical kingdom of God is the supreme end of God himself in the world, if we admit that historically this idea first received shape through Christ, and if we are not satisfied with the vague conception of a wholly accidental relation between God and the world, especially the moral world. Now the freedom and independence of a man's conduct in pursuit of the supreme end of the kingdom of God is proof that at bottom, and in a way suited to the human spirit, we are dependent upon God; therefore Christ, in the exercise of his particular vocation must certainly be regarded, not merely as independent of all the world, but as upheld by God. Since, however, as the founder of the kingdom of God in the world, in other words, as the bearer of God's ethical lordship over men, he occupies a unique position toward all who have received a like aim from him, therefore he is that being in the world in whose self-end God makes effective and manifest after an original manner his own eternal self-end, whose whole activity, therefore, is discharge of his vocation, forms the material of that complete revelation of God which is present in him, in whom, in short, the word of God is a human person.

The problem here presented to theology is solved when we have shown that there is no contradiction between the ethical and the religious apprehension of Christ, that the former finds its necessary complement in the latter, and that there is nothing here inconsistent either with the Christian idea of God, or with the complete conception of moral freedom. The origin of the person of Christ—how his person attained the form in which it presents itself to our ethical and religious apprehension—is not a subject of theological inquiry, because the problem transcends all inquiry. What ecclesiastical tradition offers us in this connection is obscure in itself, and there is not fitted to make anything clear. As bearer of the perfect revelation, Christ is given to us that we may believe on him. When we do believe on him, we find him to be the revealer of God. But the correlation of Christ with God his Father is not a scientific explanation. And as a theologian one ought to know that the fruitless clutching after such explanations only serves to obscure the recognition of Christ as the perfect revelation of God. . . .

Faith in Christ is neither belief in the truth of his history nor assent to a scientific judgment of knowledge such as that presented by the Chalcedonian Formula (451). It is not a recognition of his divine nature of such a kind that, in affirming it, we disregard his lifework and his action for the salvation of those who have to reckon themselves as belonging to his community. In so far as trust in him includes a knowledge of him, this knowledge will determine the value of his work for our salvation. This value is to be decided by the fact that Christ, as bearer of the perfect revelation of God, through his solidarity with the Father, in the right exercise of his love and patience over the world, demonstrated his Godhead as man for the salvation of those whom, as his community, he at the same time represented before the Father by his obedience and still represents.

▲ ▲ ▲

Ritschl's theological aim was to justify religion in an age of positivistic science. He sought to achieve this justification by the total severance of religion from theoretical knowledge. To resolve the intellectual problem religion poses—the tension within a human being who is of the natural world but has a spiritual personality—is not a matter of abstract necessity, according to Ritschl. The test of faith is pragmatic; what humans seek in religion is a personal good. All speculative concern is irrelevant. He agreed with Immanuel Kant that the essential truth of things in themselves is beyond our grasp, making it impossible for us to move from the "phenomenal" to the "noumenal," but Ritschl nevertheless believed that the reality of the noumenal is not open to doubt. If we do not understand God in God's own inner nature, we can nevertheless discern God by God's actions. In the same way we can recognize the work of Jesus the Christ without resorting to some metaphysical explanation of his person. The real importance of Jesus the Christ is the impact of his moral personality, testified to historically, upon our own. Thus the one sure standard or basis for our faith is the example of the historical Jesus, whose unique consciousness of God is our only model. (Here we can also see some similarity to the views of Friedrich Schleiermacher.) Ritschl relied heavily on the testimony of history, and while he was aware of the work of Strauss impugning the credibility of the gospel tradition, he assumed that biblical authority is sufficient to give us the needed insight into the mind of Jesus. Not the Bible, not dogma, not the church—Christ is the believer's authority as he is met in a positive historical record.

In *The Doctrine of Justification and Reconciliation,* his most outstanding work, Ritschl departed from traditional expositions by giving centrality to the doctrine of Christ's work. He broke with the traditional method of expounding theological ideas in a logical sequence and, like his predecessor Schleiermacher, made his case on the facts of experience.

25. ADOLF VON HARNACK (1851–1930)

During the nineteenth century, historical research was one of the most important developing fields related to the study of Christian thought. Among researchers of Christian history Adolf von Harnack was unparalleled. Born in Dorpat, Russia, he was professor of church history successively at Leipzig, Giessen, Marburg, and Berlin, where his fame spread far and wide. Particularly interested in the early church period, since he regarded it as normative, Harnack wrote an impressive series of books and monographs on the era.

As a historian, he was intrigued by the effect of social and cultural mores upon Christianity. Heretofore it had been assumed that Christianity sprang of a piece from the New Testament and remained unchanged throughout at least its early history. Harnack highlighted the contrast between the Christianity of the Gospels and the effect upon early Christianity of the Hellenistic point of view. On the whole, he felt that history had been unkind to the religion of Jesus, hardening it into dogmas that expressed the Greek spirit of speculation but falsified the simple gospel of Jesus of Nazareth.

At the turn of the century Harnack gave a series of lectures in Berlin on the subject "The Essence of Christianity" (translated into English under the title *What Is Christianity?* in 1901). Suggestive of his powers as a historical critic, these lectures were deliberately provocative. In seeking the essence or simple gospel of Christianity, Harnack isolated three possible definitions, the most important being "God the Father and the infinite value of the human soul." This was later reduced in the masculinist language of the day to "the Fatherhood of God and the brotherhood of man," and as such it became a slogan for early twentieth-century Protestant liberalism.

Source: What Is Christianity? *translated by T. B. Saurdles (Philadelphia: Fortress Press, 1986), 6, 10, 14, 51, 63, 124–25, 142–44.*

▼ ▼ ▼

What is Christianity? It is solely in its historical sense that we shall try to answer this question here; that is to say, we shall employ the methods of historical science, and the experience of life gained by witnessing the actual course of history. . . .

Where are we to look for our materials? The answer seems to be simple and at the same time exhaustive: Jesus Christ and his gospel. . . .

We shall see that the gospel in the gospel is something so simple, something that speaks to us with so much power, that it cannot easily be mistaken. No far-reaching directions as to method, no general introductions, are necessary to enable us to find the way to it. . . .

If, however, we take a general view of Jesus' teaching, we shall see that it may be grouped under three heads. They are each of such a nature as to contain the whole, and hence it can be exhibited in its entirety under any one of them. *Firstly, the kingdom of God and its coming. Secondly, God the Father and the infinite value of the human soul. Thirdly, the higher righteousness and the commandment of love.* That Jesus' message is so great and so powerful lies in the fact that it is so simple and on the other hand so rich; so simple as to be exhausted in each of the leading thoughts which he uttered; so rich that every one of these thoughts seems to be inexhaustible and the full meaning of the sayings and parables beyond our reach. But more than that—he himself stands behind everything that he said. His words speak to us across the centuries with the freshness of the present. . . .

To our modern way of thinking and feeling, Christ's message appears in the clearest and most direct light when grasped in connection with the idea of God the Father and the infi-

nite value of the human soul. . . . But the fact that the whole of Jesus' message may be reduced to these two heads—God as the Father, and the human soul so ennobled that it can and does unite with him—shows us that the gospel is . . . *religion itself.* . . .

What position did Jesus himself take up towards the gospel while he was proclaiming it, and how did he wish himself to be accepted? We are not yet dealing with the way in which his disciples accepted him, or the place which they gave him in their hearts, and the opinion which they formed of him; we are now speaking only of his own testimony of himself. But the question is one which lands us in the great sphere of controverted questions which cover the history of the church from the first century up to our own time. In the course of this controversy men put an end to brotherly fellowship for the sake of a nuance; and thousands were cast out, condemned, loaded with chains and done to death. It is a gruesome story. On the question of "Christology" men beat their religious doctrines into terrible weapons and spread fear and intimidation everywhere. This

Pop Quiz

attitude still continues: Christology is treated as though the gospel had no other problem to offer, and the accompanying fanaticism is still rampant in our own day. Who can wonder at the difficulty of the problem, weighed down as it is with such a burden of history and made the sport of parties? Yet anyone who will look at our Gospels with unprejudiced eyes will not find that the question of Jesus' own testimony is insoluble. . . .

With the recognition of Jesus as the Messiah the closest possible connection was established, for every devout Jew, between Jesus' message and his person; for it is in the Messiah's activity that God himself comes to his people, and the Messiah who does God's work and sits at the right hand of God in the clouds of heaven has a right to be worshipped. But what attitude did Jesus himself take up towards his gospel? Does he assume a position in it? To this question there are two answers; one negative and one positive.

In those leading features of it which we described in the earlier lectures the whole of the gospel is contained, and we must keep it free from the intrusion of any alien element: God and the soul, the soul and its God. There was no doubt in Jesus' mind that God could be found, and had been found, in the law and the prophets. "He hath showed thee, O man, what is good; and what doth the Lord require of thee, but to do justly, and to love mercy, and to walk humbly with thy God?" [Mic. 6:8]. He takes the publican in the temple, the widow and her mite, the lost son, as his examples; none of them know anything about "Christology," and yet by his humility the publican was justified. These are facts which cannot be turned and twisted without doing violence to the grandeur and simplicity of Jesus' message in one of its most important aspects. To contend that Jesus meant his whole message to be taken provisionally, and everything in it to receive a different interpretation after his

death and resurrection, nay, parts of it to be put aside as if no account, is a desperate supposition. No! his message is simpler than the churches would like to think it; simpler, but for that very reason sterner and endowed with a greater claim to universality. A man cannot evade it by the subterfuge of saying that as he can make nothing of the "Christology" the message is not for him. Jesus directed men's attention to great questions; he promised them God's grace and mercy; he required them to decide whether they would have God or Mammon, an eternal or an earthly life, the soul or the body, humility or self-righteousness, love or selfishness, the truth or a lie. The sphere which these questions occupy is all-embracing; the individual is called upon to listen to the glad message of mercy and the Fatherhood of God, and to make up his mind whether he will be on God's side and the eternal's, or on the side of the world and of time. *The gospel, as Jesus proclaimed it, has to do with the Father only and not with the Son.* This is no paradox, nor, on the other hand, is it "rationalism," but the simple expression of the actual fact as the evangelists give it.

But no one had ever yet known the Father in the way in which Jesus knew him, and to this knowledge of him he draws other men's attention, and thereby does "the many" [Matt. 20:28] an incomparable service. He leads them to God, not only by what he says, but still more by what he is and does, and ultimately by what he suffers.

▲ ▲ ▲

In *What Is Christianity?* Harnack set himself the task as a historian to employ the objective methods of that discipline to examine the central themes of Christianity. Harnack's answer to the question, What is Christianity? is straightforward and simple: The essence of Christianity is the gospel as found in the historic life and teaching of Jesus of Nazareth. Here we have the core of Christianity from which must be removed the layers of dogma and church polity.

According to Harnack, the burden of the preaching of Jesus of Nazareth can be stated in a few words: God is our Father and the human soul may be so enabled that it can and does unite with him. What Jesus sought to inspire was personal faith. What Jesus had in mind was the individual and the abiding disposition of a heart of love.

For Harnack the metaphysical theology of the early church's Christology must be discounted. Jesus was Son of God in that no one has ever attained a like consciousness of God within himself or herself. Rightly understood, the name of Son means nothing but the knowledge of God for Harnack. This is the manner in which Jesus' messiahship is to be explained: the sense of divine Sonship led him to come naturally to a conviction of his own messianic role. The gospel is not a theoretical system of doctrine or philosophy of the universe; it is doctrine only insofar as it proclaims the reality of God the Father.

26. KARL BARTH (1886–1968)

Friend and foe—and Karl Barth had many of both—agreed that he was the theologian's theologian of the middle years of the twentieth century. His initial publication, a story commentary on the Pauline Epistle to the Romans, appeared in 1919. Subsequently, a steady stream of books from his pen made his name famous in and out of religious circles throughout the world.

Although Barth addressed himself to a great diversity of topics from Communism to Mozart, his consuming passion for thirty years went into the volumes containing more than 7,500 pages known as the *Church Dogmatics* (1936–1962). He would doubtless wince at the suggestion, but the only comparison would be Thomas Aquinas's *Summa Theologiae* in the Middle Ages. A theology in the grand manner, its sprawling contents covered the spectrum of doctrinal interpretation that stirred theological discussion for fifty years and more.

Born in Basel, Switzerland, and educated at Swiss and German universities, Barth took a pastorate for ten years, from 1911 to 1921, in the Swiss village of Safenwil. He taught theology and New Testament at Göttingen, Münster, and Bonn, where his unstinting opposition to Nazism and its religious policies led to his dismissal in 1934. Returning to his native Basel in 1935, Barth retired in 1961 at the age of seventy-five. In the meantime the heavy volumes of the *Dogmatics* appeared on schedule. In addition, he wrote on assorted topics and traveled to Scotland in 1937 to give the Gifford Lectures and to the United States in 1962, where he lectured at Princeton and the University of Chicago.

Church Dogmatics was originally planned to comprise five main topics:

the Word of God, God, Creation, Reconciliation, and Redemption. The first volume appeared in 1932 and twelve more followed up to the Doctrine of Redemption, at which point Barth retired, suggesting that he might never finish the work. In his early days Barth was called the theologian of crisis, neoorthodoxy, and dialectical theology. These labels suggested a shift in gears from one theological method to another, and at first Barth was eager to distinguish himself from practically all his predecessors, especially those of the nineteenth century. In later years he was less concerned about defining his trademark and seemed content to talk simply about evangelical theology.

Certain distinguishable features in his theology persisted over the years. Always anxious to rehabilitate the preliminary doctrine of the Word of God after the disintegrating influences of modern liberalism, Barth exhibited a lively interest in the whole matter of revelation. Here he antagonized both liberals and conservatives by insisting, on the one hand, that the Bible is authoritative in its own right regardless of our understanding, or the scholar's criticism, and, on the other hand, that the Word of God must not be identified with the written words of Scripture. Indeed, the Word of God can be considered in three ways, as proclaimed, as revealed, and as written. But in these distinctions, as in their unity, the main point is that Jesus Christ is the Word made flesh.

Increasingly it became clear that Barth's governing norm was Christology. Wherever he dipped into doctrine, he always came up with christocentric implications. Even in the case of the bristling and speculative doctrine of election, Barth approached the question from the novel view that Christ himself is the elect. At a time when few theologians could find anything positive to say for the doctrine, Barth affirmed in his first proposition, "The doctrine of election is the sum of the Gospel because of all words that can be said or heard it is the best: God elects man."

In still another important instance, namely, in the doctrine of human nature, Barth's christocentric method provided a radical readjustment of conventional theological traditions. Instead of beginning with created human nature standing in need of Christian salvation, Barth boldly reversed the sequence and announced that theological anthropology begins with Christ. Again in his first proposition on this doctrine he asserted, "As the man Jesus is himself the revealing Word of God, he is the source of our knowledge of the nature of man as created by God."

Barth never worried himself over criticisms about his ponderous style, highly technical vocabulary, irritatingly long paragraphs, detours in fine print into the byways of theological history and biblical exegesis, private feuds with former friends, aloofness from the ecumenical movement, or strong pronouncements on political events.

One thing seems inevitable—the sheer massive weight and theological daring of the *Church Dogmatics* will ensure that future generations will still be studying the theology of Karl Barth when many of his contemporaries will no longer be remembered.

Source: The Epistle to the Romans, *translated by Edwyn C. Hoskyns (London: Oxford University Press, 1933), 28–29;* Church Dogmatics, *vol. I/1, translated by G. T. Thomson (Edinburgh: T. & T. Clark, 1936), 191, 193–94;* Church Dogmatics, *vol. II/2, translated by G. W. Bromily, et al. (Edinburgh: T. & T. Clark, 1957), 103, 161, 164, 166–67.*

▼ ▼ ▼

THE EPISTLE TO THE ROMANS
[Paul] appeals only to the authority of God. This is the ground of his authority. There is no other.

Paul is authorized to deliver—the gospel of God. He is commissioned to hand over to humanity something quite new and unprecedented, joyful and good—the truth of God. Yes, precisely—of God! The gospel is not religious message to inform humanity of their divinity, or to tell them how they may become divine. The gospel proclaims a God utterly distinct from humanity. Salvation comes from him, and because they are, as human beings, incapable of knowing him, they have no right to claim anything from him. The gospel is not

one thing in the midst of other things, to be directly apprehended and comprehended. The gospel is the Word of the primal origin of all things, the Word which, since it is ever new, must ever be received with renewed fear and trembling. . . .

Jesus Christ our Lord. This is the gospel and the meaning of history. In this name two worlds meet and go apart, two planes intersect, the one known and the other unknown. The known plane is God's creation, fallen out of its union with him, and therefore, the world of the "flesh" needing redemption. The world of human beings, and of time, and of things—our world. This known plane is intersected by another plane that is unknown—the world of the Father, of the primal creation, and of the final redemption. The relation between us and God, between this world and his world, presses for recognition, but the line of intersection is not self-evident. The point on the line of intersection at which the relation becomes observable and observed is Jesus, Jesus of Nazareth, the historical Jesus.

THE WORD OF GOD
Primarily and originally the Word of God is undoubtedly the Word that God speaks by and to himself in eternal concealment. We shall have to return to this great and inalienable truth when we develop the concept of revelation in the context of the doctrine of the Trinity. But undoubtedly, too, it is the Word which is spoken to men in revelation, Scripture and preaching. Hence we cannot speak or think of it at all without remembering at once the man who hears and knows it. The Word of God, Jesus Christ, as the being of the church, sets us ineluctably before the realization that it was and will be men who are intended and addressed and therefore characterized as recipients but as also themselves bearers of this Word. The Word of God thus sets us before the "so-to-speak" anthropological problem.

How then can men be this? Before the "so-to-speak" anthropological problem, I said, and I indicated thereby that it can be called this only with some reserve. Or is this not so? Shall we say unreservedly that the question of the possibility of the knowledge of God's Word is a question of anthropology? Shall we ask what man generally and as such, in addition to all else he can do, can or cannot do in this regard? Is there a general truth about man which can be generally perceptible and which includes within it man's ability to know the Word of God? We must put this question because an almost invincible development in the history of Protestant theology since the Reformation has led to an impressive affirmative answer to this question in the whole wing of the church that we have called modernist. . . .

The question is whether this event ranks with the other events that might enter man's reality in such a way that to be able to enter it actually requires on man's part a potentiality which is brought by man as such, which consists in a disposition native to him as man, in an organ, in a positive or even a negative property that can be reached and discovered by self-reflection, by anthropological analysis of his existence, in short, in what philosophy of the Kantian type calls a faculty.

It might also be that this event did not so much presuppose the corresponding possibility on man's part as bring with it and confer it on man by being event, so that it is man's possibility without ceasing (as such) to be wholly and utterly the possibility proper to the Word of God and to it alone. We might also be dealing with a possibility of knowledge which can be made intelligible as a possibility of man, but, in contrast to all others, only in terms of the object of knowledge or the reality of knowledge and not at all in terms of the subject of knowledge, i.e., man as such. In the light of the nature of God's Word, and especially of what we said above about its purposiveness or pertinence, of its being aimed at

man, its character as an address to man, we must decide against the first view and in favor of the second. From this standpoint, the same that concerns us here, we had to understand the Word of God as the act of God's free love and not as if the addressed and hearing man were in any way essential to the concept of the Word of God. That man is the recipient of God's Word is, to the extent that it is true, a fact, and it cannot be deduced from anything we might previously know about God's nature. Even less, of course, can it be deduced from anything we previously knew about the nature of man. God's Word is no longer grace, and grace itself is no longer grace, if we ascribe to man a predisposition towards this Word, a possibility of knowledge regarding it that is intrinsically and independently native to him. But the same results from what was said in the same passage about the content of the Word of God addressed to man.

We then made the assertion that this content, whatever it might be in concretissimo for this man or that man, will always be an authentic and definitive encounter with the Lord of man, a revelation which man cannot achieve himself, the revelation of something new which can only be told him. It will also be the limitation of his existence by the absolute "out there" of his Creator, a limitation on the basis of which he can understand himself only as created out of nothing and upheld over nothing. It will also be a radical renewal and therewith an obviously radical criticism of the whole of his present existence, a renewal and a criticism on the basis of which he can understand himself only as a sinner living by grace and therefore as a lost sinner closed up against God on his side. Finally it will be the presence of God as the one who comes, the future one in the strict sense, the eternal Lord and Redeemer of man, a presence on the basis of which he can understand himself only as hastening towards this future of the Lord and expecting him. To be sure, it is not these formulae which describe the real content of the Word of God, but the content of the Word which God himself speaks and which he does so always as these formulae indicate, the real content of the Word, that tells man also that there can be no question of any ability to hear or understand or know on his part, of any capability that the creature, the sinner, the one who waits, has to bring to this Word, but that the possibility of knowledge corresponding to the real Word of God that it represents an inconceivable novum compared to all his ability and capability, and that it is to be understood as a pure fact, in exactly the same way as the real Word of God itself.

THE ELECTION OF JESUS CHRIST

In its simplest and most comprehensive form the dogma of predestination consists then, in the assertion that the divine predestination is the election of Jesus Christ. But the concept of election has a double reference—to the elector and the elected. And so, too, the name of Jesus Christ has within itself the double reference: the one called by this name is both very God and very man. Thus the simplest form of the dogma may be divided at once into two assertions that Jesus Christ is the electing God, and that he is also elected man.

In so far as he is the electing God, we must obviously—and above all—ascribe to him the active determination of electing. It is not that he does not elect as man; i.e., elect God in faith. But this election can only follow his prior election, and that means that it follows the divine electing which is the basic and proper determination of his existence.

In so far as he is man, the passive determination of election is also and necessarily proper to him. It is true, of course, that even as God he is elected; the elected of his Father. But because as the Son of the Father, he has no need of any special election, we must add at once that he is the Son of God elected in his oneness with man, and in fulfillment of God's covenant with man. Primarily, then, electing is the divine determination of the existence of Jesus Christ, and election (being elected) the human. . . .

The eternal will of God in the election of Jesus Christ is his will to give himself for the sake of man as created by him and fallen from him. According to the Bible this is what took place in the incarnation of the Son of God, in his death and passion, in his resurrection from the dead. We must think of this as the content of the eternal divine predestination. The election of grace in the beginning of all things is God's self-giving in his eternal purpose. His self-giving: God gave—not only as an actual event but as something eternally foreordained—God gave his only begotten Son. God sent forth his own Word. And in so doing, he gave himself. He gave himself up. He hazarded himself. He did not do this for nothing, but for man as created by him and fallen away from him. This is God's eternal will. And our next task is to arrive at a radical understanding of the fact and extent that this will, as recognized and expressed in the history of doctrine, is a twofold will, containing within itself both a Yes and a No. We must consider how and how far the eternal predestination is a quality, a *praedestinatio gemina.* . . .

For if God himself became man, this man, what else can this mean but that he declared himself guilty of the contradiction against himself in which man was involved; for that he submitted himself to the law of creation by which such a contradiction could be accompanied only by loss and destruction; that he made himself the object of the wrath and judgment to which man had brought himself; that he took upon himself the rejection which man had deserved; that he tasted himself the damnation, death and hell which ought to have been the portion of fallen man? . . .

When we say that God elected as his own portion the negative side of the divine predestination, the reckoning with man's weakness and sin and inevitable punishment, we say implicitly that this portion is not man's portion. In so far, then, as predestination does contain a No, it is not a No spoken against man. In so far as it is directed to perdition and death, it is not directed to the perdition and death of man. . . . Rejection cannot again become the portion or affair of man. The exchange which took place at Golgotha, when God chose as his throne the malefactor's cross, when the Son of God bore what the son of man ought to have borne, took place once and for all in fulfillment of God's eternal will, and it can never be reversed. There is no condemnation—literally none—for those that are in Christ Jesus. For this reason, faith in the divine election as such as per se means faith in the non-rejection of man, or disbelief in his rejection. Man is not rejected. In God's eternal purpose it is God himself who is rejected in his Son. The self-giving of God consists, the giving and sending of his Son is fulfilled, in the fact that he is rejected in order that we might not be rejected. Predestination means that from all eternity God has determined upon man's acquittal at his own cost.

▲ ▲ ▲

For most of the twentieth century Karl Barth was a dominant influence in theology. As with Calvin in the Reformation period, there were those who loved him and those who were at great odds with him. Nevertheless, through his massive writings in history, his many monographs, his Romans commentary, and his well-known *Church Dogmatics,* Barth's name has been indelibly written on the pages of theological history.

Because of its vision of a dialectic between God and humanity, for example, Barth's commentary on Romans, first appearing in German in 1918, caused a sensation. One of Barth's contemporaries, Karl Adam, described the work as a bombshell landing in the playground of the theologians. Barth himself

described the event as ascending a church tower, reaching for the bannister, but instead getting hold of the bell rope and to his horror having to listen to what the great bell had sounded over him, but not him alone (see Paul Lehmann, "The Changing Course of a Corrective Theology," *Theology Today* 13, no. 3 [October 1956]: 334).

For Barth, who was in part reacting to events in the First World War and the liberal teachings of his own former teachers, including Harnack, there is a tremendous gulf between God and humanity—an insight he derived from the work of Søren Kierkegaard. This gulf may never be bridged from the human side—an insight recovered from the reformers of the sixteenth century, Augustine, and all the way back to the Apostle Paul. God's revelation is God's self-revelation and is the only source of knowledge of God. We can do nothing as a result of our own activity or insight. God is the "Wholly Other," radically distinct from all human capability.

In this movement away from his liberal roots and teachers, Barth challenged the liberal theology of the nineteenth century, from Schleiermacher to Harnack, with its naive optimism about humanity and history, and initiated something of a new reformation. He is purported to have said that to do theology correctly one must turn Schleiermacher upside down on his head. Barth has been variously described as a Neo-Protestant, a Neo-Calvinist, and a Neo-Reformer.

For Barth the Word of God has a three-fold form: the proclaimed, the written, and the revealed. In his own words, "The presupposition which makes proclamation to be proclamation and therewith the church to be the church, is the Word of God. It attests to itself in Holy Scripture in the words of the prophets and apostles to whom it was originally and once for all uttered through God's revelation" (*Church Dogmatics,* vol. I/1, 98). This is God's most gracious act toward humanity. This is what makes God's free movement toward us grace. If humanity had a predisposition toward this Word, it would no longer be grace.

Barth's fascinating reinterpretation of the ponderous doctrine of election or predestination drew many and varied responses. Simply put, this doctrine means that in the "Jesus-event," God took upon Godself both rejection and election on our behalf. As Barth puts it, ". . . Jesus Christ is the electing God and he is also the elected man" (*Church Dog-*

matics, vol. II/2, 103). In a word, in Jesus Christ God has said *yes* to humanity. This led some theologians, such as the Dutch theologian G. C. Berkouwer, to charge Barth with *apokatastasis* or universal salvation. Whether Barth is a universalist is a matter of debate, but his view is in one way a return to the views of the early Eastern theologians (such as Athanasius, Cyril of Alexandria, and Maximus the Confessor) and their understanding of reconciliation and redemption. God, in speaking God's *yes* to creation, has set the objective ground for human redemption by establishing a relationship with human nature in which we may participate. In this Jesus event God has taken on our condemnation and made redemption possible for any and all who are in Christ.

27. RUDOLF OTTO (1868–1937)

An early spokesperson for what came to be known as the science of comparative religions, Rudolf Otto provided a pioneering study on the idea of the holy. Born near Hanover, Germany, Otto studied at Erlangen and Gottingen, where he became a professor of theology. Travel in the East, particularly in India, deepened his interest in non-Christian religions.

In 1917 Otto published the first edition of *The Idea of the Holy* (translated into English in 1923). The subtitle reveals the thesis: "An inquiry into the non-rational factor in the idea of the divine and its relation to the rational." Devising a new vocabulary, Otto coined the term *numinous* to describe the peculiar character of the religious object's impact upon the believer.

The meaning of the word *holy* for Otto is something essentially ineffable, non-conceptual, akin to the "beautiful." It consists of an "overplus of meaning" and cannot be so much taught as evoked. Related to the experience of the holy is the *mysterium tremendum*—a sense of awe-fulness, majesty, urgency, and energy. The mystery in the experience stems from the wholly other nature of the religious object, a way of speaking about God that the Swiss theologian Karl Barth picked up later and redefined in his own terms.

Source: The Idea of the Holy, *translated by John W. Harvey (New York: Oxford University Press, 1923), 1–7, 12, 28, 31.*

▼ ▼ ▼

It is essential to every theistic conception of God, and most of all to the Christian, that it designates and precisely characterizes deity by the attributes Spirit, Reason, Purpose, Good Will, Supreme Power, Unity, Selfhood. The nature of God is thus thought of by analogy with our human nature of reason and personality; only, whereas in ourselves we are aware of this as qualified by restriction and limitation, as applied to God the attributes we use are "completed," i.e., thought as absolute and unqualified. Now all these attributes constitute clear and definite *concepts:* they can be grasped by the intellect; they can be analyzed by thought; they even admit of definition. An object that thus be thought conceptually may be termed *rational*. . . .

All depends upon this: in our idea of God is the non-rational overborne, even perhaps wholly excluded, by the rational? Or conversely, does the non-rational itself preponderate over the rational? Looking at the matter thus, we see that the common dictum, that Orthodoxy itself has been the mother of Rationalism, is in some measure well founded. It is not simply that Orthodoxy was preoccupied with doctrine and the framing of dogma, for these have been no less a concern of the wildest mystics. It is rather that Orthodoxy found in the construction of dogma and doctrine no way to do justice to the non-rational aspect of its subject. So far from keeping the non-rational element in religion alive in the heart of the religious experience, orthodox Christianity manifestly failed to recognize its value, and by this failure gave to the idea of God a one-sidedly intellectualistic and rationalistic interpretation. . . .

And so it is salutary that we should be incited to notice that Religion is not exclusively contained and exhaustively comprised in any series of "rational" assertions; and it is well worth whilst to attempt to bring the relation of the different "moments" of religion to one another clearly before the mind, so that its nature may become more manifest.

This attempt we are not to make with respect to the quite distinctive category of the holy or sacred. . . .

"Holiness"—"the holy"—is a category of interpretation and valuation peculiar to the sphere of religion. It is, indeed, applied by transference to another sphere—that of Ethics—but it is not itself derived from this. While it is complex, it contains a quite specific element or "moment," which sets it apart from "the Rational" in the meaning we gave to that word above, and which remains inexpressible—an *arreton* (Greek) or *ineffable*—in the sense that it completely eludes apprehension in terms of concepts. The same thing is true (to take a quite different region of experience) of the category of the beautiful. . . .

By means of a special term we shall the better be able, first, to keep the meaning clearly apart and distinct, and second, to apprehend and classify connectedly whatever subordinate forms or stages of development it may show. For this purpose I adopt a word coined from the Latin *numen. Omen* has given us *ominous,* and there is no reason why from *numen* we should not similarly form a word *numinous.* I shall speak then of a unique "numinous" category of value and of a definitely *numinous* state of mind, which is always found wherever the category is applied. This mental state is perfectly *sui generis* and irreducible to any other; and therefore, like every absolutely primary and elementary datum, while it admits of being discussed, it cannot be strictly defined. . . .

Let us consider the deepest and most fundamental element in all strong and sincerely felt religious emotion. Faith unto Salvation, Trust, Love—all these are there. But over and above these is an element which may also on occasion, quite apart from them, profoundly affect us and occupy the mind with a well-nigh bewildering strength. Let us follow it up with every effort of sympathy and imaginative intuition wherever it is to be found, in the lives of those around us, in sudden, strong ebullitions of per-

sonal piety and the frames of mind such ebullitions evince, in the fixed and ordered solemni-
ties of rites and liturgies, and again in the
atmosphere that cling to old religious monu-
ments and buildings, to temples and churches.
If we do so we shall find we are dealing with
something for which there is only one appropriate expression, *mysterium tremendum*. . . .

It might be objected that the mysterious is
something which is and remains absolutely and
invariably beyond our understanding, whereas
that which merely eludes our understanding
for a time but is perfectly intelligible in principle should be called, not a "mystery," but
merely a "problem." But this is by no means an
adequate account of the matter. The truly
"mysterious" object is beyond our apprehension and comprehension, not only because our
knowledge has certain irremovable limits, but
because in it we come upon something "wholly
other," whose kind and character are incom-
mensurable with our own, and before which we
therefore recoil in a wonder that strikes us chill
and numb. . . .

The qualitative *content* of the numinous
experience, to which "the mysterious stands
firm as *form*, is in one of its aspects the element
of daunting "awefulness" and "majesty," which
has already been dealt with in detail; but it is
clear that it has at the same time another
aspect, in which it shows itself as something
uniquely attractive and *fascinating*.

These two qualities, the daunting and the
fascinating, now combine in a strange harmony
of contrasts, and the resultant dual character of
the numinous consciousness, to which the
entire religious development bears witness, at
any rate from the level of the "daemonic dread"
onwards, is at once the strangest and most
noteworthy phenomenon in the whole history
of religion. The daemonic-divine object may
appear to the mind an object of horror and
dread, but at the same time it is no less something that allures with a potent charm, and the
creature, who trembles before it, utterly cowed

and cast down, has always at the same time the
impulse to turn to it, nay even to make it
somehow his own, The "mystery" is for him
not merely something to be wondered at but
something that entrances him; and beside that
in it which bewilders and confounds, he feels a
something that captivates and transports him
with a strange ravishment, rising often enough
to the pitch of dizzy intoxication; it is the
Dionysiac-element in the numen.

▲ ▲ ▲

Rudolf Otto stands in the tradition of
Friedrich Schleiermacher, who held that
God is apprehended only in feeling and
that we can never really know God as
God *really is*. All attempts at knowing
God, in God's essence, by means of sci-
entific or metaphysical analysis, are
doomed to failure.

In his *The Idea of the Holy*, Otto endeavors to describe the non-conceptual elements of religion. It is Otto's view that
religion is rational in that it ascribes
definable attributes to the deity and that
it is non-rational or suprarational in that
the essence of the deity is not exhaustively defined by any such ascription.
The non-rational is the innermost core of
religion; it is the experience of the holy,
which can only be evoked but not
defined. To describe this experience Otto
coined the term *numinous*.

The numinous is felt to be objective
and outside the self. It is more than
merely a feeling of dependence, as
Schleiermacher would have expressed it.
To be understood it must be experienced
in oneself, in creature-consciousness or
creature-feeling, for example, when a
person is overwhelmed by and responds
to an overpowering might. The numinous is not identical with feeling; rather,
it is that which evokes certain affective
states.

The most basic and the deepest element of strong religious emotion is the feeling that Otto describes by the term *mysterium tremendum. Tremendum,* as the English derivative "tremendous" suggests, involves ideas of power, majesty, and might. Otto further suggests that *tremendum* involves elements of "awefulness," overpoweringness, and energy. Corresponding to these qualities are the subjective responses of dread, insignificance, and impotence.

If any of this is difficult to understand, this should be expected, for, as the adjective *mysterium* suggests, there is something "wholly other" about the numinous that reason with its limited power can never grasp. Scientifically educated and oriented modern human beings have difficulty with this because they do not like mystery; they believe and think more in terms of problems and difficulties that are measurable and conquerable by an increase in human knowledge and technique. But mystery, as Otto describes it, is entirely different from a problem or mere difficulty. With mystery there is something that will forever elude human attempts to understand it.

This awareness of the non-rational is found, according to Otto, in every religion, for every religion is endowed with a pure *a priori* (inherent, self-evident) capacity for experiencing the holy. But for him, also, the numinous has been most fully realized in Christianity, for here the holy has been made manifest in the person of Jesus the Christ.

28. RUDOLF BULTMANN (1884–1976)

In 1941 a scholarly, technical study of nearly fifty pages on biblical interpretation was published in Germany; it has since become a document of extreme importance. The essay was titled *New Testament and Mythology,* and the author was Rudolf Bultmann. The thesis of Bultmann's discussion had to do with the disentangling of the essential meaning of the New Testament gospel from incidental factual data and fanciful mythological images and language. The term Bultmann used to describe his method was demythologization.

Assuming that the New Testament is the vehicle and the medium by and through which the gospel is made available to the believer and the church, how is the modern person to be confronted by the living reality of Jesus Christ without becoming hopelessly bogged down in ancient mythology and prescientific ways of thinking? This is a question, Bultmann insisted, not only for biblical expositors and theologians but for practical preachers and pastors. Bultmann's answer to the question involved an honest and bold "demythologizing" of the New Testament in order to disclose its living truth and message. He believed that the gospel is too often presented as if acceptance of the mythology were a prerequisite for the decision of faith. Bultmann argued that the main import of the gospel was not to authenticate the historical event but to open believers to the challenge of being crucified with Christ here and now.

By mythology, Bultmann understood the ancient cosmology that took the universe to be three-storied: (1) a heaven above, (2) a hell beneath, (3) and an earth in between. As for space, so for time: the New Testament speaks in simple linear images of (1) a past, (2) a present, and (3) a future. Bultmann's concern was to reinterpret the biblical mythology in existentialist terms, so that the faith-event in Jesus Christ is not needlessly obscured by assumptions and the trappings of another age.

Approaching the problem from a long career as a New Testament scholar, Bultmann published his essay only a few years before his retirement at the University of Marburg. Born in Wiefelstede, Oldenburg, he was educated at Tübingen, Berlin, and Marburg. He taught at Breslau, Giessen, and Marburg, and was the author of many books and articles on biblical criticism. *New Testament and Mythology* stirred up a debate of major proportions. His critics thought he simply revived the negative mythological position of Strauss's *Life of Jesus* (1835); his disciples interpreted the demythologizing process as a giant step into a totally new kind of biblical theology.

Sources: Jesus Christ and Mythology *(New York: Scribner, 1958), 15–16, 32–33, 51–52;* "New Testament and Mythology: The Problem of Demythologizing the New Testament Proclamation," *in* New Testament and Mythology and Other Basic Writings, *selected, edited, and translated by Schubert M. Ogden (Philadelphia: Fortress Press, 1989), 1–2, 9–10, 25–26, 31, 41–42.*

▼ ▼ ▼

[God cannot be introduced as a factor to explain this-worldly events, for] . . . modern science does not believe that the course of nature can be interrupted or, so to speak, perforated, by supernatural powers. . . . The same is true of the modern study of history, which does not take into account any intervention of God or of the devil or of demons in the course of history. . . .

The Quest for Meaning

Modern men take it for granted that the course of nature and of history, like their own inner life and their practical life, is nowhere interrupted by the intervention of supernatural powers. . . .

The decisive step was taken when Paul declared that the turning point from the old world to the new was not a matter of the future but did take place in the coming of Jesus Christ. . . . To be sure, Paul still expected the end of the world as a cosmic drama, the parousia of Christ on the clouds of heaven, the resurrection from the dead, the final judgment, but with the resurrection of Christ the decisive event has already happened. The church is the eschatological community of the elect, of the saints who are already justified and are alive because they are in Christ, in Christ who as the second Adam abolished death and brought life and immortality to light through the gospel (Rom. 5:12-14; 2 Tim. 1:10). "Death is swallowed up in victory" (1 Cor. 15:54).

After Paul, John de-mythologized the eschatology in a radical manner. For John the coming and departing of Jesus is the eschatological event. "And this is the judgment, that the light has come into the world, and men loved darkness rather than light, because their deeds were evil" (John 3:19). "Now is the judgment of this world, now shall the ruler of this world be cast out" (12:31). For John the resurrection of Jesus, Pentecost and the parousia are one and the same event, and those who believe have already eternal life. . . . "He who believes in the Son has eternal life; he who does not obey the Son shall not see life, but the wrath of God rests upon him."

Now, when we interpret the Bible, what is our interest? Certainly the Bible is an historical document and we must interpret the Bible by the methods of historical research. . . . But what is our true and real interest? Are we to read the Bible only as an historical document in order to reconstruct an epoch of past history for which the Bible serves as a "source"? Or is it

more than a source? I think our interest is really to hear what the Bible has to say for our actual present, to hear what is the truth about our life and our soul.

DEMYTHOLOGIZING THE NEW TESTAMENT

The world is a three-story structure, with earth in the middle, heaven above it, and hell below it. Heaven is the dwelling place of God and of heavenly figures, the angels; the world below is hell, the place of torment. But even the earth . . . is a theater for the working of supernatural powers, God and his angels, and Satan and his demons. . . . This age stands under the power of Satan, sin, and death (which are precisely "powers"). It is hastening toward its imminent end, which will take place in a cosmic catastrophe. . . .

"When the time had fully come" God sent his Son. The Son, a preexistent divine being, appears on earth as a man (Gal. 4:4; Phil. 2:6ff.; 2 Cor. 8:9; John 1:14; etc.); his death on the cross, which he suffers as a sinner (2 Cor. 5:21; Rom. 8:3), makes atonement for the sins of men (Rom. 3:23-25; 4:25; 8:3; 2 Cor. 5:14, 19; John 1:29; 1 John 2:2; etc.). His resurrection is the beginning of the cosmic catastrophe through which death brought into the world by Adam is annihilated (1 Cor. 15:21-22; Rom. 5:12ff.); the demonic powers of the world have lost their power (1 Cor. 2:6; Col. 2:15; Rev. 12:7ff.; etc.). The risen one has been exalted to heaven at the right hand of God (Acts 1:6ff.; 2:33; Rom. 8:34; etc.); he has been made "Lord" and "King" (Phil. 2:9-11; 1 Cor. 15:25). He will return on the clouds of heaven in order to complete the work of salvation; then will take place the resurrection of the dead and the last judgment (1 Cor. 15:23-24, 50ff.; etc.); finally, sin, death, and all suffering will be done away (Rev. 21:4; etc.). And this will all happen at any moment; Paul supposes that he himself will live to experience this event (1 Thess. 4:15ff.; 1 Cor. 15:51-52; see also Mark 9:1). . . .

The real point of myth is not to give an objective world picture; what is expressed in it, rather, is how human beings understand ourselves in our world. Thus, myth does not want to be interpreted in cosmological terms but in anthropological terms—or, better, in existentialist terms. . . .

What is expressed in myth is the faith that the familiar and disposable world in which we live does not have its ground and aim in itself but that its ground and limit lie beyond all that is familiar and disposable and that this is all constantly threatened and controlled by the uncanny powers that are its ground and limit. In unity with this myth also gives expression to the knowledge that we are not lords of ourselves, that we are not only dependent within the familiar world but that we are especially dependent on the powers that hold sway beyond all that is familiar, and that it is precisely in dependence on them that we can become free from the familiar powers. . . .

The question, then, is whether our "nature" as human beings can be realized, that is, whether we are already brought to ourselves simply in being shown what our authentic "nature" is (or in reflecting on it ourselves). That we have become lost or gone astray to some degree, or, at least, are constantly in danger of doing so by misunderstanding ourselves, obviously is and always has been presupposed by philosophy as well as theology. . . . But philosophy is convinced that all that is needed to bring about the realization of our "nature" is that it be shown to us. . . .

Is this self-confidence on philosophy's part justified? In any case, here is its difference from the New Testament, which claims that we can in no way free ourselves from our factual fallenness in the world but are freed from it only by an act of God. . . .

This, then, is the decisive point that distinguishes the New Testament from philosophy, Christian faith from "natural" self-understanding. . . .

We have sought to carry out the demythologizing of the New Testament proclamation. Is there still a mythological remainder? For anyone who speaks of mythology as soon as there is any talk of God's act, of God's decisive eschatological act, there certainly is. But such mythology is no longer mythology in the old sense, so that it would have now become obsolete with the passing away of the mythical world picture. For the salvation occurrence about which we talk is not some miraculous, supernatural occurrence but rather a historical occurrence in space and time. . . . We have intended to follow the intention of the New Testament itself and to do full justice to the paradox of its proclamation—the paradox, namely, that God's eschatological emissary is a concrete historical person, that God's eschatological act takes place in a human destiny, that it is an occurrence, therefore, that cannot be proved to be eschatological in any worldly way. . . .

The preachers, the apostles, are human beings who can be understood historically in their humanity. The church is a historical, sociological phenomenon, whose history can be understood historically as a part of the history of culture. And yet they are all eschatological phenomena, eschatological occurrence. . . .

The transcendence of God is not made immanent as it is in myth; rather, the paradox of the presence of the transcendent God in history is affirmed; "the word became flesh."

▲ ▲ ▲

For a great many contemporary human beings the New Testament comes to us with an "incredible" pre-scientific view of the world and the attendant picture of a God acting in a mythological way, that is, an other-worldly being intervening supernaturally in the course of human events. This New Testament drama is pictured in an elaborate cosmological and eschatological *mythos* with its three-storied world—

the heaven above, the earth below, and the underworld.

In Bultmann's view, this mythological understanding of the world is impossible in our day and age. To call upon contemporary persons to accept this form of belief is to ask them to carry out a sacrifice of intellect and to isolate their religious beliefs from their daily experience.

This is not necessary, according to Bultmann, for the Christian message is not inextricably bound to this ancient cosmic mythology. He believes that an examination of the mythical conceptions will reveal a deeper meaning concealed under the mythological cover. Thus, what Bultmann calls for is not elimination of the New Testament mythology, but interpreting its underlying intention. Mythical imagery is a natural vehicle for expressing transcendent power and action in terms of this world and human life; what is important is not the imagery but the understanding of existence that the myths enshrine.

Bultmann argues that the process of interpreting New Testament mythology, of demythologization, begins in the New Testament itself, in the writings of Paul, and most decisively with the Johannine tradition. For example, the Johannine concept of "eternal life" is already a demythologization of earlier futuristic eschatology. Consequently, on the basis of this New Testament precedent, Bultmann considers the contemporary task of demythologization to be entirely justified.

But how is this to be carried out? It was Bultmann's position that myths are an objectification of humanity's own existential self-understanding, and, therefore, should be interpreted existentially. To interpret means to translate, that is, to make understandable. We simply cannot

eliminate myth. This was the great mistake of liberal theology, which eliminated the *kerygma* (the original apostolic preaching) along with the myth. Rather our task, said Bultmann, is to reinterpret mythos—*existentially!*

The New Testament teaches that humans lose their true life inasmuch as they try to depend upon the material world in which they live, because authentic life must be based on intangible elements. Asceticism is not a viable answer. Rather, we should live in the world as if not in the world.

If the right questions to be asked of the Bible are concerned with the possibilities of authentic human existence, then it is important to discover a philosophical anthropology that will most adequately conceptualize our human situation and bring to expression the real intention of the biblical texts. Bultmann was convinced that existentialist philosophy provides us with just the needed conceptual framework to carry out the task of demythologization in our time. More particularly, Martin Heidegger's existential analysis can give new significance to such time-worn terms as "sin," "faith," "spirit," "flesh," "death," and "freedom." In response to some of his critics (Karl Barth, for example), who argued that the Bible is not about human existence but rather God's self-revelation, Bultmann called on no less an authority than St. Augustine, who also rejected any separation between God and humanity. This was classically expressed in Augustine's famous words at the beginning of his *Confessions:* "Thou hast made us for Thyself, and our hearts are restless until they find their rest in Thee." For Bultmann, the question of God and myself are identical.

Existentialism has afforded theology a contemporary language and an analysis of the human condition that is remarkably akin to that of classical Christianity, argued Bultmann. It has posed those questions about existence that Christianity has perennially sought to answer. Even more, it has offered religious thought a categorical scheme and style of doing theology that hit a particularly responsive chord in our contemporary

"age of anxiety." In speaking of the irrational and the absurd, human fallenness, depersonalization, anxiety, inauthenticity, and the demands of radical decision-making, existentialism has expressed the mood of modern times. In using existentialism as a tool of interpretation, Christian religious thought has once again given evidence of its resilience and ability to meet the challenge of modern secular culture.

29. PAUL TILLICH (1886–1965)

The word that is probably most associated with Paul Tillich's theology is *correlation*. It is a term that Tillich himself used in relation to his theological method, but it also suggests other interesting traits of this comprehensive thinker. Correlation is establishing a relationship among independent concepts and phenomena; Tillich's method of correlation attempted to bridge the gap between Christian tradition and modern culture. Tillich's concern was not to synthesize opposites so that they merge their differences but to accept distinctions in such a manner as to give depth to the complexity of reality.

Tillich was himself an illustration of his own principle. Born in Germany, he did his teaching and writing in the United States beginning in 1933; trained in nineteenth-century thought, he engaged the developments, controversies, and issues of the twentieth century; something of a Prussian professor, he became involved in socialist political movements; equally at home with philosophy or theology, he liked to remind philoso-

phers of theology, and theologians of philosophy; a classicist and a Platonist, he showed affinities for modern art, depth psychology, and existentialism.

Although he had written several books during his German teaching career, it was after he came to Union Theological Seminary in New York City that he began to articulate his method of correlation as his primary approach to theology. In a prolific output of publications, he produced a dozen books and numerous articles on all sorts of theological, philosophical, and cultural topics, including three volumes of his *Systematic Theology* and three series of sermons. After retiring from Union Seminary in New York, he was appointed university professor at Harvard and then accepted a similar position at the University of Chicago in 1963.

The *Systematic Theology* volumes are the most precise and substantial of Tillich's theological writings and best represent his method of correlation. There are, he argued, two kinds of traditional theologies, the apologetic and the kerygmatic. Kerygmatic theology's focus is to proclaim the gospel (*kerygma*), to make it known, to communicate its content. Apologetic theology seeks to relate the gospel to the problems of life and to the crucial questions asked by those who are outside the traditional theological circle. The one operates from the vantage point of revelatory answers; the other from the restless anxiety of existential questions.

Tillich sought to correlate revelatory answers and existential questions. Though he was widely misinterpreted at this point, he did not suggest that the questions will of themselves imply the answers. The correlation is one of independence and interdependence so that questions and answers are related and not reduced to an oversimplified synthesis.

The method determined much of Tillich's theological system. The existential question about knowledge is related to the doctrine of revelation; the question of being and non-being is related to the "ground of all being," God; human existential estrangement is related to the New Being as it is in Jesus as the Christ; the question about the meaning of history is related to the kingdom of God. Not only are our questions illumined by the revelatory answers, but the contemporary meaning of Christian faith is sharpened in the process of correlation.

Tillich developed a distinctively technical and metaphysical language for his theology, and his critics accused him of philosophizing and impersonalizing the biblical message. But those who are especially eager to translate the traditional doctrines of the faith into terms intelligible to moderns see Paul Tillich as a serious voice, one that should be heeded.

Source: Systematic Theology, *vol. 1 (Chicago: University of Chicago Press, 1951), 11–14, 49–50.*

▼ ▼ ▼

Ultimate Concern is the abstract translation of the great commandment: "The Lord, our God, the Lord is one; and you shall love the Lord your God with all your heart, and with all your soul, and with all your mind, and with all your strength" (Mark 12:29). The religious concern is ultimate; it excludes all other concerns from ultimate significance; it makes them preliminary. The ultimate concern is unconditional, independent of any conditions of character, desire, or circumstance. The unconditional concern is total: no part of ourselves or our world is excluded from it; there is no "place" to flee from it (Ps. 139). The total concern is infinite: no movement of relaxation and rest is possible in the face of a religious concern which is ultimate, unconditional, total, and infinite.

The word "concern" points to the "existential" character of religious experience. We cannot speak adequately of the "object religion" without simultaneously removing its character as an object. That which is ultimate gives itself only to the attitude of ultimate concern. It is the correlate of an unconditional concern but not a "highest thing" called "the absolute" or the "unconditioned," about which we could argue in detached objectivity. It is the object of total surrender, demanding also the surrender of our subjectivity while we look at it. It is a matter of infinite passion and interest (Kierkegaard), making us its object. . . . This, then, is the first formal criterion of theology: The object of theology is what concerns us ultimately. Only those propositions are theological which deal with their object in so far as it can become a matter of ultimate concern for us. . . .

The question now arises: What is the content of our ultimate concern? What does concern us unconditionally? The answer, obviously, cannot be a special object, not even God, for the first criterion of theology must remain formal and general. If more is to be said about the nature of our ultimate concern, it must be derived from an analysis of the concept "ultimate concern." Our ultimate concern is that which determines our being or not-being. Only those statements are theological which deal with their object in so far as it can become a matter of being or not-being for us. This is the second formal criterion of theology.

Nothing can be of ultimate concern for us which does not have the power of threatening and saving our being. The term "being" in this context does not designate existence in time and space. Existence is continuously threatened and saved by things and events which have no ultimate concern for us. But the term "being" means the whole of human reality, the structure, the meaning, and the aim of existence. All this is threatened; it can be lost or saved. Man is ultimately concerned about his being and meaning. "To be or not to be" in this sense is a matter of ultimate, unconditioned, total, and infinite concern. . . .

It is not an exaggeration to say that today man experiences his present situation in terms of disruption, conflict, self-destruction, meaninglessness, and despair in all realms of life. This experience is expressed in the arts and literature, conceptualized in existential philosophy, actualized in political cleavages of all kinds, and analyzed in the psychology of the unconscious. It has given theology a new understanding of the demonic-tragic structures of individual and social life. The question arising out of this experience is not, as in the Reformation, the question of a merciful God and the forgiveness of sins; nor is it, as in the early Greek church, the question of finitude, of death and error; nor is it the question of personal religious life or of the Christianization of culture and society. It is the question of a reality in which the self-estrangement of our existence is overcome, a reality of reconciliation and reunion, of creativity, meaning and hope. We shall call such a reality the "New Being." . . .

But this answer is not sufficient. It leads immediately to the further questions, "Where

To Be or Not to Be

is this New Being manifest?" Systematic theology answers this question by saying: "In Jesus the Christ." This answer also has presuppositions and implications which it is the main purpose of the whole system to develop. Only this must be said here—that this formula accepts the ancient Christian baptismal confession of Jesus as the Christ. He who is the Christ is he who brings the new eon, the new reality. And it is the man Jesus who in a paradoxical assertion is called the Christ. Without this paradox the New Being would be an ideal, not a reality, and consequently not an answer to the question implied in our human situation.

▲ ▲ ▲

The intellectual sources of Paul Tillich's theological system were many. They included, for example, Platonism, late medieval mysticism, German Idealism, and existentialists from Kierkegaard to Heidegger. Because of this diversity, Tillich is hard to place on the theological spectrum, although he himself admitted to standing in the existentialist movement. While his theology was governed by an ontological structure, he correlated that structure with human existential questions and concerns. This existential stance seems to dominate Tillich's method and system.

Tillich pointed out that the modern study of religion has been characterized by attempts to reduce religion to some other natural aspect or condition of human experience. The philosopher tends to equate religion with metaphysics, the sociologist explains religious experience on the basis of the certain needs of society, the psychologist may reduce religion to certain forms of projection or rationalization. While Tillich did not deny that these analyses have a place, he suggested that they do not get to the heart of religion as a dimension of the human spirit.

A major theme in Tillich's writing is the idea that religion is a human being's *ultimate concern*. Human beings are curious in their capacity to look beyond their immediate and preliminary interests to those concerns that undergird and give meaning to their existence. Religious faith then grows out of those experiences that we invest with ultimate value and to which we give our ultimate allegiance. Behind Tillich's assertion that religious faith is ultimate concern lie two assumptions: (1) that ultimate concern is common to all religions, that is, no matter what the difference may be, a religious experience is precisely that which makes an ultimate claim on our loyalties and (2) that no one is without some kind of "faith" in the sense of something that concerns them ultimately.

Tillich's view is suggestive on several levels. His view enables us to understand the intensity of viewpoints that we would perhaps not ordinarily classify as religious; it allows us also the power to speak of "gods" of various sorts—wealth, power, and a whole variety of ideologies and "isms." A dedicated Marxist, for example, has a commitment to a philosophical point of view that may reject traditional belief in God, yet the Marxist's commitment may be as intense as that of a religious zealot. We can speak of an individual consumed with the desire for monetary gain, another person with an almost fanatical desire for power, and yet another totally consumed with the goal of national liberation or with the overthrow of the current political regime. All have in common an intense desire for the success of the cause that claims their ultimate allegiance. To state it in Tillich's terms, their "faith" is their ultimate concern, and like all faiths it makes a total demand of the individual committed to it.

When one examines the history of religions, one discovers that there is such a wide variety of objects to which human beings have attached importance at some time or another that virtually everything has in some culture been considered worthy of worship and veneration. A social scientist studying this diversity would probably not want to make any judgments about these religious commitments. Tillich, on the other hand, did suggest a way of judging rival faith commitments by distinguishing between true and false ultimacy. By *ultimacy*, Tillich meant that which will be normative for our lives and demand our unqualified response. If the object of faith is not itself ultimate, then such a faith is idolatrous and can give rise to the demonic. The term *demonic* is one Tillich used frequently to describe an ultimate commitment to that

which is not ultimate, as when an individual submits to the demand of a totalitarian state for total allegiance. The demonic events unleashed on the world by the Nazis, witnessed by Tillich before he left Germany in 1933, are a prime example of how an ideology can claim ultimacy only to produce the most savage kind of human activity.

It should also be noted that a person's "real" faith (in the sense of ultimate concern) may not be the same as the religion to which lip service is given. A professing Christian's real faith, that is, ultimate concern, may be entirely different from the Christian religion. (One is reminded here of Søren Kierkegaard's *Attack upon Christendom*.) Tillich's point is that when we give our ultimate allegiance to something that is not ultimate, we take the risk of being disappointed, perhaps even destroyed, by the failure of our "faith." It is only when we commit ourselves to that which is truly ultimate that faith can be said to be genuine.

30. Reinhold Niebuhr (1892–1971)

From the time that Reinhold Niebuhr wrote *Moral Man and Immoral Society* (1927), he became the recognized prophet of the new biblical and dialectical theology, which reintroduced the doctrine of sin and put a question mark over the optimism that had been so apparent in liberal theology and American "Social Gospel" thought.

Born in Wright City, Missouri, and of German background, Niebuhr was brought up in the Evangelical and Reformed Church

and attended college at Elmhurst and divinity school at Eden Theological Seminary in St. Louis. For a decade and a half he was the pastor of the Bethel Evangelical Church in Detroit, Michigan, and the experience of dealing with problems in the industrial world remained with him always. In 1928 he was called to Union Theological Seminary in New York City to teach Christian ethics, and in that position his name became known around the world.

If reports are accurate, he was a vigorous and explosive lecturer, and he gathered successive circles of students around him. At the same time he was writing books and actively participating in many social action groups and committees. Heavily weighted on the liberal side of politics and social justice, his theology became increasingly more biblical. It was not inconsistent, according to Niebuhr, to be theologically to the right of center and politically to the left.

In fact, Reinhold Niebuhr cannot be categorized so easily. He belonged neither to the left nor to the right. His statements and his books were essentially critical in nature. He was expert in evaluating trends, drawing generalizations, and comparing modern with classical views. His approach was dialectical in principle and related to the ambiguity or tension constantly at work in all kinds of extremes and opposing factions. Convinced that this was deeply rooted in biblical thinking, Niebuhr began to proclaim the Christian perspective on social problems as representing a fuller dimension than either idealistic or naturalistic positions.

Invited to give the prestigious Gifford lectures at the University of Edinburgh in 1938, Niebuhr dedicated himself to what was to be his major work, *The Nature and Destiny of Man*. In this work, which marked a major shift in Niebuhr's understanding of human nature, all Niebuhr's powers of historical criticism, biblical interpretation, and social analysis were given full expression. Niebuhr's anthropological point was to demonstrate that the Christian view was more realistic, and therefore more adequate, than other views of human nature. By taking both a higher and lower view of human nature (in other words, his dialectical approach), the Christian position could include more data and make a more comprehensive judgment about human self-transcendence, on the one hand, and the inevitable human limitations on the other.

Source: The Nature and Destiny of Man, *vol. 1 (New York: Charles Scribner's Sons, 1941; reprint, Macmillan), 4–5, 12–14, 16–18.*

▼ ▼ ▼

Though man has always been a problem to himself, modern man has aggravated that problem by his too simple and premature solutions. Modern man, whether idealist or naturalist, whether rationalist or romantic, is characterized by his simple certainties about himself. He has aggravated the problem of understanding himself because these certainties are either in contradiction with each other or in contradiction with the obvious facts of history, more particularly of contemporary history; and either they have been controverted by that history or they are held in defiance of its known facts. It is not unfair to affirm that modern culture, that is, our culture since the Renaissance, is to be credited with the greatest advances in the understanding of nature and with the greatest confusion in the understanding of man. Perhaps this credit and debit are logically related to each other.

To appreciate fully the modern conflicts in regard to human nature, it is necessary to place the characteristically modern doctrines of man in their historic relation to the traditional views of human nature which have informed western culture. All modern views of human nature are adaptations, transformations and varying compounds of primarily two distinctive views of man: (a) The view of classical antiquity, that is of the Greco-Roman world, and (b) the biblical view. It is important to remember that while these two views are distinct and partly incompatible, they were actually merged in the thought of medieval Catholicism. (The perfect expression of this union is to be found in the Thomistic synthesis of Augustinian and Aristotelian thought.) The history of modern culture really begins with the destruction of this synthesis, foreshadowed in nominalism, and completed in the Renaissance and Reformation. In the dissolution of the synthesis, the Renaissance distilled the classical elements out of the synthesis and the Reformation sought to free the biblical from the classical elements. Liberal Protestantism is an effort (on the whole an abortive one) to reunite the two elements. There is, in fact, little that is common between them. What was common in the two views was almost completely lost after modern thought had reinterpreted and transmuted the classical view of man in the direction of a greater naturalism. Modern culture has thus been a battleground of two opposing views of human nature. This conflict could not be resolved. It

ended in the more or less complete triumph of the modernized classical view of man, a triumph which in this latter day is imperiled not by any external foe but by confusion within its own household. . . .

The Christian faith in God as Creator of the world transcends the canons and antinomies of rationality, particularly the antinomy between mind and matter, between consciousness and extension. God is not merely mind who forms a previously given formless stuff. God is both vitality and form and the source of all existence. He creates the world. This world is not God; but it is not evil because it is not God. Being God's creation, it is good.

The consequence of this conception of the world upon the view of human nature in Christian thought is to allow an appreciation of the unity of body and soul in human personality which idealists and naturalists have sought in vain. Furthermore it prevents the idealistic error of regarding the mind as essentially good or essentially eternal and the body as essentially evil. But it also obviates the romantic error of seeking for the good in man-as-nature and the

Marketing Meets Theology

evil in man-as-spirit or as reason. Man is, according to the biblical view, a created and finite existence in both body and spirit. Obviously a view which depends upon an ultra-rational presupposition is immediately endangered when rationally explicated; for reason which seeks to bring all things into terms of rational coherence is tempted to make one known thing the principle of explanation and to derive all other things from it. Its most natural inclination is to make itself that ultimate principle, and thus in effect to declare itself God. Christian psychology and philosophy have never completely freed themselves from this fault, which explains why naturalists plausibly though erroneously regard Christian faith as the very fountain source of idealism.

This is also the reason why the biblical view of the unity of man as body and soul has often seemed to be no more than the consequence of primitive Hebraic psychology. In Hebrew thought the soul of man resides in his blood and the concept of an immortal mind in a mortal body remains unknown to the end. It is true that certain distinctions are gradually made. At first both *ruach* and *nephesh* mean little more than "breath"; but they are gradually distinguished and *ruach* becomes roughly synonymous with spirit or *nous* and *nephesh* with soul or *psyche*. But, unlike Greek thought, this distinction does not lead to dualistic consequences. The monism of the biblical view is something other than the failure to differentiate *physis, psyche* and *nous*, which characterized Greek thought before Anaxagoras; nor is it merely the consequence of an undeveloped psychology. It is ultimately derived from the biblical view of God as the Creator and of the biblical faith in the goodness of creation.

The second important characteristic of the Christian view of man is that he is understood primarily from the standpoint of God, rather than the uniqueness of his rational faculties or his relation to nature. He is made in the "image of God." It has been the mistake of many Christian rationalists to assume that this term is no more than a religious-pictorial expression of what philosophy intends when it defines man as a rational animal. We have previously alluded to the fact that the human spirit has the special capacity of standing continually outside itself in terms of indefinite regression. Consciousness is a capacity for surveying the world and determining action from a governing centre. Self-consciousness represents a further degree of transcendence in which the self makes itself its own object in such a way that the ego is finally always subject and not object. The rational capacity of surveying the world, of forming general concepts and analyzing the order of the world is thus but one aspect of what Christianity knows as "spirit." The self knows the world, insofar as it knows the world, because it stands outside both itself and the world, which means that it cannot understand itself except as it is understood from beyond itself and the world. . . .

This conception of man's stature is not, however, the complete Christian picture of man. The high estimate of the human stature implied in the concept of "image of God" stands in paradoxical juxtaposition to the low estimate of human virtue in Christian thought. Man is a sinner. His sin is defined as rebellion against God. The Christian estimate of human evil is so serious precisely because it places evil at the very center of human personality: in the will. This evil cannot be regarded complacently as the inevitable consequence of his finiteness or the fruit of his involvement in the contingencies and necessities of nature. Sin is occasioned precisely by the fact that man refuses to admit his "creatureliness" and to acknowledge himself as merely a member of a total unity of life. He pretends to be more than he is. Nor can he, as in both rationalistic and mystic dualism, dismiss his sins as residing in that part of himself which is not his true self, that is, that part of himself which is involved in physical necessity. In Christianity it is not the eternal man who judges the finite man; but the eternal and holy God who judges sinful man. Nor is redemption in the power of the eternal man who gradually sloughs off finite man. Man is not divided against himself so that the essential man can be extricated from the nonessential. Man contradicts himself within the terms of his true essence. His essence is free self-determination. His sin is wrong use of his freedom and its consequent destruction.

Man is an individual but he is not self-sufficing. The law of his nature is love, a harmonious relation of life to life in obedience to the divine center and source of his life. This law is violated when man seeks to make himself the center and source of his own life. His sin is therefore spiritual and not carnal, though the infection of rebellion spreads from the spirit to the body and disturbs its harmonies also. Man, in other words, is a sinner not because he is one limited individual within a whole but rather because he is betrayed by his very ability to survey the whole to imagine himself the whole. . . . The essence of man is his freedom. Sin therefore cannot be attributed to a defect in his essence. It can only be understood as a self-contradiction, made possible by the fact of his freedom but not following necessarily from it.

Christianity, therefore, issues inevitably in the religious expression of an uneasy conscience. Only within terms of the Christian faith can man not only understand the reality of the evil in himself but escape the error of attributing that evil to anyone but himself. It is possible of course to point out that man is tempted by the situation in which he stands. He stands at the juncture of nature and spirit. The freedom of his spirit causes him to break the harmonies of nature and the pride of his spirit prevents him from establishing a new harmony. The freedom of his spirit enables him to use the forces and processes of nature cre-

atively; but his failure to observe the limits of his finite existence causes him to defy the forms and restraints of both nature and reason. . . . It must suffice at this point to record the fact that the Christian view of human nature is involved in the paradox of claiming a higher stature for man and of taking a more serious view of his evil than other anthropology.

▲ ▲ ▲

Neither of the two volumes of *The Nature and Destiny of Man*, titled *Human Nature* and *Human Destiny*, can be considered apart from the other without seriously distorting the author's purpose. For Niebuhr the structures of freedom, sin, judgment, and redemption, which find application in the historical process, are defined by human nature. At the same time, human destiny is the drama of history in which human nature is acted out.

Niebuhr begins his argument by observing that humanity is a problem to itself. Classical Greek views such as those found in Plato and Aristotle tend to define humanness in terms of rationality or spirit. Distinctively modern views, while shifting between naturalism and philosophical idealism, tend to be optimistic about human nature and human progress, emphasizing autonomy, reason, and virtue. In Niebuhr's view all understandings of humanity, whether ancient or modern, have significant problems attached to them. If humanity is defined, as it was in antiquity, in terms of rationality or mind or spirit, we are confronted with its involvement with nature. On the other hand, if we use nature or the natural process as definitive for humanness, as is characteristic of much of modern thought, the question of how we will understand human consciousness and self-transcendence arises.

In critical contrast to both of these views, Niebuhr's Christian interpretation was that the key to human fulfillment is in humanity's relation to God. In biblical fashion Niebuhr emphasized the integral unity of body and spirit, of creatureliness and freedom, in human nature. So, for Niebuhr, the Christian view combines the truths and avoids the errors and failures of the alternative views of what it means to be human. This was the consistent thesis of Niebuhr's work and life.

The biblical view of humanness is seen to be rooted in the idea of the God who is revealed to humanity and in whose presence alone humanity sees itself for what it truly is. Thus God defines what it means to be human. This view comes to explicit formulation in Niebuhr's exposition of the *imago dei*—the idea that humans are created in the image of God. At the same time, human beings are self-venerating sinners. Niebuhr disagrees with many of the early church theologians who sought, under the influence of Greek philosophy, to identify the image of God with human reason. Instead, he argued, as did Augustine, that the image of God is the self-conscious and self-transcendent character of the human mind and self. This is what pushes human beings beyond every fixed structure or context, forcing distinctively human questions such as: Who am I? What is the meaning and purpose of life? and so forth. These questions are formulated by a self-conscious and centered being with the capacity for self-determination.

At the same time, however, we are sinners, by which Niebuhr meant the human tendency toward self-centeredness and egotism. Sin is our attempt at "playing God," that is, making ourselves the center of all things. Such arrogance in the language of the traditional Christian vices is pride. The account of the fall in the Book of Genesis is simply a mythical way of describing humanity's observable behavior. This egotism is not limited to individuals; it has serious social, economic, and political implications as well. Niebuhr was well-known for his political activity and his social consciousness, including his role in labor and civil rights causes and in the formation of the State of New York's Liberal Political Party. Niebuhr was truly neoorthodox: while holding fast to traditional doctrines, he was not trapped by their traditional interpretations.

31. DIETRICH BONHOEFFER (1906–1945)

An unsystematic theologian in the tradition of Søren Kierkegaard who has spoken to successive generations of religiously questing young people is the Nazi-martyred Dietrich Bonhoeffer. At the age of thirty-nine he was executed for his implication in the abortive March 13, 1943, assassination plot on Adolf Hitler. His fragmentary writings have had an astonishing circulation and ready acceptance in many parts of the world.

Bonhoeffer was born in Breslau, Germany. He studied at Tübingen and Berlin and, in 1930, at Union Theological Seminary, New York. He taught theology and held brief pastorates in such scattered places as Barcelona, Berlin, and London. In America again in 1939, he decided to return to Germany to participate in the German church resistance movement. Arrested in 1943 and imprisoned for nearly two years, he was hanged at Flossenburg only a few days before the concentration camp was liberated by the advancing American army.

Most of Bonhoeffer's essays, papers, and letters, as well as his few completed books, have been translated, and a considerable library of interpretation about him and his views has grown up since his death. His mind was alert to the changing theological times. He was deeply influenced by Karl Barth, but later turned away from what he called Barth's "positivism of revelation." Committed to the Christian faith and to Jesus Christ, he worked on behalf of the ecumenical movement and helped to train young pastors. Yet he was restless with conventional religion and the institutional church.

Bonhoeffer became involved in the movement against Adolf Hitler when he began working with the Confessing Church in opposition to the Nazi-backed German Christians. At the height of the struggle, when Bonhoeffer was the leader of a clandestine seminary in Finkenwalde, he wrote *The Cost of Discipleship* (1949; the English translation of *Nachfolge*, 1939), which firmly established his reputation as a talented theologian. The work juxtaposed two concerns, the superlative demands of Christian obedience and the perfunctory, cheap forms of grace so prevalent and tawdry. In an age when many were searching for something authentic to which total allegiance could be given, this book spoke a powerful and meaningful message by italicizing the high cost of Christian living. Bonhoeffer questioned whether the modern church had so obscured the gospel by adding man-made dogmas, burdensome rules, and irrelevant demands that to make a genuine decision for Christ has become extremely difficult, if not impossible.

Bonhoeffer proposed to tell how Jesus of Nazareth called us to be disciples; his intention was not to impose still harder demands but to show how anyone who follows the command of Jesus single-mindedly and unresistantly finds the burden or yoke easy. Discipleship, argued Bonhoeffer, means joy, and it is not limited to a spiritual elite but is for everyone. In pursuing this idea, Bonhoeffer distinguished between "cheap grace" and "costly grace." Cheap grace is self-bestowed as doctrine, a general truth for which there is no need for a life of obedience. But happy are they, Bonhoeffer asserted, who discover the truth that grace is costly just because it is the "grace of God in Jesus Christ." And certainly Bonhoeffer's life was evidence of this commitment.

While in prison Bonhoeffer was able to sustain remarkable correspondence with family and friends on all sorts of personal and theological subjects. Toward the end of his confinement he began to hint at a radically daring idea he termed "religionless Christianity." To be a true Christian in the modern world, he speculated, involved first of all being altogether in the world. Would that not imply, he asked, the need for a secular theology for a "world come of age," a world that no longer depends on religious supports?

Although Bonhoeffer was not permitted to work out these bold proposals, his questions just prior to his death struck responsive sparks in the minds of many. The fervor of his devotion and the genius of his perception that the long neglected doctrine of the Christian life needed to be lifted up for fresh assessment help to explain how this young theologian in prison could speak so effectively to his own and the next generation of seekers.

Source: Letters and Papers from Prison, *enlarged edition, edited by Eberhard Bethge (New York: Macmillan, 1971), 279–82, 285–86, 341–42, 360–61, 369–70;* The Cost of Discipleship, *translated by R. H. Fuller (London: SCM Press, 1959), 35–41.*

▼ ▼ ▼

RELIGIONLESS CHRISTIANITY

What is bothering me incessantly is the question of what Christianity really is, or indeed who Christ really is, for us today. The time when people could be told everything by means of words, whether theological or pious, is over, and so is the time of inwardness and conscience and that means the time of religion in general. We are moving towards a completely religionless time; people as they are now simply cannot be religious anymore. Even those who honestly describe themselves as "religious" do not in the least act up to it, and so they presumably mean something quite different by "religious."

Our whole nineteen-hundred-year-old Christian preaching and theology rest on the "religious *a priori*" [presupposition] of mankind. Christianity has always been a form—perhaps the true form—of "religion." But if one day it becomes clear that this a priori does not exist at all, but was a historically conditioned and transient form of human self-expression, and if therefore man becomes radically religionless—and I think that that is already more or less the case (how else is it, for example, that this war, in contrast to all previous ones, is not calling forth any "religious" reaction?) what does that mean for "Christianity"? . . .

How can Christ become the Lord of the religionless as well? Are there religionless Christians? If religion is only a garment of Christianity—and even this garment has looked very different at different times—then what is a religionless Christianity? . . .

The questions to be answered would surely be: What do a church, a community, a sermon, a liturgy, a Christian life mean in a religionless world? How do we speak of God—without religion, i.e., without the temporally conditioned presuppositions of metaphysics, inwardness, and so on? How do we speak (or perhaps we cannot now even "speak" as we used to) in a "secular" way about "God"? . . .

Religious people speak of God when human knowledge (perhaps simply because they are too lazy to think) has come to an end. . . . I've come to be doubtful of talking about any human boundaries (is even death, which people now hardly fear, and is sin, which they now hardly understand, still a genuine boundary today?). It always seems to me that we are trying anxiously in this way to reserve some space for God; I should like to speak of God not only on the boundaries but at the center, not in weakness but in strength; and therefore not in death and guilt but in man's life and goodness. As to the boundaries, it seems to me better to be silent and leave the insoluble unsolved. Belief in the resurrection is not the "solution" of the problem of death. God's "beyond" is not the beyond of our cognitive faculties. . . . God is beyond in the midst of our life. The church stands, not at the boundaries where human powers give out, but in the middle of the village. That is how it is in the Old Testament, and in this sense we still read the New Testament far too little in light of the Old. How this religionless Christianity looks, what form it takes, is something that I am thinking about a great deal.

"CHEAP GRACE—COSTLY GRACE"

Cheap grace is the deadly enemy of our church. We are fighting today for costly grace.

Cheap grace means grace sold on the market like cheapjacks' wares. The sacraments, the forgiveness of sin, and the consolations of religion are thrown away at cut prices. Grace is represented as the church's inexhaustible treasury, from which she showers blessings with generous hands, without asking questions or fixing limits. Grace without price; grace without cost! The essence of grace, we suppose, is that the account has been paid in advance; and, because it has been paid, everything can be had for nothing. Since the cost was infinite, the possibilities of using and spending it are infinite. What would grace be if it were not cheap?

Cheap grace means as a doctrine, a principle, a system. It means forgiveness of sins proclaimed as a general truth, the love of God taught as the Christian "conception" of God. An intellectual assent to that idea is held to be of itself sufficient to secure remission of sins. The church which holds the correct doctrine of grace has, it is supposed, *ipso facto* a part in that grace. In such a church the world finds a cheap covering for its sins; no contrition is required, still less any real desire to be delivered from sin. Cheap grace therefore amounts to a denial of the living Word of God, in fact, a denial of the Incarnation of the Word of God.

Cheap grace means the justification of sin without the justification of the sinner. Grace alone does everything they say, and so everything can remain as it was before. "All for sin could not atone" (from the hymn *Rock of Ages* by Augustus Toplady). The world goes on in the same old way, and we are still sinners "even in the best life" as Luther said. Well, then, let the Christian live like the rest of the world, let him model himself on the world's standards in every sphere of life, and not presumptuously aspire to live a different life under grace from his old life under sin. That was the heresy of the enthusiasts, the Anabaptists and their kind. Let the Christian beware of rebelling against the free and boundless grace of God and desecrating it. Let him not attempt to erect a new religion of the letter by endeavoring to live a life of obedience to the commandments of Jesus Christ! The world has been justified by grace. The Christian knows that, and takes it seriously. He knows he must not strive against this indispensable grace. Therefore—let him live like the rest of the world! Of course he would like to go and do something extraordinary, and it does demand a good deal of self-restraint to refrain from the attempt and content himself with living as the world lives. Yet it is imperative for the Christian to achieve renunciation, to practice self-effacement, to distinguish his life from the life of the world. He must let grace be grace indeed, otherwise he will destroy the world's faith in the free gift of grace. . . . Cheap grace is not the kind of forgiveness of sin which frees us from the toils of sin. *Cheap grace is the grace we bestow on ourselves* [emphasis added].

Cheap grace is the preaching of forgiveness without requiring repentance, baptism without church discipline, Communion without confession, absolution without personal confession. Cheap grace is grace without discipleship, grace without the cross, grace without Jesus Christ, living and incarnate.

Costly grace is the treasure hidden in the field; for the sake of it a man will gladly go and sell all that he has. It is the pearl of great price which in order to buy the merchant will sell all his goods. It is the kingly rule of Christ, for whose sake a man will pluck out the eye which causes him to stumble, it is the call of Jesus Christ at which the disciple leaves his nets and follows him.

Costly grace is the gospel which must be sought again and again, the gift which must be asked for, the door at which a man must knock. Such grace is costly because it calls us to follow, and it is grace because it calls us to follow Jesus Christ. It is costly because it costs a man his life, and it is grace because it gives a man the only true life. It is costly because it condemns sin, and grace because it justifies the sinner. Above all, it is costly because it cost God the life of his Son: "You were bought at a great price," and what has cost God much cannot be cheap for us. Above all, it is grace because God did not reckon his Son too dear a price to pay for our life, but delivered him up for us. Costly grace is the Incarnation of God.

▲ ▲ ▲

The vision of Dietrich Bonhoeffer of a "this-worldly, secular" Christianity has had an enduring influence on a large number of Christian theologians and laypeople. Bonhoeffer's vision is a type of manifesto of a new lifestyle for the Christian. Significant to this new way is an affirmation of this world, the world in which we carry out our daily tasks. Bonhoeffer was disinterested in another world, opposed to setting apart so-called

In Heaven, Bonhoeffer and Luther Discuss Grace

religious activities, such as prayer and church-going, from the everyday activities of earning a living or engaging in politics. We can see in Bonhoeffer's writings challenges that brought religion into such activities as civil rights, the war on poverty, and war resistance, and more generally those attitudes and ideas associated with political and liberation theology. Religion, if it is to be vital, must lead to the amelioration of social problems. In this way, secular, this-world theology is the proper concern of humanity. The concrete context, not some heteronomous authority such as biblical revelation or church tradition, becomes the basis for normative judgments. These ideas and convictions are strikingly reminiscent of the ideas that were influential during the Enlightenment.

Part Five

The Contemporary Period

Earlier sections of this book generally fall into what Robert Bellah terms the "historic stage" of Christian religion or what the philosopher Karl Jaspers called the "axial age," a pivotal point in the development of religious thought. In this formative period, logical systems of thought, both philosophical and theological, prevailed, reflecting the strong influence of classical Greek thought. During this time, "official scriptures" emerged along with a universalistic view of religion, that is, the idea that all everywhere should live by the one true way. This view is coincidental with a universalistic morality: moral laws and principles are for all. In this epoch human beings may yet be weak or even "fallen" but should nevertheless follow the universal order of things. The ultimate goal is to escape from this imperfect world into heaven or nirvana. The modern period, from Immanuel Kant's lifetime through the twentieth century, begins with critique of the historic stage's assumptions. It is often characterized as liberalism, together with its antithesis, neoorthodoxy, and it has as its foundation such giants as Schleiermacher, Ritschl, Strauss, Barth, and Tillich.

In our age, some of the historic and modern characteristics are extended. Classical or orthodox theology continues, especially in large measure in the Eastern Orthodox and classical Roman Catholic tradition. But significant new developments occur in response to the characteristics of the contemporary world. First and foremost, contemporary religion is characterized by its willingness to move away from the historic quest for unity. Religion, in particular, has had to learn to live with pluralism. Contemporary theology reflects pluralism and the challenge put before it by secularism.

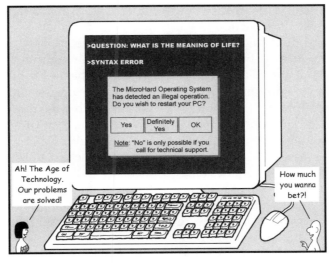

Computerized Theology

The idea that all of reality may be grasped either by the human mind, through some philosophical–theological system or by some ritualistic practice has been seriously challenged, if not discarded or replaced. Contemporary theology also takes seriously the continuing challenges of the sciences, which seek to pursue their respective disciplines unimpeded by religious authority or any all-embracing system of thought.

Characteristic of this stage is recognition of the validity as well as the limits of logic and acknowledgment of the important function of religious language. Theologies of liberation and ecology have a desire to humanize the world and deal constructively with environmental issues. In the modern world many worldviews, many visions of life, can be appreciated, and the individual is challenged to be open to this diversity of perspective.

As illustrative of the characteristics central to this stage in Christian history and our own era, we have selected some writers who represent dramatic, exciting, challenging change in theology and who reflect and have responded to central features of our time in various forms of liberation theology. Here following we shall briefly consider: Gustavo Gutiérrez, the progenitor of liberation theology; feminist theologians Mary Daly, Letty Russell, and Rosemary Radford Ruether; and black theologians Martin Luther King Jr. and James H. Cone.

32. Latin American Liberation Theology

Liberation theology in its Latin American form emerged as a religious response to large-scale human suffering and poverty. It began as a reaction to the pain, suffering, and political oppression assailing so many human beings there and arose as a theology of and for the poor, with a total commitment to the freedom of the oppressed. Liberation theology addresses not only personal salvation but also the personal and social well-being of the masses.

This is not simply a "knee-jerk" reaction. Liberation theology makes a significant theological statement about the reality of this finite world and the nature of human life. Why should some human beings, all created in God's image and all therefore children of God, be charac-

terized and treated as "subhuman"? Poverty, political and social oppression, or anything that attacks human life is itself to be challenged and attacked. Human existence is constituted as free, self-determining, reflective, critical, and creative. The freedom and integrity of the human person are sacred, and the gospel addresses the whole person, not just his or her "spiritual" condition.

As Gustavo Gutiérrez, the "father" of liberation theology, has frequently argued, theology in the developed nations is different from liberation theology. Developed nations argue about the relation between faith and reason, the ability to maintain faith in a secularized world, and a host of other familiar doctrinal issues. While much modern Western theology since Friedrich Schleiermacher has been "apologetic," intent to make Christian faith intelligible and credible to the skeptical modern mind, liberation theology is understood as a "second act," by which one reflects on one's firm commitment to the God who sides with the poor. Liberation theology's issue is how to address, in light of Christian faith, the problem of being a non-person in the world today, or how to empower the disenfranchised and oppressed of the world today. How should Christianity respond to these issues? Christianity's role is especially difficult to define in light of the fact that religious authority has been substantially weakened in our secular world.

Oppression and the problem of dehumanization pose an intrinsic challenge to any faith in God. Latin American liberation theology has demonstrated that massive poverty and social oppression on a continent dominated by the Christian faith and the Christian church are in fact a scandal to that very faith and church. Christian theology must go deeper; it must go beyond sentimental faith.

Emerging simultaneously, other forms of liberation theology have developed in the last thirty years: feminist theology, black theology, womanist and *mujerista* theologies, and indigenous theologies from Asia and Africa. Each has contributed a critical reading of Christianity's history and theology and sought to affirm the full humanity of marginalized persons. Liberation theologies preclude investigating the idea of God or faith in God in abstraction. Theologians must deal with the concept of God as it relates to human suffering and oppression of any type. Simply put: the prob-

lem of human suffering, whether in Latin America, North America, or elsewhere, is the problem of God. Theological issues in our time come to a focus as a history of suffering, oppression and liberation. And, if Christian faith is anything at all, it is a faith that liberates—the form of which is shaped by the historical context in which the faith is proclaimed.

Gustavo Gutiérrez

Latin American liberation theology perceives great evil in socio-economic structures that give wealth and power to a privileged class while maintaining both peasants and the urban poor in deprivation and powerlessness. Some liberation theology focuses its efforts on the creation of "base communities" in which the poor can find mutual support and perhaps develop political influence. Other liberation theologies preach a more active political agitation along socialist lines. There is no program on which all liberation theology agrees.

Gustavo Gutiérrez, a Peruvian Roman Catholic priest, gave the movement its name with his book *A Theology of Liberation*. In this work Gutiérrez redefines salvation more inclusively as liberation, and he formulates God's "preferential option" for the poor, by which he asserts that God's care for *all* creation implies a special priority for standing in solidarity with those traditionally excluded or oppressed.

In the following passages, Gutiérrez discusses liberation and secularization. "Secularization" was originally a late medieval word for the process of handing over church property to the civil authorities, to place it under secular control. Within the context of liberation theology, secularization is the process whereby ideas, values, and practices once aligned with the church's traditional "otherworldly" focus (offering heaven as the reward for suffering on earth) have been shifted towards a concern to take care of this world for the sake of others, including generations yet to come.

Western culture as a whole has undergone a high degree of secularization in the last few centuries with the notion that no single idea or institution—political, religious, economic, or otherwise—can contain all of reality. The "historic" or classical form of religion perceives this as unreligiousness, a falling away from the true, otherworldly religion. Modern religion, however, argues that concern for this world can be quite religious.

Gutiérrez believes that the purpose of the Roman Catholic Church and, by implication, of all religious bodies, should be to serve the world. So the purpose of the church becomes "secular," in a sense. It is a religious obligation, according to Gutiérrez, to engage in the kind of political, economic, and social activity that will decrease human suffering and liberate the poor from the dehumanizing conditions under which they often suffer.

Source: A Theology of Liberation: History, Politics, and Salvation *(Maryknoll, N.Y.: Orbis Books, 1973, 1988), 33, 41–42.*

▼ ▼ ▼

AN ENTIRELY DIFFERENT WORLD
In all the different responses we are considering, the world has gradually been acknowledged as existing in its own right. Autonomous with regard to both ecclesiastical authority and the mission of the church, the world has slowly asserted its secularity. Acknowledgment by the church of this autonomy manifested itself first with timidity and distrust—hence the expressions "healthy," "just," and "legitimate" autonomy which frequently appear in documents from the magisterium of the church. (Magisterium means "teaching authority" in the Roman Catholic Church, asserting that the pope, the bishops, have final authority for teaching the truth of Christ.) But gradually and especially in theological circles, the values and irreversibility of the process to which we now refer as secularization have become more obvious.

Secularization appeared as a breaking away from the tutelage of religion, as a desacralization. This is the most common way of characterizing this process. Harvey Cox (Harvard professor of Church and Society and author of *The Secular City*) writes: "We have defined secularization as the liberation of man from religious and metaphysical tutelage, the turning away from other worlds and toward this one" (p. 17). This is how the process of secularization has historically been presented. It was an initial attempt to deal with the problem, valid albeit incomplete.

There is a second and more positive approach to this subject, which is already suggested in the final part of the text quoted above. Secularization is, above all, the result of a transformation of the self-understanding of man. From a cosmological vision, man moves to an anthropological vision, due especially to scientific developments. Man perceives himself as a creative subject. Moreover man becomes aware—as we have noticed above—that he is an agent of history, responsible for his own destiny. His mind discovers not only the laws of nature, but also penetrates those of society, history, and psychology. This new self-understanding of man necessarily brings in its wake a different way of conceiving his relationship with God.

In this sense, secularization—and this has been recalled often lately—is a process which not only coincides perfectly with a Christian vision of man, of history, and of the cosmos; it also favors a more complete fulfillment of the Christian life insofar as it offers man the possibility of being more fully human. This realization has engendered efforts to search for the biblical roots of secularization, efforts at times somewhat "concordist." Biblical faith does indeed affirm the existence of creation as distinct from the Creator; it is the proper sphere of man, whom God himself has proclaimed lord of this creation. *Worldliness,* therefore, is a must, a necessary condition for an authentic relationship between man and God.

All this has important ramifications. In the first place, rather than define the world in relation to the religious phenomenon, it would seem that religion should be redefined in relation to the profane. The worldly sphere appears in fact in every way more consistent in itself. This is Bonhoeffer's world come of age, *Mundig,* the source of his anguished question, "How can we speak about God in this adult world?" (Bonhoeffer you will recall was the German Lutheran pastor who feared that the church was too unworldly and too dependent on God to handle a monster like Hitler and needed to promote more involvement by religious people as mature adults responsible for this history, not leaving it to God to take care of it.)

On the other hand—on a very concrete level in which we are particularly interested—if formerly this tendency was to see the world in terms of the church, today almost the reverse is true: the church is seen in terms of the world. In the past, the church used the world for her own ends; today many Christians—and non-Christians—ask themselves if they should, for example, use the influence of the church to accelerate the process of transformation of social structures.

FAITH AND THE NEW HUMAN PERSON

It is not our purpose to deal with all the complex questions which this heading suggests, but only to consider briefly some of the aspects of the subject which concerns us.

From the viewpoint of faith, the motive which in the last instance moves Christians to participate in the liberation of oppressed peoples and exploited social classes is the conviction of the radical incompatibility of the evangelical demands with an unjust and alienating society. They feel keenly that they cannot claim to be Christians without a commitment to liberation. But the articulation of the way in which this action for a more just world is related to a life of faith belongs to the level of intuition and groping—at times in anguish.

If theology is a critical reflection—in the light of Word accepted in faith—on historical praxis (praxis is a word that arose in socialist-Marxist thought. If you translate it as simply "practice," this would not be in error. But it is used to suggest the interplay between practice and theory, between what a person does and what a person believes. In religious terms it stands for action informed by faith or belief. You are what you do!) and therefore on the presence of Christians in the world, it should help us to establish this relationship. Theological reflection should attempt to discern the positive and negative values in this presence. It should make explicit the values of faith, hope, and charity contained in it. And it should contribute to correcting possible aberrations as well as the neglect of other aspects of Christian life, pitfalls into which the demands of immediate political action, regardless of how generous it is, sometimes allow us to fall. This too is the task of critical reflection, which by definition should not be simply a Christian justification a posteriori (i.e., after the fact). Basically this reflection should contribute in one way or another to a more evangelical, more authentic, more concrete, and more efficacious commitment to liberation.

It is important to keep in mind that beyond—or rather, through—the struggle against misery, injustice, and exploitation the goal is the creation of a new man. Vatican II has declared, "We are witnesses of the birth of a new humanism, one in which man is defined first of all by his responsibility toward his brothers and toward history" (*Gaudium et Spes,* No. 55). This aspiration to create a new man is the deepest motivation in the struggle which many have undertaken in Latin America. This fulfillment of this dream (if it can ever be completely fulfilled) can be only vaguely by this generation, but this aspiration even now inspires their commitment.

This quest poses questions and challenges to the Christian faith. What the faith says about itself will demonstrate its relationship to the goal of the people who are struggling for the emancipation of others and of themselves. Indeed, an awareness of the need for self-liberation is essential to a correct understanding of the liberation process. It is not a matter of "struggling for others," which suggests a paternalism and reformist objectives, but rather of becoming aware of oneself as not completely fulfilled and as living in an alienated society. And thus one can identify radically and militantly with those—the people and the social class—who bear the brunt of oppression.

DEVELOPMENT AND LIBERATION

Although we will consider the liberation from a theological perspective more extensively later, it is important at this time to attempt an initial treatment in the light of what we have just discussed.

The term *development* is relatively new in the texts of the ecclesiastical magisterium. Except for a brief reference by Pius XII, the subject is broached for the first time by John XXIII in the encyclical letter *Mater et Magistra. Pacem in Terris* gives the term special attention. *Gaudium et Spes* dedicates a whole section to it, though the treatment is not original. All these documents stress the urgency of eliminating the existing injustices and the need for an economic development geared to the service of man. Finally, [Pope Paul VI's] *Populorum Progressio* discusses development as its central theme. Here the language and ideas are clearer; the adjective *integral* is added to development, putting things in a different context and opening new perspectives.

These new viewpoints were already hinted at in the sketchy discussion of Vatican Council II on dependence and liberation. *Gaudium et Spes* points out that "nations on the road to progress . . . continually fall behind while very often their dependence on wealthier nations deepens more rapidly; even in the economic sphere" (no. 9). Later it acknowledges that "although nearly all the people have gained their independence, it is still far from true that they are free from excessive inequalities and from every form of undue dependence" (no. 85).

These assertions should lead to a discernment of the need to be free from dependence, to be liberated from it. The same *Gaudium et Spes* on two occasions touches on liberation and laments the fact that it is seen exclusively as the fruit of human effort: "Many look forward to a genuine and total emancipation of humanity brought solely by human effort. They are convinced that the future rule of man over the earth will satisfy every desire of his heart" (no. 10). Or it is concerned that liberation be reduced to a purely economic or social level: "Among the forms of modern atheism is that which anticipates the liberation of man especially through his economic and social emancipation" (no. 20). These assertions presuppose, negatively speaking, that liberation must be placed in a wider context; they criticize a narrow vision. They allow, therefore, for the possibility of a "genuine and total" liberation.

Unfortunately, this wider perspective is not elaborated. We find some indications, however, in the texts in which *Gaudium et Spes* speaks of the birth of a "new humanism, one in which man is defined first of all by his responsibility toward his brothers and toward history" (no. 55). There is a need for men who are makers of history, "men who are truly artisans of a new humanity" (no. 30), men moved by the desire to build a really new society. Indeed, the conciliar document asserts that beneath economic and political demands "lies a deeper and more widespread longing. Persons and societies thirst for a full and free life worthy of man— one in which they can subject to their own welfare all that the modern world can offer them so abundantly" (no. 9)

All this is a beginning. It is an oft-noted fact that *Gaudium et Spes* in general offers a rather ironic description of the human situation; it touches up the uneven spots, smoothes the rough edges, avoids the more conflictual aspects, and stays away from the sharper confrontations among social classes and countries.

The encyclical *Populorum Progressio* goes a step further. In a somewhat isolated text it speaks clearly of "building a world where every man, no matter what his race, religion, or nationality, can live a fully human life, freed from servitude imposed on him by other men or by natural forces over which he has not sufficient control" (no. 47). It is unfortunate, however, that this idea is not expanded in the encyclical. From this point of view, *Populorum Progressio* is a transitional document. . . . The outright use of the language of liberation, instead of its mere suggestion, would have given a more decided and direct thrust in favor of the oppressed, encouraging them to break with their present situation and take control of their own destiny.

The theme of liberation appears more completely discussed in the message from the eighteen bishops of the Third World, published as a specific response to the call made by *Populorum Progressio*.

The product of a profound historical movement, this aspiration to liberation is beginning to be accepted by the Christian community as a sign of the times, as a call to commitment and

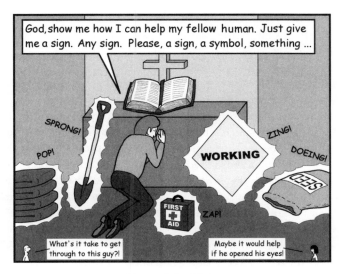

Signs of the Times

interpretation. The biblical message, which presents the work of Christ as liberation, provides the framework for this interpretation. Theology seems to have avoided for a long time reflection on the conflictual character of human history, the confrontations among men, social classes, and countries. St. Paul continuously reminds us, however, of the paschal core of Christian existence and of all of human life: the passage from the old man to the new, from sin to grace, from slavery to freedom. . . .

Summarizing what has been said above, we can distinguish three reciprocally interpenetrating levels of meaning of the term *liberation,* or in other words, three approaches to the process of liberation.

In the first place, liberation expresses the aspiration of oppressed peoples and social classes, emphasizing the conflictual aspect of the economic, social, and political process which puts them at odds with wealthy nations and oppressive classes. In contrast, the word *development,* and above all the policies characterized as developmentalist *{desarrollistra}*, appear somewhat aseptic, giving a false picture of a tragic and conflictual reality. The issue of development does in fact find its true place in the more universal, profound, and radical perspective of liberation. It is only within this framework that development finds its true meaning and the possibilities of accomplishing something worthwhile.

At a deeper level, liberation can be applied to an understanding of history. Man is seen as assuming conscious responsibility for his own destiny. This understanding provides a dynamic context and broadens the horizons of the desired social changes. In this perspective the unfolding of all man's dimensions is demanded—a man who makes himself throughout his life and throughout history. The gradual conquest of true freedom leads to the creation of a new man and a qualitatively different society. This vision provides, therefore, a better understanding of what in fact is at stake in our lives.

Finally, the word *development* to a certain extent limits and obscures the theological problems implied in the process designated by this term. On the contrary the word *liberation* allows for another approach leading to biblical sources which inspire the presence and action of man in history. In the Bible, Christ is presented as the one who brings us liberation. Christ the Savior liberates man from sin, which is the ultimate root of all disruption of friendship and of all injustice and oppression. Christ makes man truly free, that is to say, he enables man to live in communion with him; and this is the basis for all human brotherhood.

This is not a matter of three parallel or chronologically successive processes, however. There are three levels of meaning of a single, complex process, which finds its deepest sense and its full realization in the saving work of Christ. These levels of meaning, therefore, are interdependent. A comprehensive view of the matter presupposes that all three aspects can be considered together. In this way two pitfalls will be avoided: first, idealist or spiritualist approaches, which are nothing but ways of evading a harsh and demanding reality, and second, shallow analyses and programs of short-term effect initiated under the pretext of meeting immediate needs.

▲ ▲ ▲

Liberation theology is based on a political interpretation of the gospel of Jesus of Nazareth. It is a specific protest against a common understanding in Christian theology that the history of the world, along with its political structures, is irrelevant to redemption because the saving intervention of God affects only a narrow strand of life and history, that is, the history of the Jewish people up to the time of Jesus of Nazareth and of the internal affairs of the churches since the time of Jesus. Liberation theologians see the term *political* in a comprehensive sense that includes "all" dimensions of life, building up the "city of man" (to borrow an old phrase). Christian theology is not simply about saving individuals, and it cannot be so limited; it is rather about saving the world—the tangled and sinful complex of human relations that in large measure preclude the possibilities of becoming fully human. Liberation theology is thus secular, this-world theology.

Liberation theology arises directly out of the experience of the oppressed and emphasizes a concrete and personal identification with the oppressed in their struggle for liberation. It is a practical implementation of a theology of the cross. Only in the experience of the disenfranchised, the oppressed, the marginalized, the vanquished of the earth is the need for redemption clearly evident. The cross symbolizes the need to write human history "upside down," from the perspective of the oppressed.

The proper method that derives from this approach is to critique the praxis of the life of the believing community. The community's continuity with the authentic gospel of Jesus and with the ecclesial tradition is not simply rational or logical, but spiritual. It is not merely a theological system (of any type) to be handed on intact so that the Christian life of the community may result from some intellectual exercise. Rather, the Christian life of faith and hope, together with action appropriate to that hope, is extended from person to person and from community to community. Reflection on that praxis follows and constitutes theology, by bringing the praxis into juxtaposition with the love of God revealed in Jesus. This is not really new! What is new is that for liberation theologians the critique of Christian

praxis requires a much closer relationship between theology and the social and human sciences than is generally acknowledged by traditional theology. In a sense liberation theology recovers a part of the gospel that has become lost in the massive abstract tomes of traditional dogma and rediscovers the disturbing nature of the gospel's claim that the proclamation of the love of God in Jesus is for all. This claim has serious implications for all structures of life: social, economic and political.

Liberation theology is partisan theology, but so is all theology. Every theology arises out of the perspective of a particular experience and a particular pattern of response within the experience. There is no such thing as a general, objective, or universal perspective for theology. Following in the tradition of the Hebrew prophets, liberation theology claims it must address the issues raised by the poor, the disenfranchised, and the marginalized.

Liberation theology is in one sense a response to so-called First-World theologians who write it off as being "partisan" without giving it much consideration. But it is also an understanding intimately related to other points of liberation theology: the theology of the cross as a question rather than an answer; the understanding of the Lord's Supper as a focus for the Christian task in the world but not identical with that task; the doctrine of redemption interpreted in terms of its roots in the Hebrew scriptures; and the teaching of the imitation of Jesus re-examined in light of Christian spiritual traditions.

Some central theological issues raised by the efforts of liberation theologians are: What is redemption? What is the content of Christian hope? What is the relation of eschatology to history? What is the relation between creation and history, that is, between God's creation and human creation? What has Christian hope to contribute to politics and public affairs? How does the Christian stand in relation to class struggle, situations of conflict, and violence? How is Jesus properly proposed for imitation? And what are the implications for ecclesiology, the church?

33. FEMINIST LIBERATION THEOLOGY

Who's Got the Handbasket?!

The movement to end the oppression of women did not begin in the twentieth century, as many might suppose. We can observe it in many places, not the least of which is the words of Mary Wollstonecraft and Elizabeth Cady Stanton, who wrote during the last decades of the nineteenth century. Yet what did develop in the latter portion of the twentieth century was the explicit and thoroughgoing critique of Christian traditions in relation to women. Pioneered by Mary Daly's *Beyond God the Father* and other texts, feminist theology focuses on ways in which patriarchal Christianity both marginalized women and distorted its own axial commitments of faith. Rich in historical and theological work, feminist theologians have explored women's experience as a signal source of theological reflection. Thus Letty Russell and Rosemary Radford Ruether, as well as many others, are inheritors of a long tradition.

In American feminist theology the emphasis has been on the experience of women, who have been given nominally high status as "mothers" and "nurturers," but who have usually been deprived of full opportunities to be self-determining and self-defining as free creative persons. Feminist theology is a "liberation" theology, for it is an attempt to reflect upon the experience of oppression and our actions for the new creation of a more humane society—which includes the rights of women.

Daly, Russell, and Ruether argue that women and men have been captives to certain roles that society assigns to each gender. Unspoken and unnoticed assumptions have dominated people and have deprived them of the freedom to make caring, responsible, and constructive choices in their lives. Daly highlights the way language induces prejudice in us all, not by teaching hate or explicit discrimination, but more subtly, by forming our concepts in such a way that we do not even notice what prejudicial assumptions are built into our consciousness. Russell argues for a feminist theology that encourages people to contribute to the meaning of faith from their own perspective. In turn, Ruether reflects on the axial insights of feminist theology and the personhood of women and their explosive implications for revisioning traditional Christian doctrines of sin, Christology, and redemption.

Mary Daly

Source: "After the Death of God the Father: Women's Liberation and the Transformation of Christian Consciousness," Womanspirit Rising: A Feminist Reader in Religion, *edited by Carol P. Christ and Judith Plaskow (New York: Harper and Row, 1979), 53–57.*

▼ ▼ ▼

The women's liberation movement has produced a large deluge of books and articles. Their major task has been the exposition and criticism of our male-oriented heritage. In order to reveal and drive home to readers the oppressive character of our cultural institutions, it was necessary to do careful research, to trot out passages from leading philosophers, psychologists, statesmen, poets, historians, saints, and theologians which make the reader's hair stand on end by the blatancy of the misogynism. Part of the task also has been the tracing of the subtle psychological mechanisms by which society has held men up and women down. This method of exposition and analysis reached its crescendo within the past year when Kate Millet's *Sexual Politics* rocketed her into the role of American counterpart to Simone de Beauvoir.

As far as the level of creative research is concerned, that phase of the work is finished. The skeletons in our cultural closet have been hauled out for inspection. I do not mean to imply that there are not countless more of the same to be uncovered (just the other day I noticed for the first time that Berdyaev blandly affirms there is "something base and sinister in the female element" et cetera). Nor do I mean that the task of communicating the message is over. Millions have yet to hear the news, let alone to grasp its import. Certainly it would be a mistake and betrayal to trivialize the fact that our culture is so diseased. That has always been a major tactic in the fine art of suppressing the rage of women. No, what I am saying is that Phase One of critical research and writing in the movement has opened the way for the logical next step in creative thinking. We now have to ask how the women's revolution can and should change our whole vision of reality. What I intend to do here is to sketch some of the ways in which it can influence Western religious thought.

The Judaic-Christian tradition has served to legitimate sexually imbalanced patriarchal society. Thus, for example, the image of the Father God, spawned in the human imagination and sustained as plausible by patriarchy, has in turn rendered service to this type of society by making its mechanisms for the oppression of women appear right and fitting. If God in "his" heaven is a father ruling "his" people, then it is in the "nature" of things and according to divine plan and the order of the universe that society be male dominated. Theologian Karl Barth found it appropriate to write that woman is "ontologically" subordinate to man. Within this context a mystification of roles takes place: the husband dominating his wife represents God himself. What is happening, of course, is the familiar mechanism by which the images and values of a given society are projected into a realm of beliefs, which in turn justify the social infra-structure. The belief system becomes hardened and objective, seeming to have an unchangeable independent existence and validity of its own. It resists social change which would rob it of its plausibility. Nevertheless, despite the vicious circle, change does occur in society, and ideologies die, though they die hard.

As the women's revolution begins to have its effect upon the fabric of society, transforming it from patriarchy to something that never existed before—into a diarchal situation that is radically new—it will, I believe, become the greatest single potential challenge to Christianity to rid itself of its oppressive tendencies or go out of business. Beliefs and values that have held sway for thousand of years will be questioned as never before. It is also very possibly the greatest single hope for survival of religious consciousness in the West.

At this point, it is important to consider the objection that the liberation of women will only mean that new characters will assume the same old roles, but that nothing will change essentially in regard to structure, ideology, or values. This objection is often based upon the observation that the very few women in "masculine" occupations seem to behave very much as men do. This is really not to the point for it fails to recognize that the effect of tokenism is not to change stereotypes or social systems but

to preserve these. What I am discussing here is an emergence of women such as has never taken place before. It is naive to assume that the coming of women into equal power in society generally and in the church in particular will simply mean uncritical acceptance of values formerly given priority by men. Rather, I suggest, that it will be a catalyst for transformation of our culture.

The roles and structures of patriarchy have been developed and sustained in accordance with an artificial polarization of human qualities into the traditional sexual stereotypes. The image of the person in authority and the accepted understanding of "his" role have corresponded to the eternal masculine stereotype, which implies hyper-rationality, "objectivity," aggressivity, the possession of dominating and manipulative attitudes toward persons and environment, and the tendency to construct boundaries between the self (and those identified with the self) and "the other." The caricature of a human being which is represented by this stereotype depends for its existence upon the opposite caricature—the eternal feminine (hyperemotional, passive, self-abasing, etc.). By becoming whole persons, women can generate a counterforce to the stereotype of the leader as they challenge the artificial polarization of human characteristics. There is no reason to assume that women who have the support of their sisters to criticize the masculine stereotype will simply adopt it as a model for themselves. More likely they will develop a wider range of qualities and skills in themselves and thereby encourage men to engage in a comparably liberating procedure (a phenomenon we are beginning to witness already in men's liberation groups); this becoming of *whole* human beings will affect the values of our society, for it will involve a change in the fabric of human consciousness.

Accordingly, it is reasonable to anticipate that this change will affect the symbols which reflect the values of our society, including religious symbols. Since some of these have functioned to justify oppression, women and men would do well to welcome this change. Religious symbols die when the cultural situation that supported them ceases to give them plausibility. This should pose no problem to authentic faith, which accepts the relativity of all symbols and recognizes that fixation upon any of them as absolute is in itself idolatrous.

The becoming of the new symbols is not a matter that can arbitrarily be decided around a conference table. Rather, they grow out of a changing communal situation and experience. This does not mean that theologically we are consigned to the role of passive spectators. We are called upon to be attentive to what the new experience of the becoming of women is revealing to us, and to foster the evolution of consciousness beyond the oppressiveness reflected and justified by symbols and doctrines throughout the millennia of patriarchy.

The imbalance is apparent first of all in the biblical and popular image of the great patriarch in heaven who rewards and punishes according to his mysterious and arbitrary will. The fact that the effects of this image have not always been humanizing is evident to any perceptive reader of history. The often cruel behavior of Christians toward unbelievers and even toward dissenters among themselves is shocking evidence of the function of that image in relation to values and behavior.

Sophisticated thinkers, of course, have never intellectually identified God with an elderly parent in heaven. Nevertheless it is important to recognize that, even when very abstract conceptualizations of God are formulated in the mind, images have a way of surviving in the imagination in such a way that a person can function on two different and even apparently contradictory levels at the same time. Thus one can speak of God as a spirit and at the same time imagine "him" as belonging to the male sex. Such primitive images can profoundly affect conceptualizations which appear to be very refined and abstract. Even the Yahweh of the future, so cherished by the theology of hope, comes through on an imaginative level as exclusively a He-God, and it is perhaps consistent with this that theologians of hope have attempted to develop a political theology which takes no explicit cognizance of the devastation wrought by sexual politics.

The widespread conception of the "Supreme Being" as an entity distinct from the world but controlling it according to plan and keeping human beings in a state of infantile subjection has been a not too subtle mask of the divine patriarch. The Supreme Being's plausibility, and that of the static world view which accompanies this projection, has, of course, declined. This was a projection grounded in specifically patriarchal infrastructures and sustained as subjectively real by the usual processes of generating plausibility. The sustaining power of the social infrastructures has been eroded by a number of developments in recent history, including the general trend toward democratization of society and the emergence of technology with the accompanying sense of mastery over the world and man's destiny. However, it is the women's movement which appears destined to play the key role in the overthrow of such oppressive elements in traditional theism, precisely because it strikes at the source of the imbalance reflected in traditional beliefs.

The women's movement will present a growing threat to patriarch religion less by attacking it than by simply leaving it behind. Few of the leaders in the movement evince an interest in institutional religion, having recognized it as an instrument of betrayal. Those who see their commitment to the movement as consonant with concern for the religious heritage are aware that the Christian tradition is by no means bereft of elements which foster genuine experiences and intimations of transcendence. The problem is that their liberating potential is choked off in the surrounding atmosphere of the images, ideas, values, and structures of patriarchy. What will, I think, become possible through the social change coming from radical feminism is a more acute and widespread perception of qualitative differences between those conceptualizations of God and of the human relationship to God which are oppressive in their implications and those which encourage self-actualization and social commitment.

The various theologies that hypostatize transcendence [make the transcendent concrete] invariably use this "God" to legitimate oppression, particularly that of women. These are irredeemably antifeminine and therefore antihuman. In contrast to this, a more authentic language of transcendence does not hypostatize or objectify God and consequently does not lend itself to such use. So, for example, Tillich's way of speaking about God as ground and power of being would be very difficult to use for the legitimation of any sort of oppression. It grows out of awareness of that reality which is both transcendent and immanent, not reducible to or adequately represented by such expressions as *person, father, supreme being.*

▲ ▲ ▲

Letty Russell

Source: Human Liberation in a Feminist Perspective—A Theology *(Philadelphia: Westminster Press, 1974), 18–21.*

▼ ▼ ▼

The gospel is a message of liberation in Jesus Christ. It is good news to all people in every situation. Concretely, and in every place of external or internal oppression, liberation has arrived in the form of one sent as the bringer of a new humanity.

Yet today, in a world of revolutionary change, the freedom chorus is constantly growing in a symphony of the groaning of creation. It is heard, not only in the streets of San Diego, Harlem, or Prague, but also along the boulevard of Rio de Janeiro, Djkarta, or Johannesburg. It is even echoed in our own hearts. We all wish we knew how it would feel to be free! We all are beginning to sense a restlessness in our bones as we try to take steps toward liberation *now,* liberation for others and for ourselves.

These are especially exciting and challenging times for women. Exciting, because so many new ideas, life-styles, and ways of service are opening up. Challenging, because women are often moving away from old securities along new paths where there are many questions and few answers. Every field of learning, every skill, every life-style becomes a new arena of experiment as women seek out their own perspectives, the contribution that they would make in building a new house of freedom.

Certainly, theology is no exception to this excitement and challenge. Women are voicing their search for liberation by rejecting oppressive and sexist religious traditions that declare that they are socially, ecclesiastically, and personally inferior because of their sex. They are digging deeper into their traditions, raising questions about the authority of the church "father," and searching out the hidden evidence of the contributions of the church "mothers" to the life and mission of the church. They are looking for truly authentic and liberating roots as they search a *usable past.* At the same time, women are joining other oppressed groups in seeking out a clear vision of a new society of justice and *shalom,* so that they can join the global struggle for a *usable future.*

These women are *feminists* because they advocate changes that will establish political, economic, and social equality of the sexes. In a Christian context they reflect on the way in which theology can become more complete, as all people are encouraged to contribute to the meaning of faith from their own perspective.

Such action and theory form the basis of *feminist theology*. It is "feminist" because the women involved are actively engaged in advocating the equality and partnership of women and men in church and society.

It is not *feminine theology* because femininity refers to a culturally defined set of roles and personal characteristics that elaborate the biological ability of women to bear children. According to the stereotypes of Western culture, some theology is masculine and some is feminine. One theology might contain elements of aggression, assertion, and analytical thinking; another might have elements of holistic and contextual sensitivity and a concern for interrelationships of persons and of human nurture. But, as Mary Daly has stated, all theology must be "concerned with the problems of persons in relation to others" and not with preconceived notions about the nature of women around which an isolated theology is developed. For this reason feminist theology strives to be *human* and not just *feminine,* as other forms of theology should strive to be *human* and not just *masculine.*

Feminist theology today is, by definition, *liberation theology* because it is concerned with the liberation of all people to become full participants in human society. *Liberation is an attempt to reflect upon the experience of oppression and our actions for the new creation of a more humane society.* In the words of Gustavo Gutiérrez, a Latin-American theologian:

> Theology of liberation attempts to reflect on the experience and meaning of faith based on the commitment to abolish injustice and to build a new society; this theology must be verified by the practice of that commitment, by active, effective participation in the struggle which the exploited classes have undertaken against their oppressors.

This perspective on theology is an elaboration of political theology or theology of hope as seen in such writers as Jürgen Moltmann or Johannes Metz. According to Moltmann, Christian political theology is an attempt to relate the eschatological message of freedom to sociopolitical reality. The focus of Christian hope is not simply on the open future but on the future of the hopeless.

Feminist theology has common roots with many so-called Third World liberation theologies. Third World is used here to refer to people living outside the United States and Western Europe (First World) and of the Communist bloc countries (Second World), and includes their descendants living in racial oppression in any country. Third World has economic as well as racial overtones pointing toward experiences of economic exploitation and colonialism. The term is presently used by groups in North America as a way of emphasizing that nonwhite groups are a majority of the world's population. They make up two thirds of the world's population, although they are a minority among those who hold political, social, and economic power. Women belong to all these various "worlds," and as such they are numbered among the oppressed and oppressors. Yet in relation to the male domination of the social structures of most societies women have a growing consciousness of their own oppression. In speaking of themselves as an oppressed world majority some women have adopted the term *Fourth World.* In this sense, Barbara Burris writes: "We identify with all women of all races, classes, and countries all over the world. The female culture is the Fourth World."

Like Third World liberation theology, feminist theology is written out of an experience of oppression in society. It interprets the search for salvation as a journey toward freedom, as a process of self-liberation in community with others in the light of hope in God's promise. Together with other people searching for freedom, women wish to speak of the hope that is in them. They want to tell the world that they are part of God's plan of human liberation.

▲ ▲ ▲

Rosemary Radford Ruether

Source: Women and Redemption: A Theological History *(Minneapolis: Fortress Press, 1998), 273–79.*

▼ ▼ ▼

The classical Christian paradigm defines women as created to be dominated and blames women as deserving redoubled domination for resisting it, while feminism defines women and men as originally equal and denounces male domination of women as sin. Redemption then becomes transformed gender relations that overcome male domination, rather than a call to women to submit to it as their means of salvation. From this foundational paradigm shift [among Quakers in the seventeenth century], a series of additional developments unfolded in nineteenth- and twentieth-century Christian feminism.

A second key shift took place from the seventeenth to the nineteenth centuries with a turn from an otherworldly to a this-worldly view of redemption. For traditional Christianity redemption means the reconciliation of the fallen soul with God, won by Christ in the cross, applied to the soul in baptismal regeneration, and developed through the struggle to live virtuously sustained by grace. Salvation is completed after death in eternal contemplative union with God (joined by the spiritual body in the resurrection).

Although hope for life after death remains a residual idea in modern Christianity, the focus of redemptive hope shifted (or returned) to a Hebraic hope for a this-worldly transformation of unjust relationships that would bring about a time of justice and peace within history (the reign of God). Nineteenth- and twentieth-century social gospel and liberation theologies have focused on this-worldly redemptive hope through some combination of personal conversion and progressive or revolutionary reform of social structures that will overcome poverty, tyranny, and war. Ecological sustainability has recently been integrated into this vision of a just and livable future.

Feminist theology developed within this modern tradition of this-worldly progressive hope, redefining the analysis of injustice in the context of gender hierarchy. Gender hierarchy is seen as central to a total system and ideology of patriarchy. Feminism sees patriarchy as a multilayered system of domination, centered in male control of women but including class and race hierarchy, generational hierarchy, and clericalism, and expressed also in war and in domination of nature. Elisabeth Schüssler Fiorenza has coined the phrase "kyriarchy" (the rule of the lord) for this multilayered system of top-down power, rooted in the religious hierarchy (which in Christianity sees itself as representing Christ as Lord). Redemption means overcoming all forms of patriarchy. . . .

BEING HUMAN

The shift from otherworldly to this-worldly redemptive hope also entails a revised anthropology and Christology. Feminists reject the classical notion that the human soul is radically fallen, alienated from God, and unable to make any move to reconcile itself with God, therefore needing an outside mediator who does the work of reconciliation for us. Instead the human self is defined through its primary identity as image of God. This original goodness and communion with its divine "ground of being" continue to be our "true nature."

Evil is serious, but it is defined in terms of external structures and cultures of domination to which human persons fall victim or identify with as victimizers. Although some powerful humans invented these systems and ideologies for their own advantage, and many people victimized by them have acceded to them through socialization, this does not change our potential for good.

We are alienated or out of touch with this potential, but experiences of consciousness-raising, starting with those who are disprivileged, begin a process of conversion, getting back in touch with a better self and reconstructing personal and social relations. An external redeemer is not necessary for this process of conversion, since we have not lost our true self rooted in God. But "grace events" of loving outreach from others and shocks of rampant evil can awaken our awareness of inauthentic distortions, put us in touch with our authentic self and set us on the path of struggle for just and loving relations.

THE FIGURE OF JESUS

The role of Jesus becomes quite different in feminist theology. His is a root story for the redemptive process in which we must all be engaged, but he does not and cannot do it for us. Redemption cannot be done by one person for everyone else. No one person can become the "collective human" whose actions accomplish a salvation that is then passively applied to everyone else. His story can model what we need to do, but it happens only when all of us do it for ourselves and with one another.

Yet there is a remarkable persistence in the attachment of Christian feminists to the Jesus story. Across many cultures—Western European and Euroamerican, African and Hispanic American, Latin American, Asian, and African—feminists, womanists, *mujeristas* continue to affirm their relation to Jesus, even as they reject the christological superstructure that has been erected by classical Christianity in his name. Only one feminist discussed in this book, Mary Daly, has definitively rejected an appropriation of Jesus, saying, "Even if Jesus wasn't a feminist, I am." By implication, if Jesus could be

shown to be "pro-woman," for Daly it would be irrelevant. Is the decisive step to being post-Christian the repudiation of any relevance of the Jesus story?

The other feminist theologians . . . across many cultures remain "Christian," however radical in their repudiation of doctrines about Christ as redeemer, in their continued affiliation with the Jesus story as foundationally paradigmatic for their feminist theology. Why is this? Does this indicate some residual need for male authority? Some fear of breaking the final tie with Christianity? There may be an element of these fears and dependencies, but not enough to explain the resiliency of the Jesus figure for feminist theology.

Modern Jesus scholarship has radically stripped the Jesus story of its dogmatic accretions, revealing a Jesus whose life continues to strike a responsive chord for feminist liberation theology; namely, a man (not lord, but brother) who dissented from the religious and social systems of domination that marginalized the poor and the despised, most notably women. He incurred the wrath of religious and political authorities for these subversive teachings and practices, and the authorities sought to silence him by publicly torturing him to death.

But, just as the cross failed to silence his story, for Jesus rose to live on in a religious movement that kept his memory alive, so all the appropriations of him into constructions of ecclesial domination through the centuries also have failed to silence the subversive power of his name. The Jesus story, continually reenvisioned, still rises, beyond the deaths of patriarchal Christianities, and still lives as a touchstone for feminists who continue to seek and celebrate their liberation in "memory of him."

The Jesus story continues to be paradigmatic for Christian feminists because it is understood as exemplifying the redemptive paradigm of feminist liberation: dissent against oppressive religious and political structures;

taking the side of the oppressed, particularly women; living a praxis of egalitarian relations across gender, race, class, and other status differences imposed by the dominant society; pointing toward a new time when these hierarchies will be overcome and anticipating redeemed relations in a community of celebration here and now.

Skeptics might wonder whether Christians in search of a "Jesus" to ground our faith are not, once again, looking down a long well and seeing our own face reflected in the bottom. However one construes the complex relation between "objective history" and subjective constructions reflective of our own desires, the Jesus story, told even by the minimalists of the Jesus Seminar, reflects this paradigm. Christian feminists resonate with this reading of the Jesus story as reflecting and grounding their own story.

If the Jesus story is claimed because it echoes our own story, why not discard it and tell our own story? The resistance to doing this, I believe, is due to several reasons. Most basically it expresses a desire to continue to belong to the church, not as a hierarchical structure, but as a community of faith; to have historical roots, to lay claim to a people, while at the same time calling that people to repent of its patriarchy and to understand its calling to redemption as liberation from patriarchy. A Jesus whose life message and praxis were redemption from patriarchy pulls the rug out from under Christian patriarchy and grounds a feminist Christianity as the "true" gospel of Jesus.

This is a powerful claim, powerful in a different way from telling our own individual stories in small communities. However paradigmatic for us in those small communities our stories may be, they do not have the historical weight of being claimed as the root story for two thousand years and by two billion people around the world today. To ground our liberative stories in the Jesus story is to lay claim to

that whole people in prophetic judgment and call to repentance.

Yet the fact that Jesus was a male, and his maleness has been used by the patriarchal church to insist that women are not christomorphic—that they cannot, as women, represent Christ—is a major problem for claiming the Jesus story as the root story for feminist theology. One answer is to deconstruct the assumption of patriarchal theology that maleness is normative for being fully human and the image of God. Jesus' maleness is declared to be one "accident" of his historical reality among others, such as being Jewish, and a first-century Galilean. What distinguishes Jesus as normative is not his maleness but the quality of his humanness as one who loves others and opts for those most vulnerable and oppressed, namely women. One imitates Christ by living in a like manner, not by possessing male genitalia.

While this deconstruction goes a long way toward answering the problem, it does not overcome the basic social-symbolic structure in which Jesus, a male, opts for women as objects of concern. This makes women paradigmatic as recipients of Jesus' liberative praxis, but not as agents of liberative action for themselves and other women (and men). Thus Christian feminist theology is pushed to go beyond the telling of the Jesus story as that of a "good man who really cared about us," and to dare to parallel the Jesus story with the stories of women who acted as liberators. Women become fully christomorphic only when one can tell stories of women who acted redemptively as parallel with the Jesus story. . . .

SUFFERING AND REDEMPTION
Many Christian feminists also question the focus on suffering and the cross as central to redemption. Others parallel Jesus and women as sufferers, a way of making women christomorphic found already in the medieval women mystics. Women are like Jesus because they suffer, and Jesus opts for women as those who

suffer. But some want to ask, "What kind of suffering is redemptive?" Is the passive suffering of victims redemptive, or does the mandate for women to suffer in this way in order to be Christlike simply a justification and prolongation of evil?

Some theologians, like Delores Williams, have answered this question by a decisive rejection of victimized suffering as redemptive. What is redemptive is action to extricate ourselves from unjust suffering and changing the conditions that cause it. It is not Jesus' suffering and death that are redemptive, but his life as a praxis of protest against injustice and solidarity in defense of life. The praxis of Jesus we need to imitate is this protest and defense of life, not acquiescence to being crucified, which represents the victory of oppressors who sought to silence him.

Suffering is a factor in the liberation process, not as a means of redemption, but as the risk that one takes when one struggles to overcome unjust systems whose beneficiaries resist change. The means of redemption is conversion, opening up to one another, changing systems of distorted relations, creating loving and life-giving communities of people here and now, not getting oneself tortured to death.

This dismantling of the patterns of patriarchal Christianity, reconstructing a radically different understanding of the key touchstones of Christian theology—God, humanity, male and female, sin and fall, Christ, redemption—raises the questions of how feminist theology relates to Scripture and tradition. . . .

▲ ▲ ▲

More than any other social development in recent years, the women's movement has made a very clear, direct, and immediate impact on religious attitudes and practices. This is not to suggest the women's movement is necessarily of greater importance than other developments; it simply indicates it is more easily traced in its effect on religious consciousness.

When viewing this movement, it is clear that feminist theology is not unified; it moves in many directions. Yet for all its diversity, there is a sense of camaraderie, goodwill, and good humor among feminist theologians. There is also shared rage among them, rage at their exclusion from participation in the full life of religious and other institutions of modern society—economic, social, and political. They respond, each in her own way, to this exclusion—a scenario that has dominated our Western culture for centuries with its partriarchal power.

Mary Daly, for example, who originally simply wished to be a faithful daughter of her church, pursuing a theological career, was excluded from any real participation in the intellectual life of the Roman Catholic Church and moved out in her own directions. For Daly, to describe God in male terms, even when denying that there was any real sexual identification being claimed, was to reflect patterns of exclusion reaching to the very core of religious faith. This tendency is dramatically increased when we see God as incarnated, that is, literally embodied, in the male human Jesus of Nazareth. The power of these symbols for the legitimation of sexual stereotypes is enormous and has prevented women from full, real, participation in the life of the faith. For Rosemary Radford Ruether, by contrast, Christian commitment entails both working for justice and life and rethinking core Christian ideas in a radically new way.

Feminist theologians have recognized for some time that if sexual inequality on the one hand and women's experience on the other are to be taken seriously, then such a whole recasting of religious concepts is necessary. Not only will the "maleness" of God, Christ, and the church have to be reassessed, but also the exclusivity and rigidity in religious circles will have to be uncovered and addressed. Despite considerable work already done by feminist scholars such as Rosemary Radford Ruether, Letty Russell, and Mary Daly, much has yet to be done.

34. BLACK LIBERATION THEOLOGY

Black theology is liberation theology that forcefully addresses the situation of those oppressed socially, economically, politically, and religiously on the basis of race. It grows out of the experience of those being oppressed and is articulated for the oppressed. In this regard the work of James Cone, for example, *Black Theology and Black Power* and *A Black Theology of Liberation*, is a significant statement for both black and white communities. Black liberation theology is not confined to academia, nor to Christianity for that matter; it is a theology of action as testified to by the tremendous influence of such persons as Dr. Martin Luther King Jr. and Malcolm X. Its focus on black consciousness is more than mere self-assertion and more than the retrieval of all that is of value in black history and culture. It locates and rejects, as well, all that represents enslavement, racism, and the dehumanization of black people, just as Gustavo Gutiérrez's liberation theology does for the people of the barrios of Peru and elsewhere in Latin America.

James Cone's work is often described as hostile, outrageous, angry, but he uses his theological insights in the service of black theology. His theological norms, however, are different from tradition. What is of normative value to him is not Scripture, tradition, or great theological systems, but black experience. At the center of black theology are the encounter with and struggle against oppression. This struggle continues today; although we have made advances in expunging oppression, racism and other "isms" still exist in our society. In light of all this, black theology reads Scripture and approaches the person of Jesus of Nazareth as liberator and his work as liberation.

Cone explores a new theological dimension with which we may formalize the relationship between experience and Jesus as the Christ. For the African American, there is a past, a present, and a future with which to contend. The past is the gritty humanity of Jesus, always very real in black Christian culture; the present is the vibrant presence of Jesus in the current struggles in which African Americans find themselves engaged; the future is bound up with hope, but not the general, philosophical hope of the European theologians, but the hope that has appeared over and over again in black life—seen particularly in spirituals.

Black theologians like Cone and King are particularly sensitive to the story of the United States, to American history. While their desire to integrate a vision of America with Christian perceptions is not something new, they place a specific emphasis on the need to create a new America. This vision necessarily excludes much of what is "old America," which systematically dehumanized and debased African Americans. Black theologians are striving to promote a new view of the United States that will force white Americans to reevaluate their own understanding of their country and its history.

Since the time of the civil rights movement, black liberation theology has added its strong voice to the contemporary theological scene. And it shares this role with its colleagues in "theological arms" in this regard, feminist theology and the liberation theology of Latin America.

Martin Luther King Jr.

Source: "Letter from Birmingham Jail," The Christian Century *(June 12, 1963): 767–73.*

▼ ▼ ▼

My Dear Fellow Clergymen:
While confined here in the Birmingham city jail I came across your recent statement calling my present activities "unwise and untimely." . . . You deplore the demonstrations taking place in Birmingham. But your statement, I am sorry to say, fails to express a similar concern for the conditions that brought about the demonstrations. . . .

THE CUP OF ENDURANCE

You may well ask, "Why direct action? Why sit-ins, marches, etc.? Isn't negotiation a better path?" You are quite right in calling for negotiation. Indeed, this is the very purpose of direct action. Nonviolent direct action seeks to foster such a tension that a community which

has constantly refused to negotiate is forced to confront the issue. It seeks to so dramatize the issue that it can no longer be ignored. . . . We know through painful experience that freedom is never voluntarily given by the oppressor; it must be demanded by the opposed. Frankly, I have yet to engage in a direct action campaign that was "well timed" in the view of those who have not suffered unduly from the disease of segregation. For years now I have heard the word "Wait!" It rings in the ear of every Negro with piercing familiarity. This "Wait!" has almost always meant "Never." As one of our distinguished jurists once said, "Justice too long delayed is justice denied." . . .

We have waited for more than 340 years for our constitutional and God-given rights. The nations of Asia and Africa are moving with jet-like speed toward gaining political independence, but we still creep at horse-and-buggy pace toward gaining a cup of coffee at a lunch counter. Perhaps it is easy for those who have never felt the stinging darts of segregation to say "Wait." But when you have seen vicious mobs lynch your mothers and fathers at will and drown your sisters and brothers at whim; when you have seen hate-filled policemen curse, kick and even kill your black brothers and sisters with impunity; when you see the vast majority of your 20 million Negro brothers smothering in an air-tight cage of poverty in the midst of an affluent society; when you suddenly find your tongue twisted as you seek to explain to your six-year-old daughter why she can't go to the public amusement park that has just been advertised on television, and see tears welling up when she is told that Funtown is closed to colored children, and see ominous clouds of inferiority beginning to form in her little mental sky, and see her beginning to distort her personality by unconsciously developing a bitterness toward white people; when you have to concoct an answer for a five-year-old son asking, "Daddy, why do white people treat colored people so mean?"; when you take a cross-country drive and find it necessary to sleep night after night in the uncomfortable corners of your automobile because no motel will accept you; when you are humiliated day in and day out by nagging signs reading "white" and "colored"; when your first name becomes "nigger," your middle name becomes "boy" (however old you are) and your last name becomes "John," and your wife and mother are never given the respected title "Mrs."; when you are harried by day and haunted by night by the fact that you are a Negro, never quite knowing what to expect next, and are plagued with inner fears and outer resentments; when you are forever fighting a degenerating sense of "nobodiness"— then you will understand why we find it difficult to wait. There comes a time when the cup of endurance runs over, and men are no longer willing to be plunged into an abyss of injustice where they experience the bleakness of corroding despair. I hope, sirs, you can understand our legitimate and unavoidable impatience.

THE LAW THAT IS NO LAW

You express a great deal of anxiety over our willingness to break laws. This is certainly a legitimate concern. Since we so diligently urge people to obey the Supreme Court's decision of 1954 outlawing segregation in the public schools, at first glance it may seem rather paradoxical for us consciously to break laws. One may well ask, "How can you advocate breaking some laws and obeying others?" The answer lies in the fact that there are two types of laws: just and unjust. I agree with St. Augustine that "an unjust law is no law at all."

Now what is the difference between the two? How does one determine whether a law is just or unjust? A just law is a man-made code that squares with the moral law or the law of God. An unjust law is a code that is out of harmony with the moral law. To put it in the terms of St. Thomas Aquinas, an unjust law is a human law that is not rooted in eternal law and natural law. Any law that uplifts human personality is just. Any law that degrades human personality is unjust. All segregation statutes are unjust because segregation distorts the soul and damages the personality. It gives the segregator a false sense of superiority and the segregated a false sense of inferiority. Segregation, to use the terminology of the Jewish philosopher Martin Buber, substitutes an "I–it" relationship for an "I–thou" relationship and ends up relegating persons to the status of things. Hence, segregation is not only politically, economically and sociologically unsound, it is sinful. Paul Tillich has said that sin is separation. Is not segregation an existential expression of man's tragic separation, his awful estrangement, his terrible sinfulness? Thus it is that I can urge men to disobey segregation ordinances, for such ordinances are morally wrong. . . . I hope you are able to see the distinction I am trying to point out. In no sense do I advocate evading the law, as would the rabid segregationist. That would lead to anarchy. One who breaks an unjust law must do so *openly, lovingly,* and with a willingness to accept the penalty. I submit that an individual who breaks a law that conscience tells him is unjust and who willingly accepts the penalty of imprisonment in order to arouse the conscience of the community over its injustice is in reality expressing the highest respect for law.

Of course, there is nothing new about this kind of civil disobedience. It was evidenced sublimely in the refusal of Shadrach, Meshach and Abednego to obey the laws of Nebuchadnezzar, on the ground that a higher moral law was at stake. It was practiced superbly by the early Christians who were willing to face hungry lions rather than submit to certain unjust laws of the Roman empire. To a degree, academic freedom is a reality today because Socrates practiced civil disobedience. We should never forget that everything Adolf Hitler did in Germany was "legal" and everything the Hungarian freedom fighters did in Hungary was "illegal." It was "illegal" to aid and comfort a Jew in Hitler's Germany. Even so, I am sure that had I lived in Germany at the time I would have aided and comforted my Jewish brothers. If today I lived in a communist country where certain principles dear to the Christian faith are suppressed, I would openly advocate disobeying that country's antireligious laws.

WHERE ARE THE CHURCHES?

Let me take note of my . . . major disappointment. Though there are some notable exceptions, I have also been disappointed with the white church and its leadership. . . . We are moving toward the close of the twentieth century with a religious community largely adjusted to the status quo—a taillight behind other community agencies rather than a headlight leading men to higher levels of justice. . . . There was a time when the church was very powerful—in the time when the early Christians rejoiced at being deemed worthy to suffer for what they believed. In those days the church was not merely a thermometer that recorded the ideas and principles of popular opinion; it was a thermostat that transformed the mores of society. Whenever the early Christians entered a town the power structure immediately sought to convict them for being "disturbers of the peace" and "outside agitators." But the Christians pressed on, in the conviction that they were "a colony of heaven," called to obey God rather than man. Small in number, they were big in commitment. By their effort and example they brought an end to such ancient evils as infanticide and gladiatorial contest. . . .

Things are different now. So often the contemporary church is a weak, ineffectual voice with an uncertain sound. So often it is an archdefender of the status quo. Far from being disturbed by the presence of the church, the power structure of the average community is consoled by the church's silent—and often even vocal—sanction of things as they are.

But the judgment of God is upon the church as never before. If today's church does not recapture the sacrificial spirit of the early church, it will lose its authenticity, forfeit the loyalty of millions, and be dismissed as an irrelevant social club with no meaning for the twentieth century. Every day I meet young people whose disappointment with the church has turned into outright disgust.

Perhaps I have once again been too optimistic. Is organized religion too inextricably bound to the status quo to save our nation and the world? Perhaps I must turn my faith to the inner spiritual church, the church within the church, as the true *ecclesia* and the hope of the world. But again I am thankful to God that some noble souls from the ranks of organized religion have broken loose from the paralyzing chains of conformity and joined us as active partners in the struggle for freedom. They have left their secure congregations and walked the streets of Albany, Georgia, with us. They have gone down the highways of the south on torturous rides for freedom. Yes, they have gone to jail with us. Some have been kicked out of their churches, have lost the support of their bishops and fellow ministers. But they have acted in the faith that right defeated is stronger than evil triumphant. Their witness has been the spiritual salt that has preserved the true meaning of the gospel in these troubled times. They have carved a tunnel of hope through the dark mountain of disappointment.

I hope the church as a whole will meet the challenge of this decisive hour.

▲ ▲ ▲

James Cone

Source: A Black Theology of Liberation *(Maryknoll, N.Y.: Orbis Books, 1990), xi–xii, xv–xvi, xvii, 1, 3–4, 6–7, 19.*

▼ ▼ ▼

PREFACE TO THE 1986 EDITION

Theology is not universal language about God. Rather, it is human speech informed by historical and theological traditions, and written for particular times and places. Theology is *contextual* language—that is, defined by the human situation that gives birth to it. . . .

A Black Theology of Liberation was first published in 1970, and it was written for and to Black Christians (and also to whites who had the courage to listen) in an attempt to answer the question that I and others could not ignore, namely, "what has the gospel of Jesus Christ to do with the black struggle for justice in the United States?" This book cannot be understood without a keen knowledge of the civil rights and black power movements of the 1960s and a general comprehension of nearly four hundred years of slavery and segregation in North America, both of which were enacted into law by government and openly defended as ordained of God by most white churches and their theologians.

I can remember clearly when I first sat down to write this text. It was immediately following the publication of my first book, *Black Theology and Black Power* (1969). Although *Black Theology and Black Power* appealed to many black and white radicals who were interested in the theological implications of black power, I knew that most Christians, black and white, especially theologians and preachers, would need a deeper analysis of Christian doctrine, using traditional theological concepts, before taking black theology seriously. When I began to write *A Black Theology of Liberation,* I was deeply involved in the black struggle for justice and was *still* searching for a perspective on Christian theology that would help African-Americans recognize that the gospel of Jesus is not only consistent with their fight for liberation but is its central meaning for twentieth-century America.

I was completely unaware of the beginnings of liberation theology in the Third World, especially in Latin America. Neither did I know much about the theme of liberation in African-American history and culture. Unfortunately, my formal theological education and historical knowledge was primarily limited to the dominant perspectives of North America and Europe. But, despite these limitations, I was determined to speak a liberating word for and to African-American Christians, using the theological resources at my disposal. I did not have time to do the theological and historical research needed to present a "balanced" perspective on the problem of racism in America. Black men, women, and children were being shot and imprisoned for asserting their right to a dignified existence. Others were wasting away in ghettoes, dying from filth, rats, and dope, as white and black ministers preached about a blond, blue-eyed Jesus who came to make us all just like him. I *had* to speak a different word, not just as a black person but primarily as a *theologian.* I felt then, as I still do, that if theology had nothing to say about black suffering and resistance, I could not be a theologian. I remembered what Malcolm X had said: "I believe in a religion that believes in freedom. Any time I have to accept a religion that won't let me fight a battle for my people, I say to hell with that religion."

The passion with which I wrote alienated most whites (and some blacks too). But I felt that I had no other alternative if I was to speak forcefully and truthfully about the reality of suffering and of God's empowerment of blacks to resist it. It was not my task to interpret the gospel in a form acceptable to white racists and their sympathizers. Theology is not only rational discourse about ultimate reality; it is also a prophetic word about the righteousness of God that must be spoken in clear, strong, and uncompromising language. Oppressors never like to hear the truth in a socio-political context defined by their lies. That was why *A Black Theology of Liberation* was often rejected as racism in reverse by many whites, particularly theologians. For example, Father Andrew Greeley referred to my perspective on black theology as a "Nazi mentality," "a theology filled with hatred for white people and the assumption of a moral superiority of black over white." White reactions to black theology never disturbed me much, because Malcolm X had prepared me for them. "With skillful manipulating of the press," said Malcolm, "they're able to make the victim look like the criminal and the criminal look like the victim. . . ."

Although my view of white theology is generally the same today as it was in 1970, there are several significant shifts in my theological perspective since the publication of this text. . . .

The most glaring limitation of *A Black Theol-ogy of Liberation* was my failure to be receptive to the problem of sexism in the black community and society as a whole. I have become so embarrassed by that failure that I could not reissue this volume without making a note of it and without changing the exclusive language of the 1970 edition to inclusive language. . . .

Another serious limitation was my failure to incorporate a global analysis of oppression into *A Black Theology of Liberation*. Unlike my moral blindness in relation to sexism, the absence of Third World issues in my perspective was due more to my lack of knowledge and personal exposure. Being so concerned about the problem of racism in the United States and being strongly influenced by the analysis of it made by the civil rights and black power movements, it was easy for me to overlook Third World problems. . . .

The third weakness of *A Black Theology of Liberation* was the absence of a clearly focused economic, class analysis of oppression. This limitation is unquestionably the result of my strong identification with the common tendency in the black community of defining racism as a domestic problem, largely associated with the exclusion of blacks from the benefits of American capitalism. Racism was primarily identified as social exclusion with disastrous political and economic consequences. I assumed that if blacks were creatively integrated into all aspects of American society the issue of racism would be essentially solved. This was faulty analysis, because I failed to see that the problem of the human condition involved much more than simply the issue of racism. . . . My strong negative reaction to the racism of many white socialists in the United States distorted my vision and prevented me from analyzing racism in relation to capitalism. . . .

The fourth and last weakness that I wish to comment on was my inordinate methodological dependence upon the neoorthodox theology of Karl Barth. Many of my critics (black and white) have emphasized this point. It is a legitimate criticism, and I can offer no explanation except to say that neoorthodoxy was to me what liberal theology was to Martin Luther King Jr.—the only theological system with which I was intellectually comfortable and which seemed compatible with the centrality of Jesus Christ in the black church community. . . .

If I were to be writing *A Black Theology of Liberation* today, I would not follow the theological nurturing that begins with a methodology based on divine revelation. . . . There is no "abstract" revelation independent of human experiences, to which theologians can appeal for evidence of what they say about the gospel. God meets us in the human situation, not as an idea or concept that is self-evidently true. God encounters us in the human condition as the liberator of the poor and the weak, empowering them to fight for freedom because they were made for it. Revelation as the word of God, witnessed in scripture and defined by the creeds and dogmas of Western Christianity, is too limiting to serve as an adequate way of doing theology today. Theology, as Latin American liberation theologians have stressed, is the second step, a reflective action taken in response to the first act of a practical commitment in behalf of the poor. . . .

THE TASK OF BLACK THEOLOGY

Christian theology is a theology of liberation. It is a rational study of the being of God in the world in light of the existential situation of an oppressed community, relating forces of liberation to the essence of the gospel, which is Jesus Christ. This means that its sole reason for existence is to put into ordered speech the meaning of God's activity in the world, so that the community of the oppressed will recognize that its inner thrust for liberation is not only consistent with the gospel but is the gospel of Jesus Christ. There can be no Christian theology that is not unreservedly with those who are humiliated and abused. . . . It is impossible to speak of the God of Israelite history, who is the God revealed in Jesus Christ, without recognizing that God is the God of and for those who labor and are over laden.

In view of the biblical emphasis on liberation, it seems not only appropriate but necessary to define the Christian community as the community of the oppressed which joins Jesus Christ in his fight for the liberation of humankind. The task of theology, then, is to explicate the meaning of God's liberating activity so that those who labor under enslaving powers will see that the forces of liberation are the very activity of God. Christian theology is never just a rational study of the being of God. Rather it is the study of God's liberating activity in the world, God's activity in behalf of the oppressed. . . . Herein lies the universal note implied in the gospel message of Jesus. The resurrection-event means that God's liberating work is not only for the house of Israel but for all who are enslaved by principalities

and powers. The resurrection conveys hope in God. Nor is the "hope" that promises a reward in heaven in order to ease the pain of injustice on earth. Rather it is the hope which focuses on the future in order to make us refuse to tolerate present inequities. To see the future of God, as revealed in the resurrection of Jesus, is to see also the contradiction of any earthly injustice with existence in Jesus Christ. That is why Camilo Torres was right when he described revolutionary action as "a Christian, a priestly struggle."

Unfortunately, American white theology has not been involved in the struggle for black liberation. It has been basically a theology of the white oppressor, giving religious sanction to the genocide of Amerindians and the enslavement of Africans. From the very beginning to the present days, American white theological thought has been "patriotic," either by defining the theological task independently of black suffering (the liberal northern approach) or by defining Christianity as compatible with white racism (the conservative southern approach). In both cases theology becomes a servant of the state, and that can only mean death to blacks. It is little wonder that an increasing number of black religionists are finding it difficult to be black and be identified with traditional theological thought forms.

The task of black theology, then, is to analyze the nature of the gospel of Jesus Christ in the light of oppressed blacks so they will see the gospel as inseparable from their humiliated condition, and as bestowing on them the necessary power to break the chains of oppression. This means that it is a theology of and for the black community, seeking to interpret the religious dimensions of the forces of liberation in that community. . . .

Black theology is Christian theology because it centers on Jesus Christ. There can be no Christian theology which does not have Jesus Christ as its point of departure.

It is to be expected that some will ask, "Why black theology? Is it not true that God is color blind? Is it not true that there are others who suffer as much as, if not in some cases more than, blacks?" These questions reveal a basic misunderstanding of black theology, and also a superficial view of the world at large. There are at least three points to be made here.

First, in a revolutionary situation there can never be nonpartisan theology. Theology is always identified with a particular community. It is either with those who inflict oppression or those who are its victims. A theology of the latter is authentic Christian theology, and a theology of the former is a theology of the Antichrist. . . .

Second, in a racist society, God is never color-blind. To say God is color-blind is analogous to saying that God is blind to justice and injustice, to right and wrong, to good and evil. Certainly this is not the picture of God revealed in the Old and New Testaments. Yahweh takes sides. . . . In the New Testament Jesus is not for all, but for the oppressed, the poor and unwanted of society and against oppressors. The God of the biblical tradition is not uninvolved or neutral regarding human affairs; God is decidedly involved. God is active in human history, taking sides with the oppressed of the land. If God is not involved in human history, then all theology is useless, and Christianity itself is a mockery, a meaningless diversion. . . .

Thirdly, there are, to be sure, many who suffer, and not all of them black. Many white liberals derive a certain joy from reminding black militants that two-thirds of the poor in America are white. Of course I could point out that this means that there are five times as many poor blacks as there are poor whites, when the ratio of each group to the total population is taken into account. But it is not my intention to debate white liberals on this issue, for it is not the purpose of black theology to minimize the suffering of others, including whites. Black theology merely tries to discern the activity of the Holy One in achieving the purpose of liberation of humankind from the forces of oppression.

Poster Boy

Because black theology is survival theology, it must speak with a passion consistent with the depths of the wounds of the oppressed. Theological language is passionate language, the language of commitment, because it is language which seeks to vindicate the afflicted and condemn the enforcers of evil. Christian theology cannot afford to be an abstract, dispassionate discourse on the nature of God in relation to humankind; such an analysis has no ethical implications for the contemporary forms of oppression in our society. Theology must take the risk of faith, knowing that it stands on the edge of condemnation by the forces of evil. Paul Tillich calls this an "existential risk." . . .

The sin of American theology is that it has spoken without passion, it has failed miserably in relating its work to the oppressed in society by refusing to confront the structures of this nation with the evils of racism. . . .

My characterization of black theology as passionate theology is analogous to Paul Tillich's analysis of "the existential thinker." Quoting Feuerbach, he writes:

Do not wish to be a philosopher in contrast to being a man. . . . Do not think as a thinker. . . . Think as a living, real being. . . . Think in Existence. Love is passion, and only passion is the mark of Existence. (Tillich, *Theology of Culture,* pp. 89–90)

In fact, Tillich quotes Feuerbach as saying, "Only what is as an object of passion—really is" (Tillich, *Theology of Culture,* p. 90). The existential thinker is a thinker who not only relates thought to existence but whose thought arises out of a passionate encounter with existence. . . .

Relating this to black theology, we can say that the definition of truth for the black thinker arises from a passionate encounter with black reality. Though that truth may be described religiously as God, it is not the God of white religion but the God of black existence. There is no way to speak of this objectively; truth is not objective. It is subjective, a personal experience of the ultimate in the midst of degradation. Passion is the only appropriate response to this truth.

▲ ▲ ▲

Although it extends back to Augustine, at least since the time of Anselm, theology has been described as *fides quarens intellectum,* faith seeking understanding. Perhaps a more fitting description of theology for the black community might be "experience seeking understanding."

With all their diversity, black theologians repeatedly emphasize how their theology grows out of the black experience in America. The experience to which Cone and others refer is often recent, such as the black power movement of the 1960s, but is also deep and textured, reaching back to slavery and, even further, to Africa. In this theology, the basis of faith is the truths that have been laboriously uncovered in the cotton fields, in factories, in the home, and on the streets. The church and the seminaries have their roles, but these roles are secondary and derivative.

To describe what has emerged theologically from the black experience is perhaps to call it "a sense of humanity," or a "deeper, fuller sense of what it means to be human." African Americans have been forced to probe this idea, and in the process their theology has taken on new dimensions. In this understanding of being human we can detect a few qualities: (1) profound humiliation—having to absorb that white society has judged one to be "something less than human"; (2) self-esteem—the recognition that no one can take away a person's basic dignity when one is prepared to hold on to it and claim it; (3) a determination to struggle—the understanding that only resistance and courage can overcome the dehumanization and debasement that are the consequences of deep-seated bigotry; and hope—a commitment to the notion that one can overcome enormous obstacles, or, as the spiritual popularized during the civil rights movement says, "We shall overcome."

In this context, religious ideas such as the divine are not alternatives to this perception of humanity but emerge within its context. God, Jesus of Nazareth, the cross, the Holy Spirit, the Scriptures, the church, and so forth are all seen with a unique vividness and intensity. And since black theology is experiential theology, it shares certain advantages with evangelical, liberal, and Latin American liberation theologies. With the evangelicals, it insists on the immediacy and directness of revelation; with the liberals it stresses the humane and reformative nature of Christian faith; with the liberation theologians, it stresses the need to advocate identification with the oppressed. Unlike the liberals, however, it does not fall prey to abstract theology; unlike the evangelicals, it does not fall prey to fundamentalism; and unlike Latin American liberation theologians, it keeps a focus on the broad range of theological reflections. Black theology has a remarkable vitality that challenges all traditional forms of theology. It is vital simply because it is close to the lives of African Americans—where they have been, where they are now, and where they are going.

EPILOGUE

At the outset of this volume, we indicated that theology (or religion) never occurs in a vacuum, that the world in which we live is not a neutral place. We hope to have demonstrated this hypothesis by our brief excursion into the works of Christian theologians through history. We saw in the works of Justin Martyr a man, who like Ignatius of Antioch died a martyr's death, took Christianity to a new level of understanding with the coalescence of his philosophical skills and religious convictions.

The works of Irenaeus of Lyons gave us a somewhat different perspective; we saw a man who was elevated to the episcopate (bishop) at a time of great strife, not only from external sources, but from divisive elements within the early Christian community itself, the Gnostics. As a champion of the faith, Irenaeus established the validity of the Christian sources, both Scripture and tradition, while at the same time providing the church with strong and valuable leadership.

With Origen of Alexandria, and such persons as Arius and Athanasius, we experienced the tremendous intellectual struggles that resulted in the establishment of religious standards called "creeds" by which the validity and authenticity of religious statements were judged. We also witnessed the severe divisions that these discussions caused within the developing church, for example, the Antiochene and Alexandrine versions of Christianity and the ever-present Latin or Roman version as well. These traditions have their descendants even in this modern era, for debates over the person of Jesus of Nazareth and the meaning of his work for our lives continue today.

With these developments within the church, yet another interesting phenomenon appeared on the scene: the active participation or "interference," if you will, of the secular authority in the life of the religious community. With the conversion, of sorts, of Constantine, the emperor who called the Council of Nicea to resolve the most pressing issue in the early church (the nature of the second person of the Trinity), the religious community in many ways became another "department of the state." The Christian church moved from being persecuted, to being accepted, to being favored, to intense arguments within the church itself with various theological adversaries declaring each other to be heretics. Nevertheless, this was a time of energy, creativity, and excitement, phenomena we have largely lost in the present age. The creativity and excitement of these early theologians, who were not university professors but bishops and pastors, is extremely useful for us.

Reinhold Niebuhr once commented on the lack of impact of Christianity on contemporary society, stating that the problem with both is that modern Christianity and modern Christians suffer from "a failure of nerve" and a "paralysis of will." In Niebuhr's opinion we just do not allow the dynamic character of the gospel to speak to us and to our worlds. Certainly there are exceptions to

this weakness. One can point to people such as Dietrich Bonhoeffer, who returned to his native Germany in the 1930s to challenge the Nazis; Archbishop Oscar Romero, slain in 1980 in his cathedral because he challenged the political and economic oppression of his people by the Salvadoran government; James Reeb, a little-known former mainline Protestant turned Unitarian, slain for his efforts to secure dignity for all human beings during the civil rights movement of the 1960s; and Martin Luther King Jr., who was known for his monumental efforts in the pursuit of justice and dignity for all. These are all individual expressions of the religious impact on our society, and in many ways these efforts are not unlike those of the early centuries of Christianity.

So that one does not get the impression that only individuals grasped the critical reality of the Christian faith, we should remember that at times even the institutional church has risen to the occasion. In 1967 the Presbyterian Church (USA) (then the United Presbyterian Church in the USA) adopted a new confession of faith simply called *The Confession of 1967*. What is unique about this statement is that (1) it spoke clearly, forcefully, and specifically to a particular time and the problems of that time and (2) it addressed several critical issues of a moral nature facing the United States and the church of Jesus Christ. In devastating critical fashion, it addressed the rampant racism of our society and the exploitation of human beings in terms of economics and sexuality. It even addressed the "sacred cow" of our land, seriously questioning the international political policies and motives of our government and the motives of "any nation" claiming that God was "on their side."

The U.S. Catholic bishops addressed these issues with equal fervor. For the Presbyterians the consequences were severe: significant losses in revenue and membership (people voted with their feet and joined less socially conscious and more fundamentalist churches). The power and demand of the gospel of Jesus proved to be too much for many Presbyterians. The Catholic bishops received sarcastic and simplistic dismissals of their critique as coming from incompetent and irrelevant men who were just out of touch with the "real" world. Many, if not most, Christians preferred that their faith and their ethics had relatively little (preferably nothing) to do with the world in which they lived and moved and had their being. Unfortunately, most of the Christians either were hostile to these challenges from the church or just ignored them. The church and the gospel were seen as something of historical interest, something to be brought out on special occasions like Christmas and Easter, but for the most part something to be ignored.

Dorothy L. Sayers, British woman of letters and theological commentator, captured the tenor of where most people are in a little book written some time ago, *Creed or Chaos*. In this work she described what most people believe about their faith, that is, if you take our literature and cinematic characterizations seriously. The Jesus we usually portray before the world is a Jesus who is somewhat ethereal, walking, as it were, without touching the ground. He is an unobtrusive, inoffensive person, to whom we refer only in times of desperate need, as a last resort. He is a Jesus without sexuality, a Jesus who is therefore safe. Thus Sayers argues that we have made Jesus out to be a classic bore in the name of one who most certainly was hardly inoffensive or boring. To which I would add, indeed, one does not get nailed like a bat to the proverbial barn door for being a weakling.

When we examine the writers of antiquity, the Middle Ages, and the rest of history up to and including the present, we see a dynamism recurring in the gospel that challenges those of us today who profess a religious faith. Real faith, Christian or otherwise, challenges all attempts to institutionalize and suffocate human spiritual development. From Ignatius of Antioch to Martin Luther King Jr., among individuals in Eastern and Western religions, examples abound of faith presenting this challenge. It is our hope that in some way this volume may help awaken readers to this part of the Christian tradition and to the potential for our continued growth as human beings toward richer, fuller lives.

STUDY QUESTIONS

1. Ignatius of Antioch

1. Why was Ignatius so concerned to affirm the reality of Christ's physical presence in the Eucharist?
2. Who were the docetists, and how did Ignatius respond to their challenges?
3. Why might Ignatius's view of Christ—that is, his Christology—be characterized as being martyriological?

2. Justin Martyr

1. Justin was one of the leading Apologists of his time. What is Apologetic theology? How effective do you think Justin was as an Apologist?
2. In what ways did Justin "intellectualize" Christian faith?
3. What role did the *Logos* play in Justin's thought? How did he modify his Neoplatonic views of God in light of Christian revelation?

3. Irenaeus of Lyons

1. Gnosticism was a major problem for Irenaeus and the church of his time. What were the essentials of Gnosticism? How well did Irenaeus address the challenge?
2. What was Irenaeus's theory of recapitulation (*anakephalaiosis*)? How did it work? Give some examples.
3. How did Irenaeus deal with the "problem of evil"?

4. Tertullian

1. What was Tertullian's attitude toward philosophy? Why?
2. What is the *regula fidei*, and how was it employed by Tertullian?
3. What was Tertullian's use of *Logos*, and in what ways may it be said that his view anticipated what was accomplished at Nicea?

5. Origen of Alexandria

1. How would you describe Origen's anthropology? What did he suggest by the *homoousion* of all minds? And how did the devil fit into this scheme?
2. What was Origen's doctrine of the *apokatastasis*?
3. Describe Origen's Christology. How did he distinguish between the *Logos* and the second person of the Trinity? What is the significance of this distinction?

6. Arius and the Arian Controversy

1. In what ways did Arius's view of the createdness of the *Logos* have an impact on redemption or salvation?
2. If you were defending Arius's view, what biblical and historical evidence might you present in that defense? How would you argue against Arius?
3. How did Arius see the relation between the Word/*Logos* and the Son, that is, the second person of the Trinity?

7. Athanasius

1. How did Athanasius, the chief respondent to Arius, answer the challenge raised by Arius?
2. In Athanasius's mind why is it not possible for us to worship a "created being" even such a "divinely created being" as the Christ?
3. Did the Christ of Athanasius have a real humanity or not? Or was Athanasius guilty of Apollinarianism?

8. The Ecumenical Councils and Creeds

1. What role did the Emperor Constantine play at the Council of Nicea? What do you think was the significance of his role for his time? for future theological resolutions?
2. The term *homoousios* was created or invented to resolve the Arian issue. What is your understanding of this term?
3. In what ways did the Councils of Constantinople and Chalcedon complete what was started at Nicea?

9. Augustine of Hippo

1. State your understanding of Augustine's view of what it means to be human, and include your understanding of his concepts of original sin, predestination, and free will.
2. Why is Augustine given the honorific title "Doctor of Grace" by the church? What role does grace play in his theology?
3. What was the Augustinian resolution to the "problem of evil"?

10. Pseudo-Dionysius

1. What was Pseudo-Dionysius' understanding of God and our ability to know God?
2. What do you understand by Pseudo-Dionysius' theological method known as the *via negativa*?
3. What is the significance of this "unknown" thinker in the history of Christian thought?

11. John Scotus Erigena

1. What did Erigena mean by *creatio ex Deo*?
2. How did Erigena use Scripture, for example, in his understanding of paradise?
3. What did Erigena mean when he suggested that all comes from God and all returns to God? And why would this view be so controversial?

12. Anselm of Canterbury

1. What role did "justice" play in Anselm's *Cur Deus Homo*? What role, if any, did the social environment of his day play in this description of redemption?
2. Present Anselm's ontological argument for the existence of God. What was the criticism offered by the monk Gaunilo? And what was Anselm's response to Gaunilo? Do you think the argument is valid or useless? Why?

3. How did Anselm use reason in his theological arguments—for example, in the ontological argument and in *Cur Deus Homo*?

13. Peter Abelard

1. Why is Abelard's theory of atonement or redemption referred to whether correctly or incorrectly as the "subjective influence theory"?
2. Compare the redemptive theologies of Anselm and Abelard.
3. What do you understand by the term, *the classic theory of atonement*?

14. Thomas Aquinas

1. What role did the philosophy of Aristotle play in Thomas's theology?
2. What were Thomas's arguments for the existence of God? How did they differ from Anselm's? Are they any more or less effective?
3. Why is Thomas often considered the most profound, most important theologian in all of Christian history before the Reformation? Do you agree or disagree? Why?

15. Johannes Meister Eckhardt

1. In what ways does the term *mysticism* fit the theology of Eckhardt?
2. Eckhardt's theology has often been described as being pantheistic. Do you agree or disagree? What evidence might you give in support of your position?
3. Is the God of Eckhardt the God of the philosophers or the God of Christianity? Why?

16. Women of the Middle Ages

1. Elaborate on the Trinity in the thought of Hildegard of Bingen. Of what significance were the insights of this talented woman for the development of theology?
2. Julian of Norwich used the idiom of God as "Mother" in her discussions of the Trinity. What was achieved by use of this metaphor?
3. According to Catherine of Siena, how does the human soul learn of its dependence upon God? What brought Catherine to this conclusion?

17. Thomas à Kempis

1. Was à Kempis an anti-intellectual? How would you support your answer?
2. Why did à Kempis place such a low value on things in this world?
3. How is Augustine's famous phrase about the restlessness of the soul manifested in the work of à Kempis?

18. Martin Luther

1. What is the foundation for Luther's concept of justification or salvation?
2. On what grounds did Luther reject the Roman Catholic Mass in his treatise *The Babylonian Captivity of the Church*?
3. In his address to the German nobility, Luther referred to three walls the papacy had erected to protect itself from reform. What were these three walls, and how accurate do you think Luther was in this criticism?

19. John Calvin

1. Calvin's theology has been described as *theocentric*. What is your understanding of this term as it applies to John Calvin?
2. Calvin has often been identified with the doctrine of double predestination. Is this doctrine preeminent in Calvin's work, as some have suggested, or is this view a distortion of Calvin's thinking? Give some evidence to support your view.
3. According to Calvin, why was the reformation of the church a necessity?

20. Immanuel Kant

1. Kant is often referred to as the "Copernicus of philosophy." Why is this so?
2. What was Kant's "categorical imperative"? How did this relate to his understanding of theology?
3. What role did Jesus of Nazareth play in Kant's moral philosophy/theology?

21. Friedrich Schleiermacher

1. In his *Speeches,* Schleiermacher addressed a group that he referred to as "the cultured despisers." Who were these "cultured despisers," and what issues were addressed by Schleiermacher in these "speeches"?
2. What did Schleiermacher mean when he referred to the "God-consciousness" of Jesus of Nazareth? How does that relate to our own "God-consciousness"?
3. Schleiermacher argued that "feeling" is the unique element of religion. What did Schleiermacher mean by *feeling*? by the "feeling of absolute dependence"?

22. David F. Strauss

1. Strauss argued in his work *The Life of Jesus, Critically Examined* that myth is real and the real is myth. What is your understanding of Strauss's use of the term *myth*? Why?
2. In his examination of the Scriptures, Strauss rejected both rationalism and supernaturalism as legitimate means of interpretation. What alternative did he offer?
3. What does Strauss's understanding of Jesus as the Christ suggest?

23. Søren Kierkegaard

1. What did Kierkegaard mean by *Christendom*? Why was he so critical of this phenomenon?
2. Kierkegaard is often referred to as the initiator of Christian existentialism. What do you think is meant by that phrase? Do you agree or disagree? Give your reasons.
3. For Kierkegaard, what did it mean to be an "authentic" Christian? Did he consider himself to be one? Why or why not?

24. Albrecht Ritschl

1. It has been suggested that Ritschl was a theologian who completely bought into the Kantian critique of religion and theology. What is meant by this?
2. What was Ritschl's understanding of God and the kingdom of God?

3. Ritschl stated that "faith in Christ is neither belief in the truth of his history nor assent to a scientific judgment of knowledge such as that presented by the Chalcedonian Formula." What is the meaning of this statement? Do you agree with it?

25. Adolf von Harnack

1. About one hundred years after Schleiermacher's *Speeches*, Harnack gave lectures published under the title *What Is Christianity?* What was Harnack's answer to that question? What is your evaluation of his answer?
2. What differences did Harnack see between the Jesus of the Gospels and the Jesus of the creeds of the early church?
3. How would Harnack answer the famous biblical question put by Jesus of Nazareth to his disciples, "Who do you say that I am?"

26. Karl Barth

1. When Barth wrote his commentary *Epistle to the Romans*, what issues was he addressing and what impact did this volume have on the development of theology in the early twentieth century?
2. When Barth used the term *the Word of God*, to whom or what was he referring?
3. Barth's theology is sometimes described as Christomonistic and even more frequently as Christocentric. What do these descriptions of Barth's theology mean?

27. Rudolf Otto

1. *Mysterium tremendum, numinous,* and *fascinans* were all terms employed by Otto in his work. How did Otto use these terms? Of what value, if any, is his approach to theology?
2. Is there any correlation between Otto's understanding of God as the "Wholly Other" and that of Barth and Kierkegaard?
3. One might describe Otto's thought as being "nonrational" but not irrational. What is the meaning of that distinction?

28. Rudolf Bultmann

1. Why did Bultmann believe that the New Testament must be demythologized?
2. What would Bultmann mean by "living authentically"?
3. Why and how did Bultmann extricate the biblical message from its cosmology? Can the New Testament "message" be separated from its cosmology?

29. Paul Tillich

1. What was Tillich's "method of correlation"?
2. What did Tillich mean by "ultimate concern"? According to Tillich, can a concern that is not really ultimate be treated as such by human beings?
3. What did Tillich mean by the term *New Being,* and how does this term relate to his understanding of Jesus as the Christ?

30. Reinhold Niebuhr

1. What was Niebuhr's understanding of the human person?
2. What was Niebuhr's understanding of the biblical concept that human beings are created in the image of God, that is, the *imago Dei*?
3. Niebuhr is often described as being neoorthodox. What does that mean, especially when related to the Reformers, such as John Calvin and Martin Luther?

31. Dietrich Bonhoeffer

1. In his work *The Cost of Discipleship*, Bonhoeffer made a distinction between "cheap grace" and "costly grace." What are the characteristics of each?
2. Bonhoeffer in his *Letters and Papers from Prison* used the term *religionless Christianity*. To what was Bonhoeffer referring? How might this be related to Kierkegaard's *Christendom*?
3. Why do you think that Bonhoeffer, who died at a young age, has had an enduring influence on secular, this-worldly Christians?

32. Latin American Liberation Theology

1. What is "liberation theology" as espoused by Gutiérrez, and why did this new theology cause such an uproar?
2. Why do you think liberation theology is aggressive in critiquing the structures and institutions of this world?
3. What is meant by the phrase God's "preferential option for the poor"?

33. Feminist Liberation Theology

1. What is Daly's critique of how the Christian tradition has supported patriarchal society?
2. What is Ruether's understanding of a feminist theological perspective on what it means to be human?
3. According to feminist liberation theology, what is the role of Jesus of Nazareth as the Christ?

34. Black Liberation Theology

1. Why was it so important for theologians such as Martin Luther King Jr. and James Cone to press home the point that what is normative for black theology is not Scripture or tradition but *black experience*?
2. Why do theologians like Cone reject the idea that God is "color-blind"?
3. In what ways, according to King and Cone, has "white liberal theology" failed the African American religious community?

Index

225